My Generation

Wisconsin Studies in American Autobiography

WILLIAM L. ANDREWS

General Editor

John Downton Hazlett

My Generation
Collective Autobiography
and Identity Politics

The University of Wisconsin Press

The University of Wisconsin Press
2537 Daniels Street
Madison, Wisconsin 53718

3 Henrietta Street
London WC2E 8LU, England

5 4 3 2 1

Library of Congress Cataloging-in-Publication Data
Hazlett, John Downton
    My generation: collective autobiography and identity politics /
John Downton Hazlett.
    278 pp.   cm. — (Wisconsin studies in American autobiography)
    Includes bibliographical references and index.
    ISBN 0–299–15780–6 (cloth: alk. paper).
    ISBN 0–299–15784–9 (pbk.: alk. paper).
    1. Autobiography.   2. Generations.   3. Intergenerational
relations.   I. Title.   II. Series.
    CT25.H39   1998
    920—dc21   97–47292

For my father and mother

The "spirit of the age" is no longer merely something that "emerges" naturally (if indeed it ever did) out of the work of a generation's intellectual elite . . . or even something that is formulated retrospectively by historians of later generations; the character of the contemporary "generation" and the "spirit" presumably created by it have become *ideological* questions *for its own members.* The problem of assessing the "spirit of the age" becomes not only a question of analyzing the works of its creators; a struggle ensues between different groups of intellectuals of the same generation (each conscious of itself not as a structurally defined group, but as a temporally located "generation") for the right *deliberately to define,* indeed to *name* the spirit of the age. For "naming" the age is not only a diagnostic function, it is an ideological one too. . . .
—Bennett M. Berger, *Looking for America: Essays on Youth,
Suburbia, and Other American Obsessions*

People are always shouting they want to create a better future. It's not true. The future is an apathetic void of no interest to anyone. The past is full of life, eager to irritate us, provoke and insult us, tempt us to destroy or repaint it. The only reason people want to be masters of the future is to change the past. They are fighting for access to the laboratories where photographs are retouched and biographies and histories rewritten.
—Milan Kundera, *The Book of Laughter and Forgetting*

Contents

Acknowledgments

In the preparation of this book, I have benefited from the suggestions and support of many people, to all of whom I owe thanks.

Some of the necessary time and funding to write this book were provided by the University of New Orleans Graduate Council, which generously supported this project with several Summer Scholar Grants. I am especially indebted to friends in the Department of English who carefully read and criticized some early chapters. Grace Tiffany, Kevin Marti, and Peter Schock all provided help in one way or another. Members of the 1987 Reader's Group—Rick Barton, John Cooke, John Gery, and Carl Malmgren—offered particularly cogent criticisms as well. Early drafts of some chapters also benefited from the reading of former teachers of mine at the University of Iowa—Robert Sayre, Albert Stone, John Raeburn, Linda Gerber, and Sherman Paul. Gordon Hutner, the editor of *American Literary History*, and the readers for that journal also contributed valuable suggestions.

Like all teachers, I have also benefited greatly from dialogues with gifted students, and I would like to thank the members of my American Autobiography seminars for their fresh insights into the genre. One graduate student, M. J. Braun, brought her own generational experience to bear on one of the later chapters, offering suggestions for its revision that were especially welcome and useful.

Among the many friends and colleagues who read chapters and offered ideas were Suzanne Qualls, Sonja Ebel, Walter Johnson, Catherine Perry, Bo Conn, Silvia San Martín, David Allen, Diana Robin, Aranzazu Usandizaga, Basia Ozieblo, Isabel Durán, Manuel Gonzalez de la Aleja Barberán, Claire Tylee, and Larry and Jane Harred. Perhaps more than any other person, Oscar Kenshur has encouraged me, provided a safe haven within which to work, served as a writing and thinking model, and advised me with regard to errant ideas.

Earlier versions of Chapters 1 and 2, and portions of Chapters 3, 4, and 5, were included in my Ph.D. dissertation, entitled "Self and History: Essays on American Historiography and Autobiography." An earlier version of Chapter 1 was published as "Generational Theory and Collective Autobiography" in *American Literary History* 4: (Spring 1992): 77–96. Its use here is by permission of Oxford University Press. Sections of Chapters 2 and 3 were published together as "The American Generational Autobiography: Malcolm Cowley and Michael Rossman" in *Prospects: An Annual Journal of American Cultural Studies*, Vol. 16., ed. Jack Salzman (New York: Cambridge UP, 1991), pp. 421–42. It is reprinted here with permission from Cambridge University Press.

At the University of Wisconsin Press, I have been given steadfast encouragement by William Andrews, General Editor of the Wisconsin Studies in American Autobiography Series, and by Mary Elizabeth Braun, Acquisitions Editor, to both of whom I am grateful. I would also like to acknowledge the insightful and careful readings of the typescript given by the Press's reviewers, Milton J. Bates and Lynn Z. Bloom. To the former, in particular, I am indebted for suggestions regarding the refinement of my ideas about the three modes of generational autobiography. The manuscript also benefited from the excellent copyediting of Susan Tarcov, who showed remarkable patience with the "trabas" involved in communicating with the author while he was teaching at the Instituto Tecnologico y de Estudios Superiores de Monterrey in Cordoba, Mexico.

Finally, I wish to acknowledge my gratitude to Morrey McElroy, whose calm presence and down-to-earth questions have made the final stages of manuscript preparation a true pleasure.

My Generation

1

Generationalism and Collective Autobiography

> Each of us moves with the men of our generation, submerged in the great anonymous multitude, and save for the final individual nucleus of our life, to ask ourselves to which generation we belong is, in large measure, to ask *who* we are.
>
> Julián Marías, *Generations: A Historical Method*

In the late 1960s and early 1970s, it was common to hear young, middle-class, white Americans referring to themselves with a self-conscious sense of shared identity and common oppression that today one associates with race, class, ethnicity, or gender. The primary collective with which those young people in the 1960s identified—the generation—is now granted attention only in popular magazines and in marketing and demographic reports on the continuing economic and social impact of the baby boomers. In the field of American autobiography, studies of works by writers who identify themselves on the basis of gender, class, race, or ethnicity have been numerous, while autobiographies in which the primary collective identity has been derived from the concept of the generation—works such as Raymond Mungo's *Total Loss Farm: A Year in the Life* (1970), Michael Rossman's *The Wedding within the War* (1971), Joyce Maynard's *Looking Back: A Chronicle of Growing Up Old in the 1960s* (1972), or David Harris' *Dreams Die Hard: Three Men's Journey through the Sixties* (1982)—have been largely ignored.

The reasons for the neglect of what I call "generational autobiographies" are not difficult to imagine. Whereas autobiographers often experience gender, race, ethnicity, and class affiliations radically and over the whole of their lives, one is most aware of one's membership in a generation during the coming-of-age years or the period that Erik Erikson refers to as the "psychosocial moratorium," when one is first entering the arena of history, rebelling against parental institutions, and experimenting with adult identities.[1] After that period, one's sense of kinship with other members of one's age group inevitably declines, and since conventional autobiographies tend to be written later in life, they rarely focus exclusively upon generational experience. Then, too, oppressed groups now enjoy a privileged position within the academy that lends an aura of moral rectitude to the study of their literatures. It is not often argued that members of specific generations are actually oppressed, whatever they themselves might say to the contrary, and when it has been argued, that oppression is generally acknowledged to be limited to the coming-of-age period itself. Once through that phase of their lives, the members of new generations within the dominant social group almost inevitably inherit the world and the power of their fathers. Given this potentially easier path to power, middle-class, alienated, and self-conscious generations do not attract the attention of critics sensitive to the moral allure of other marginalized groups. Not surprisingly, critics tend to ignore the role of the generational concept in the construction of autobiographical identity.[2]

It is not my intention to insist upon the need to recognize generational autobiographers as members of an oppressed class, but I do wish to show how their perception of the self as collective and their awareness that self-construction is inherently political bear on the theory of autobiography. One of the best reasons for studying generational autobiographies is that they so powerfully undercut the central assumption of traditional autobiographical theory—the assumption that the genre depends upon the notion of the individualized self. That assumption has been effectively attacked by writers approaching the genre from the perspective of marginalized groups. Central to the argument between traditional critics and their opponents is the model of identity formation that each group employs. The model used by traditional critics, Susan Stanford Friedman claims, is inaccurate on two counts: "First, the emphasis on individualism does not take into account the importance of a culturally imposed identity for women and minorities. Second, the emphasis on separateness ignores the differences in socialization in the construction of male and female gender identity. From both an ideological and psychological perspective . . . individualistic paradigms of the self ignore the role of collective and relational identities in the individuation process of women and minorities."[3]

American generational autobiographies help to demonstrate that the cultural pervasiveness of the myth of individualism does not prevent the self from being conceived collectively. But more important than the mere existence of generational autobiographies is the way in which they enable us to see features of the genre less visible (but nonetheless present) in more individualized works, particularly the dialogical nature, constructedness, and negotiability of the autobiographical self. The self of generational autobiography is always more or less overtly offered in the service of identity politics, but these conspicuous characteristics of collective autobiography also have, I believe, important implications for our understanding of the way in which the selves of more conventional, individualized texts are dialectically related to collectives.

Before looking at specific generational autobiographies, however, I would like to provide in this chapter a brief outline of those aspects of generational theory (as exemplified in the work of Randolph Bourne and José Ortega y Gasset) that coincide with the first example of American generational autobiography. The ideas and assumptions of these theorists will also help to clarify the conception of the self that underlies all later examples of the form.

As Karl Weintraub demonstrates in *The Value of the Individual: Self and Circumstance in Autobiography*, Western culture required a sense of the value of the individual self before it could produce texts that purported to narrate the coming-into-being of such a self.[4] The same thing holds true for texts about a collective self. Historically, of course, stories that construct the identities of groups—tribes, dynasties, nations, religious enclaves—are much older than those about individuals. Tales of the Hebrews' dealings with Yahweh and other tribes are early examples of a kind of collective autobiography. So, indeed, is the modern practice of historiography when the historiographer is writing about his own collective group.

To speak of a generational autobiography, therefore, naturally presupposes the existence of a culturally sponsored generational concept as well as the sense among particular age cohorts of a strong generational identity. Generational theorists like Karl Mannheim and Annie Kriegel, as well as generational historians like Robert Wohl, agree that the generational experience has significantly affected the development of personal identity only for a relatively restricted number of age cohorts. In America, generational consciousness has been strongest among those who came of age during and after the First World War and among those who came of age during the period of the Vietnam War. Why this should be so is open to speculation, though both Kriegel and Wohl have attempted to articulate some of the social and historical causes that have contributed to age group consciousness. Professor Wohl, whose book *The Generation of 1914* is one of the best studies of European generationalism, states that the essential element in

> the formation of a generational consciousness is some common frame of reference that provides a sense of rupture with the past and that will later distinguish the members of a generation from those who follow them in time. This frame of reference is always derived from great historical events like wars, plagues, famines, and economic crises, because it is great historical events like these that supply the markers and signposts with which people impose order on their past and link their individual fates with those of the communities in which they live.[5]

Kriegel attributes the rise of generational consciousness to peculiarly modern causes. It is the result, she says, of the "shrinkage of time" that has been caused by the lengthening of the average life expectancy, by the rise of the bourgeoisie, by the regulation of modern life according to certain well-defined stages of socialization, and by the proliferation of ideologies.[6] Other theorists point to factors such as increased social mobility, the development of mass communication, the greater numbers attending universities, and the breakdown of regional identities.[7] Generational autobiographies also reveal that such consciousness is primarily a phenomenon of the middle classes, and in particular of young, white, middle-class males who feel alienated from or oppressed by their parent institutions. In reaction, either they identify themselves with another marginalized group, or, if the feeling of alienation is sufficiently widespread, they identify themselves as a collective on the basis of that which separates them from those who control those institutions—their age.

Both the generation that came of age during the First World War and the Vietnam War generation experienced disillusionment as America engaged in the fighting of an apparently meaningless war; both groups felt a tremendous gap between their own cultural, social, and sexual values and those of their parents; and both groups enjoyed an economic security that allowed them to devote time to questions of value and meaning. The earlier group came of age during the period of America's transition from a rural to an urban society, when enormous changes were occurring in basic institutions such as the family, the church, and the school. For the most part, it was middle-class youths who were first affected by these changes and who were forced, as a group, to adopt a political stance in order to defend themselves and their values against charges of immorality.[8] The later generation came of age during a time when professed political, economic, and social ideals were radically undermined by lived experience; middle-class young people, raised on the assumption that American prosperity was permanent, prepared for the future amid the upheavals of the civil rights movement, the growth of the "multiversity," anxiety about nuclear war, the assassination of three greatly admired political leaders, and an increasing scarcity of economic opportunities.

Perhaps the most important distinction between the two generations is that the earlier group tended to express its generational consciousness in sociological or historical studies that obscured the extent to which the writers saw their own generation as the vanguard of history and themselves as members of a self-conscious generational elite. The later group expressed its generational consciousness specifically in autobiographical forms that simultaneously make explicit the personal dimension of generational thought and the collective element in autobiographical discourse. This difference can be attributed in part to the literary fashions of each period. During the first decades of the twentieth century, scientism, together with the modes of discourse that it fostered, enjoyed a prestige that it lacked in the late 1960s and seventies. During the later period, fashion favored the mode of individual witness to protest the depersonalization of mass society and established historiographical postures of objectivity. However, the distinct forms in which generational consciousness has emerged during these two periods will prove useful here, because one can use the earlier theoretical expression of the phenomenon to illuminate the assumptions about the self, about society, and about history in the later, more personal autobiographies.

As a social and historical category, the idea of the "generation" had existed in the nineteenth century; but as a theory of social change, as a form of romantic historicism, and as a means of self-conception, the idea found particularly fertile ground among young people who came of age in the first three decades of the twentieth century.[9] The conviction that a new generation had arrived upon the world scene was shared during this period by writers and intellectuals all over America and Europe. In Europe, it was accompanied by a remarkable flowering of theories that sought to explain historical change, zeitgeists, and social disorder as the result of the rhythmic pattern of generation succeeding generation. Wohl observes that

> the nineteenth century tradition of the young generation as a vanguard of cultural and political change, the emergence of youth as a clearly defined and demographically significant social group, its organization, and a growing sense of collective historical destiny all converged to create a formidable wave of generational thinking during the first few decades of the twentieth century. This swell of generationalism reached its peak between 1928 and 1933, then slowly ebbed leaving its main traces in literature and memoirs. But during the years of flow the generational idea appeared on the pens and lips of men and women of all camps and countries. All these people were struck . . . by the discovery that one's generation was a destiny whose iron shackles permitted no escape. (207–8)

In this early period of popularity, generational theorists believed that the idea would displace other historiographical concepts such as the mass and the individual—and serve as an accurate instrument for measuring and predicting social change. In this belief, they were largely disappointed. However, as a form of romantic historicism and as a means of self-conception for young people (and potential autobiographers), the idea was very powerful. It satisfied important ideological needs (much as a religion or a political philosophy might do), and it helped answer vital questions about identity: Who am I in relation to history, to the present world, to others? And it provided some young people with an ethical and political program that apparently transcended personal ambition and quotidian life.

In spite of the popularity of the idea during the first decades of this century, America produced no systematic generational theorists comparable to those found in Europe. The idea of the generation, however, had been around at least since Emerson noted in his journal that "as a vast, solid phalanx the generation comes on, they have the same features and their pattern is new in the world. All wear the same expression. . . ."[10] In the second decade of the twentieth century, the idea found a powerful spokesman in a young intellectual, Randolph Bourne, who began his career as a reformer by taking up the banner of his generation against "the rigidity of tradition." Bourne believed that the consciousness of each generation is determined by the particular portion of history that it possesses in its youth. "A man's spiritual fabric," he wrote, "is woven by that time." Bourne conceived of history itself as a series of generations, each one of which could be characterized by a collective spirit and the issues and "radicalisms" that it calls forth. The sharing of a given historical moment by distinct age groups, therefore, meant that different generational spirits inevitably clashed over the issues of "their times." This, said Bourne, is the reason there is social conflict, generational strife, and historical change.[11]

Called by Van Wyck Brooks "the flying wedge of the younger generation," Bourne anticipated many of the central tenets of European generational theory. As early as 1911, he was writing about the differences that exist between the older generation, who "sit in the saddle," and the young, who are the only people that are "actually contemporaneous." According to Bourne, who was twenty-five when he wrote his essays on youth, "very few people get any really new experience after they are twenty-five, unless there is a real change of environment."[12] Bourne was a polemicist espousing the political and cultural idealism of his own generational group, but his activism, which appears so emphatically in his early work, is frequently implicit in the more "objective" social and historical generationalism of European intellectuals. The peculiar notion that Bourne espouses in the article just quoted, that men do not "have experience" after they are twenty-five, will appear again as the historicist element of European generational theory. Implicit in the idea is the belief that each generational era has an objective spirit independent of the lives of particular individuals, but organically tied to a collective sensibility. This sensibility (in Europe, it was called a Zeitgeist or "Spirit of the Age") gives rise, in an almost mystical fashion, to tasks whose accomplishment is the burden of the generation. Generationalists like Bourne, who stood behind a youth movement, believed that only young people lived in direct relation to this spirit and could therefore "have experience." Youth is the one period in life when a person can live fully in consonance with his or her time; to avoid doing so, as a tradition-minded or "conservative" (Bourne's term) youth might choose to do, would be to live in unreality, like old men who "live only in the experience of their youthful years."[13]

Views like Bourne's are frequently encountered in generational autobiographies, in statements to the effect that one did not *really* experience the twenties or the sixties unless one was present, in some fashion, at the major symbolic rites of the generational moment. In this form, generationalism is like all forms of historicism; it contains an animism by which collective history is perceived to embody a will independent of individuals. Only when one is living in consonance with this will—the "direction of history"—is one able to take part in "real time." Those who fail to obey the generational imperatives forfeit their times; according to writers like Bourne, they have not lived.

Generational historicism, in this form, may be interestingly compared to the phenomenon observed in those religious cultures in which concrete, historical time is transcended and members of the culture achieve "reality" by participation in periodic rituals that reenact the primordial events described in creation myths.[14] The object of such rituals is to overcome the perceived unreality of individual existence and linear time. In generational historicism, the unreality of individual experience and personal history is overcome as members of the generation participate in "real" generational experience. In religious cultures, of course, reality is defined in sacred and metahistorical terms. In generationalism, reality is defined in terms of collective identity and history; that is, the individual's private existence is given significance through participation in collective, "historical" acts.

In concrete terms, generational historicism such as Bourne's often requires that youth, in order to experience historical "reality," stand behind the various progressive programs and issues made popular by generational spokesmen who make up the political or cultural avant-garde. The belief that such participation allows the transcendence of individual existence and thrusts the participant into the vanguard of history underlies many generational autobiographies that emerged from the generation that came of age in the 1960s. There it creates an authorial stance that apparently suppresses the individual self at the same time that it exalts (no doubt to the author's great individual credit) the collective self to which the author belongs. Such a posture is particularly evident in those works that are written in the midst of the coming-of-age experience. In *The Wedding within the War* (1971), Michael Rossman articulates this feeling when he comments on the importance of his own presence at the 1960 demonstrations protesting the persecutive activities of the House Un-American Activities Committee: "It is one thing to say that we are living in the middle of history; everyone is aware of this. It is quite another thing to *know* this is so, to participate in actions that one knows are in the growing-bud of the historical tree."[15] In generational autobiographies that view the coming-of-age experience retrospectively, this sense of the preeminence of the generational moment is frequently heightened by nostalgia. Dotson Rader, writing his *Blood Dues* (1973) only four or five years after the peak years of his "historical moment," comments: "The New Left was populated by ghosts. And yet if you were young and feeling and decent in the sixties, I think it was the only place to be."[16] And David Harris, one of the more analytical of the sixties generational autobiographers, says retrospectively of his 1966 commune:

We believed we were laying the foundation of a New Age. . . . We were the
"real thing." As far as we were concerned, no one had ever done what we
were doing. . . . I, for one, thrived during that summer spent with six other
young men perched together on what felt like the front bumper of reality.[17]

As a form of historicism, generationalism infuses history with a
suprapersonal meaning, but it also seeks to predict the direction of history on the basis of the continual replacement of older generations by rising generations. Since the time period over which a generation can exert
its influence ranges from ten to thirty years (depending on which theorist
one consults), generationalists must predict historical trends on the basis
of a relatively limited temporal unit. And since theorists have no solid
basis for determining how a given generation will react to historical
events or to the legacy of their predecessors, their predictions are tentative at best. In addition, the predictions of generationalism have had to
compete with those of Marxism, which are based on much longer temporal units—the duration of the rise and fall of economic classes. In this
competition, at least as it has been reflected in autobiographies, generationalism has not fared well. When autobiographers enthusiastic about
the generational idea have attempted to express the relationship of the
generation to a larger pattern of history, they have often produced a mixture of generational and Marxist historicism.

The European generationalists were more systematic and thorough
than their American counterparts like Bourne (who died in 1918). In the
1920s, writers in France, Spain, and Germany constructed the first fully
developed generational theories: In France, François Mentre's *Les généra-
tions sociales* (1920); in Spain, José Ortega y Gasset's *El tema de nuestro
tiempo* (1923) and, later, *En torno a Galileo* (1933); and in Germany,
Wilhelm Pinder's *Kunstgeschichte nach Generationen* (1926), Edward
Wechssler's *Die Generationen als Jugendgemeinschaft* (1927) and *Das
Problem der Generationen in der Geistesgeschichte* (1929), Karl Mannheim's essay "Das Problem der Generationen" (1928), and Julius Peter-
son's *Die literarischen Generationen* (1930).

Ortega, one of the more influential of these writers in America, developed his generational idea as a solution to the problem of historical
evolution. Traditional historical studies, he said, generally fell into one of
two categories: those that explained historical change as the consequence
of individual action and personality, and those that attributed it to the actions of collectives. The generation, he proposed, could serve as a compromise between the two:

the changes in vital sensibility which are decisive in history, appear under the
form of the generation. A generation is not a handful of outstanding men,
nor simply a mass of men; it resembles a new integration of the social body,
with its select minority and its gross multitude, launched upon the orbit of

existence with a pre-established vital trajectory. The generation is a dynamic compromise between mass and individual, and is the most important conception in history, . . . the pivot responsible for the movement of historical evolution.[18]

Ortega's distinction between the generation's elite "minority" and its "gross multitude" was particularly appealing to autobiographers whose political commitments were leftist and collective, but who still desired to play a role in generational history as individuals. The task of the elite, Ortega thought, was to give voice to the generation's sensibility and destiny and, "by reason of their eminent intellectual qualities," to assume "responsibility for the conduct of our age" (21).

Once Ortega had established the generation's role in historical change, he set about noting the ways in which its collective identity is produced. The members of each generation, he said, "come into the world endowed with certain typical characteristics which lend them a common physiognomy, distinguishing them from the previous generation" (15). This physiognomy is determined, in part, by the generation's response to its two historical "tasks," one of which is simply "the reception, through the agency of the previous generation, of what has had life already, e.g., ideas, values, institutions," and "the other is the liberation of the creative genius inherent in the generation concerned" (16). The responses to these tasks allow for two different types of generational identity. Generations "which felt that there was a perfect similarity between their inheritance and their own private possessions" create "ages of accumulation" and possess no particularly strong generational identity. On the other hand, generations that "have felt a profound dissimilarity between the two factors" lead to "ages of elimination and dispute, generations in conflict." These generations, in general, tend to be highly self-conscious and creative (17).

Ortega further claimed that the number of years that make up a generation is determined by the length of the various stages of the average life cycle: there are five stages of life—childhood (1–15), youth (15–30), initiation (30–45), dominance (45–60), and old age (60–75)—and each of these stages represents a generation. Each of them is also marked by a "vital sensibility," which is the result, in part, of a sharing of historical experience in the way that is only possible among coevals. In historical theory, this gives rise to a concept of "the non-coetaneity of the contemporary." The historic present, according to this concept, is not experienced by all contemporaries in the same way. There coexist in each "today" at least three different "todays": that which belongs to youth, that which is ruled by the mature man, and that which is contemplated by the aged.[19]

One of the most important aspects of generational thought for understanding generational autobiography is the notion that within given generations, there coexist generational "units" or parties that vie with each other over the issues of the times. Ortega, meeting the objection that generations cannot constitute a coherent collective because subgroups within a given age group are often at odds with one another, claims that these generational opponents nonetheless share a "general sign of identity" and that beneath the "most violent opposition of 'pros' and 'antis' it is easy to perceive a real union of interests. Both parties consist of men of their own time; and great as their differences may be their mutual resemblances are still greater" (*Modern Theme*, 15). Mannheim likewise argues that "within any generation there can exist a number of differentiated, antagonistic generation-units. Together they constitute an 'actual' generation precisely because they are oriented toward each other, even though only in the sense of fighting one another."[20] Such antagonisms constitute one of the most salient characteristics binding the group of generational autobiographies written by those who came of age in the 1960s.

Although the usefulness of generationalism to autobiographers living during periods of intense generational ferment should be readily apparent, not every autobiographer who stresses generational identity is aware of the theories discussed in this chapter. Generational theory is a useful descriptive tool not because autobiographers read it in order to write their narratives, but because it clarifies ideas already present in the attitudes of the groups it purports to describe. Like theories of the individual Romantic self, theories of a generational self are of interest to students of autobiography because they describe ways in which large numbers of people constitute themselves and their worlds. The work of generational theorists simply articulates what many people in this century have felt—that the idea of the generation (and especially the "young generation") has helped to shape our conception of who we are.[21]

The ideas of Bourne, Ortega, and other generationalists who came of age in the first decades of the twentieth century serve two purposes here. They foreshadow several of the underlying assumptions of the generational autobiographies that are my central concern in this book. Most of these theorists, for example, see in generationalism a "scientific" explanation of social conflict and change, and most share a quasi-religious belief in zeitgeists that give rise to generational tasks and historical trends. Generational autobiographers tend to hold both of these assumptions, though often in forms that downplay the scientific claims or supplement them with other kinds of historicism, such as Marxism. Nonetheless, the generational theorists should also be given credit for accurately isolating generational phenomena that manifest themselves in the later autobiographical works. The theorists recognize the concept of the generation as a crucial aspect of collective identity, and they distinguish within the generational construct a notion of a mass and an elite, the latter of which articulates generational identity, interprets generational tasks, and provides leadership in carrying them out. Finally, they all attribute internal differences within generations to arguments over the shared "reality" that both provides their common bond and separates them from other age groups.

In this book, I will look at a number of autobiographies whose authors construct a self based primarily upon the concept of the generation described here. The second chapter will examine closely a work that may well serve as a prototype for the subgenre of generational autobiography, Malcolm Cowley's *Exile's Return: A Narrative of Ideas*. Published in 1934 and written by a member of the generation that came of age in the 1920s, this book stands apart from the large body of works written by other members of Cowley's age group. My examination of it will introduce many of the primary features of the form and establish some of the major themes that I will follow in later works. I will pay particular attention to the construction of generational plots as a means of controlling the discourse by which the recent past is given meaning and values are established, and I will also focus on the problem of authorial claims of representative status. Following the examination of this seminal work, Chapters 3, 4, and 5 will examine the intragenerational and intertextual dialogue among autobiographers who came of age between 1960 and 1975. These chapters take up generational narratives in roughly chronological fashion, showing how each responds to its predecessors and to other generational voices in the culture. The method reveals, among other things, that the large number of works written by members of this age group are of three types: annunciatory, reactive, and elegiac. Each of these types is based on the kind of narrative stance and voice the writer assumes as a participant in the generational dialogue. Finally, my epilogue will discuss the implications of the book's arguments and analyses for our understanding of the nature of autobiography.

My hope is that this book will help readers appreciate the role that the idea of the generation has played in the shaping of American autobiographical writing from Malcolm Cowley to Todd Gitlin. People have so long imagined that the "rugged individualist" or the "rags-to-riches" success story is the dominant version of selfhood available to American writers that they frequently fail to recognize other versions as having their own traditions and followings. This book will demonstrate that amidst the multiplicity of autobiographical selves that have emerged in this century, the generational self has figured significantly.

2

An American Generational Autobiography

Collective Identity in Malcolm Cowley's Exile's Return

In America, fervent generational self-consciousness first emerged among writers who were born between 1890 and 1905 and who came of age during and immediately after the Great War. Dubbed the "Lost Generation" by Gertrude Stein, they produced an extensive shelf of literature dealing with the experiences of young people as they entered history in the second and third decades of the new century. F. Scott Fitzgerald is perhaps the best known of these generational writers, not only for his short stories and novels, but also for his essays, later collected in *The Crack-Up*.[1] Also contributing to the construction of that generation's now legendary identity were its numerous memoirs and reminiscences, including Vincent Sheean's *Personal History* (1934), Joseph Freeman's *An American Testament: A Narrative of Rebels and Romantics* (1936), Robert McAlmon's *Being Geniuses Together* (1938), Samuel Putnam's *Paris Was Our Mistress* (1947), Morley Callaghan's *That Summer in Paris* (1963), Ernest Hemingway's *A Moveable Feast* (1964), Lillian Hellman's *An Unfinished Woman* (1970), and John Glassco's *Memoirs of Montparnasse* (1970).[2]

There is one book, however, that clearly stands apart from the others on this shelf: Malcolm Cowley's *Exile's Return: A Narrative of Ideas*. Published in 1934 just as enthusiasm for generationalist ideas was cresting, this book virtually invents a new autobiographical genre.[3] When Cowley's contemporaries embraced the generational theme, they most often did so in order to show how their coming-of-age years influenced the development of their *unique* selves; like most conventional autobiographies, each of them focuses on the author's individual story. In *Exile's Return*, by contrast, Cowley adopts a narrative strategy that audaciously breaks with autobiographical tradition and the dominant American myth of individualism: he privileges a "we" over an "I" in a work primarily concerned with American selfhood. One need not search far to discover his reasons for doing this. A few years before writing his book, Cowley experienced a conversion to Marxism. He was not unique

14

in that, of course, but it was precisely his sense of his typicality that most prepared Cowley for the writing of this book. Born in 1898, the son of a middle-class physician in Pittsburgh, Cowley had gone to a normal "big-city high school" (Kenneth Burke was a classmate and friend) and later attended Harvard as an undergraduate. After that, his life followed a path that was, he thought, more or less like that of many of his contemporaries. Sheean's and Freeman's books even trace conversions to Marxism that are very similar to Cowley's. But Cowley's conversion, in combination with an interest in generationalism and a familiarity with Emersonian culture criticism, predisposed him not only to place a critique of individualism at the heart of his generational plot, but also to incorporate it into his conception of the form.

In the prologue to his 1951 revision of *Exile's Return*, Cowley describes the book as "the story of the lost generation" written "while its adventures were still fresh in my mind." He then adds, "since I had shared in many of the adventures I planned to tell a little of my own story, but only as an illustration of what had happened to others."[4] This modest description of his method drastically understates the importance of Cowley's personal story in the generational plot, for the first edition is, in fact, built around Cowley's entire life history from childhood up to the time during which he wrote the book. He includes chapters on his childhood, his high school and college years, his "exile" in Europe, his extended devotion to what he calls the "religion of art," his disillusionment with bohemian life, and his political conversion. These are the major elements of his own story, and they are also the major elements of the collective story he means to tell. For the story of the generation here begins, as he began, in a pastoral, Edenic America; it continues, as he continued, in a period of exile and bohemianism; and it concludes, as his own story concluded (at least temporarily), with repatriation and salvation via the political and historical insights of Marxism. The generational narrative is, in short, simply his own narrative writ large.

Because of this peculiar blend of autobiography and collective history, classifying this book has always struck me as an intriguing problem. In the past, critics have disposed of the book's genre by calling it a "literary memoir" or a "literary history." The publishers of the Viking Compass edition of 1956 list it simply as "biography." These generic labels were made somewhat more accurate by Cowley's 1951 revisions, which deleted a good bit of his "own story" and all of the first edition's enthusiastic Marxism. Cowley, of course, was not worrying about generic classification when he made his revisions—political paranoia was probably a more pressing motivation—but the editorial surgery he performed on the text clearly made it easier for autobiographical theorists to ignore what Cowley had accomplished in his 1934 book.

That *Exile's Return* is autobiography seems undeniable: it recounts a significant portion of the writer's life story, and it is a first-person retrospective construction of the writer's identity. It differs from most American autobiographies, however, in that the authorial identity constructed in it is collective and the first-person pronoun it uses is plural. Even as collective autobiography, it is rather odd, as can be seen by comparing it with other types of historical narrative that might also be termed collective autobiography. National, religious, and ethnic histories, for example, are types of collective autobiography when they are authored by persons within the group itself. In most such narratives, however, the writer stands apart from the group when narrating the major events of its past, and the writer's own experiences may or may not coincide with those that make up the collective's significant past. Indeed, such writers usually efface themselves altogether, thereby suppressing that which constitutes the autobiographical project—the (re)construction of *the writer's* identity. Historiography of the sort Cowley wrote differs from these precisely because it ties collective identity directly to the individual experiences of the author.

Cowley's generational self in *Exile's Return* is, to use Hayden White's term, an "emplotted" one.[5] That is, its meaning is ultimately determined by the kind of story in which it is embedded. White borrows his own breakdown of historiographical plot types from Northrop Frye's categories of romance, comedy, tragedy, and satire, but he concedes that other taxonomies are possible. Although one might call Cowley's plot a romance, it is most usefully classed as a conversion narrative, for both the proselytic and the quasi-religious intent of that originally Christian form underlie Cowley's secular narrative.

While the conversion plot structures the book as a whole, Cowley also makes use of subplots that underlie portions of the overall narrative and enrich its cultural resonances. There are three primary subplots, each provided by a theory of history and each concerned with particular metaphors of collectivity. The first of these theories, generationalism, focuses on a familial metaphor and provides a plot of historical progress based on conflicts between children and parents or between different age groups. As we saw in the last chapter, the "physiognomy" of self-conscious generations is determined, according to this theory, by the nature of their response to the parental worldview. The second, Emersonianism, focuses on the national metaphor and provides a plot driven by the young generation's search for authenticity of self and culture. The character of American youth, in this plot, is determined by their response to an ongoing national cultural crisis. Finally, Marxism functions in two ways in the text: it provides a subplot that narrates the decline and displacement of the bourgeois class by the ascendant working class, and it also provides the "faith" to which the overarching conversion plot turns. By embedding all three of these subplots—the generationalist, the Emersonian, and the Marxist—in an overarching conversion story, Cowley constructs a narrative that resonates with cultural and collective histories far beyond the experience of his own generation. The project involved a radical rethinking of generic boundaries and the elements of conventional autobiography. The resulting text, as we will see in the following chapters, established the profile of a new subgenre of life writing.

Cowley and Earlier Generational Thought

Although Cowley doesn't refer to specific generational theorists in *Exile's Return*, the ideas that they espoused were present everywhere in the culture of the period. As Cowley writes in the 1934 prologue:

> Everywhere after the War people were fumbling for a word to express their feeling that youth had a different outlook. The word wouldn't be found for many years; but long before Gertrude Stein made her famous remark, the young men to whom she was referring already had undergone the similar experiences and developed the similar attitude that made it possible to describe them as a literary generation. (7)

There is, however, little doubt that he was familiar with the work of Randolph Bourne and at least some of the European generationalists. Until the war, Bourne had been a well-known contributing editor to the *New Republic*, the journal for which Cowley was working while he was writing *Exile's Return*, and Cowley does devote some attention in his book to the slightly older Greenwich Village group to which Bourne belonged (76–84). Of the European writers mentioned in the previous chapter, the only one Cowley ever directly acknowledged was José Ortega y Gasset, but during the 1920s, when European generational theory was being formulated, Cowley was particularly attuned to transatlantic influences. In a later work, —*And I Worked at the Writer's Trade*, Cowley devotes an entire chapter to a reconsideration of the generational idea that informed *Exile's Return* and gives a major share of his attention to Ortega's theory.[6] One can, in fact, trace a good many of Cowley's generationalist assumptions in *Exile's Return* to Ortega's *El tema de nuestro tiempo*, which was published in America as *The Modern Theme* by the same company that one year later published Cowley's book. In his prologue, for example, Cowley constructs the general features of the "Lost Generation" and the place it occupied in the history of the twenties. Following Ortega, who asserted that every generation establishes its identity by either rejecting or accepting the legacy of its predecessors, Cowley asserts that his "generation belonged to a period of confused transition from values already fixed to values that had to be created. . . . They were seceding from the old, and yet could adhere to nothing new; they groped their way toward another scheme of life, as yet undefined" (11). He also echoes Ortega's insistence that internecine antagonisms are characteristic of generational groups. His literary generation, he says, is

> not a group or a school: as a matter of fact they include several loosely
> defined groups that are not always friendly with one another, and many in-
> dividuals who differ with every group among their contemporaries. Still,
> whatever their internal disagreements, they differ even more with writers
> older or younger than themselves, who have a different past behind them.
> (9–10)

Likewise, Cowley borrows from Ortega (and from Bourne) an idea that is the hallmark of his work on the writers who came of age during the 1920s: the idea that a generation's "common physiognomy" (Ortega) or "spiritual fabric" (Bourne) is determined by the particular slice of history it experiences in its youth. Cowley expresses the same idea when he explains the factors that set his generation apart from its predecessors: "They came to maturity during a period of violent change, when the influence of time seemed temporarily more important than that of class or locality" (7). Like many of his peers, Cowley responded ardently to generational ideas, and he was eager to catalogue those events and social changes that separated his generation from their parents. Earlier Americans, he says, had identified themselves regionally or by class, but those who came of age between 1915 and 1925 were marked by history itself. The Great War, increased social mobility, urbanization, and the standardization of culture, education, and language affected his peers with incredible rapidity and finality, snatching them forever out of the nineteenth-century world that remained their parents' spiritual home.

Cowley was also attracted to Ortega's and Bourne's notions of a generational elite, but he avoided representing his "elite" as particularly gifted leaders. Bourne, as we have seen, believed that the generational vanguard comprises those youths who live fully in consonance with the spirit of their times. These young politicos interpret the "tasks" assigned to each generation by the spirit of the age. Ortega similarly claimed that the generation is made up of a mass and an elite, the latter of whom are responsible for the "conduct" of the age. Cowley's elite, by contrast, is artistic, consisting of people whose personalities and work reflect the mood and style of their generation. They are, he writes, "more sensitive and barometric than members of other professions" (13); as "instruments" sensitive to—though often unconscious of—cultural and historical pressures, these generational representatives are more likely to behave in extreme ways than the mass of their contemporaries. Indeed, the extremity of their actions is often, according to Cowley, the best indicator of the underlying condition of an outwardly prosperous and happy nation.

It is, in fact, this division of the generation into an elite and a mass that allows Cowley to write in the collective voice even though his book's plot derives largely from his own experiences. By identifying with a "barometric" elite, he grants himself the right to employ the plural first-person pronoun. His private and public experiences stand in for collective experience. What happens to "me" represents what happens to "us."

The differences between Cowley's and Ortega's views of the elite arise, in part, from the temporal perspective from which each writer views his generational experience. Since Ortega was first formulating his theory while actively seeking political power (*El tema de nuestro tiempo* was first published in 1923), it is not surprising that he endows his elite with special historical and political insight into the "tasks" of the age. For Ortega, generationalism is a causal theory of identity *and* of social change; the generation represents a new collective identity, and the characteristics of that new identity make social change inevitable The agents of the change, logically, are those young intellectuals who most clearly understand generational tasks. Cowley's *Exile's Return*, in contrast, is largely retrospective. Since the "themes" that he and his friends had embraced during the 1920s had already proven less than vital by the time Cowley sat down to write about them, he was in no position to take the politics of youth as seriously as Ortega. "When reduced to terms of action," he writes in his epilogue, "the ideas that dominated the literary world of the 1920's . . . [led to] unsatisfactory results" (294). For Cowley, therefore, generationalism is almost exclusively a theory of identity.

While Cowley's generationalism is hardly as political as Ortega's, *Exile's Return* is no less concerned with political questions. The first edition of the book, after all, is devoted to turning the political failure of his generation's youthful period into the basis of their political triumph as fully fledged adults. That triumph, however, is made possible not by generationalism, but by another theory of social evolution, Marxism. According to this theory, the agents of social progress are produced by class experiences rather than by generational experiences. As bourgeois artists, Cowley and his friends are excluded by Marxism from membership in the proletarian vanguard, a circumstance that forces him to invent new strategies by which to secure prestige for his group. One of those strategies is precisely to construct his artist friends as "barometers," for this role relieves them of the burden of having to possess political acumen while it retains for them some small degree of distance from a despised bourgeois culture. Another strategy, outlined with naive clarity in the book's epilogue, is simply to call upon his friends to abandon their natural affiliation with the bourgeoisie to align themselves with the new, rising class of "factory workers and poor farmers and people now looking for jobs" (301), and to offer their skills as writers to "the oppressed classes all over the world" (302).

For Ortega, the shift from the vital sensibility of one generation to another causes the most important changes in history. Cowley's generationalism stops well short of this. For him, generationalism allows one to depict the superficial aspects of one's collective identity. It enables him to describe the "look" of this identity—how it acts, what it talks about, what mannerisms it adopts, what issues it obsesses about. The events that follow the Wall Street crash of 1929, however, demonstrate to Cowley that forces other than generational shifts are the real controlling factors in historical change. The crash reveals to him that the "influence of time" upon the "half-unconscious" attitudes of his generation was only "temporarily more important" (7) than the influence of those other, more deeply rooted, forces. Ultimately, this conviction leads Cowley to look for the sources of historical change in interpretations of the past that go beyond the immediate experience of the generation. He finds these interpretations in Emersonianism and Marxism. With the narrative tools provided by these two traditions, he constructs a historical context within which his collective conversion narrative makes sense.

Generational Identity and the Emersonian Tradition

In *Exile's Return*, Cowley's use of his personal narrative to construct generational identity is buttressed not only by generational theory and its belief that the central narratives of history are constructed around intergenerational conflicts, but also by the constructions of national identity suggested by Emersonian culture criticism. By the 1930s, that criticism had developed a rich tradition that included not only Emerson's work, but also the work of Walt Whitman, Henry David Thoreau, Horatio Greenough, Thorstein Veblen, Louis Sullivan, Van Wyck Brooks, Waldo Frank, and Randolph Bourne, to mention just a few. The America of this criticism suffered from a split consciousness, divided pathologically between the rhetoric of an artificial idealism and the reality of pragmatic materialism, between its highbrow and lowbrow cultures. America, according to the Emersonians, was driven by the greed of its business class, but it paid lip service to high culture by purchasing it from abroad, placing it in museums, and turning it over to the supervision of women. In short, America was still essentially a cultural colony of Europe, which produced the art that American businessmen, through the agency of their wives, consumed or put on display in their homes.

The plot that Cowley borrowed from this tradition is a simple one. In it, the youth of America, undernourished and unsupported by their own culture, develop ridiculous affectations, or go into exile, or fall into despair. Emerson himself offered the first suggestion of this plot in his famous speech "The American Scholar" (1837). "Young men of the fairest promise," he declared to the Phi Beta Kappa Society at Harvard,

> who begin life upon our shores, inflated by the mountain winds, shined upon by all the stars of God, find the earth below not in unison with these, but are

hindered from action by the disgust which the principles on which business is managed inspire, and turn drudges, or die of disgust, some of them suicides.[7]

In the Emersonian plot, American youth seeking a meaningful outlet for their creative and spiritual energies must either adopt a life of continual conflict with official, bourgeois America or embrace cultural exile. Most writers—in fact, just about every canonical writer in the nineteenth century—took this version of American realities seriously enough to opt for some form of exile. To leave America meant that one could make use of the more nurturing European environment, but it also meant cutting oneself off from one's homeland and childhood, the wellsprings of artistic inspiration. To many artists, however, such exile was preferable to living in America. In the long run, however, it mattered little whether they tried to accommodate themselves, fought back as voices of cultural opposition, or left to live and work elsewhere; the prognosis for their self-realization and productivity was a bleak one.

If one were looking for a specific literary antecedent to the Emersonian plot embedded in *Exile's Return*, a likely candidate might well be Randolph Bourne's thinly disguised autobiographical essay "History of a Literary Radical."[8] This short work characterizes Bourne's generation and the condition of American culture by presenting the life story of a representative American, the "biography" of "my friend Miro." Although the narrative represents a slightly older group than Cowley's "cohort of the damned," the misguided quest for culture that Miro undertakes and the pattern of exile and repatriation that his life follows are very similar to the generational plot narrated in Cowley's autobiography. However, Bourne's construction of a generational portrait in an individualized, third-person narrative is rejected by Cowley, who simply embraces the first-person "we" and presents his collective voice directly.

Bourne's generational plot was implicit, however, in the work of most Emersonians of the period, and one can see evidence of their influence on Cowley's thinking throughout his book. Its first section, "Mansions in the Air," for example, narrates the generation's high school and university experiences, which Cowley sums up as a "long process of deracination" that forces him and his peers into their first spiritual exile. It is a story clearly informed by the Emersonian notion that an American education promulgates cultural values that are woefully unconnected to American life. In both high school and the university, Cowley writes, he was taught that all "art and ideas" were

products manufactured under a European patent; all we could furnish toward them was raw talent, destined usually to be wasted. Everywhere, in every department of cultural life, Europe offered the models to imitate—in painting, composing, philosophy, folk music, folk drinking, the drama, sex, politics, national consciousness—indeed this country was not even a nation; it had no traditions except the fatal tradition of the pioneer. (105)

What he didn't learn in school, he says, was "the idea that culture was the outgrowth of a situation":

> that an artisan knowing his tools and having the feel of his materials might be a cultured man; that a farmer among his animals and his fields, stopping his plow at the corner to meditate over death and life and the next year's crop, might have culture without even reading a newspaper. Essentially, we were taught to regard culture as something assumed like a suit of English clothes or an Oxford accent, a uniform that made us citizens of a privileged world. (35)

One can find these same complaints in any number of Emersonian writers, including Emerson himself, who implored his "American Scholar" to turn away from "the courtly muses of Europe" and to look to the near-at-hand—"the shop, the plough, and the ledger"—for his creative inspiration.[9] Thoreau voices the complaint again in *Walden* (1854) when he inveighs against the disembodied studies of Harvard College students. Walt Whitman repeats it in *Democratic Vistas* (1871), protesting that the "sons and daughters of the New World, ignorant of its genius, [are] not yet inaugurating the native, the universal, and the near, still importing the distant, the partial, and the dead."[10] Thorstein Veblen's 1899 essay "The Higher Education" argues with ironic loquacity that the university education of an American "gentleman of leisure" is a badge of economic status rather than anything of real use. Such students, he writes, are

> currently expected to spend a certain number of years in acquiring this substantially useless information [classics and the "dead" languages], and its absence creates a presumption of hasty and precarious learning, as well as a vulgar practicality that is equally obnoxious to the conventional standards of sound scholarship and intellectual force.[11]

In the twentieth century, Bourne and his friend Van Wyck Brooks continued the Emersonian attack on American education. In his *America's Coming-of-Age* (1915), Brooks asks his readers to consider the education of the typical college student:

> Suddenly confronted during four years with just this remote influence of ideals, out of which the intellectual structure has evaporated and which never possessed a social structure, will he not find them too vague, too intangible, too unprepared-for to be incorporated into his nature? Certainly ideals of this kind, in this way presented, in this way prepared for, cannot enrich life, because they are wanting in all the elements of personal contact.[12]

Likewise, Bourne's biography of an American "literary radical" describes the fatuity of the education provided by America's "culture ministers":

No doubt ever entered [Miro's] head that four years of Latin and three years of Greek, an hour a day, were the important preparation that he needed for his future as an American citizen. No doubt ever hurt him that the world into which he would pass would be a world where, as his teacher said, Latin and Greek were a solace to the aged, a quickener of taste, a refreshment after manual labor, and a clue to the general knowledge of all human things.[13]

Cowley's borrowing from this critical tradition serves his generational autobiography in at least one important way: it allows him to infuse Gertrude Stein's characterization of his generation with something more than the ennui and devil-may-care morality that it conventionally carried.[14] They are a "lost" generation in a very Emersonian sense—because they have been "schooled away" from an organic connection with America. By thus constructing a story in which generational and Emersonian issues overlap, Cowley is able to embed his generational plot in an ongoing story about national identity.

The Emersonians did, of course, have a reform program. They called for the creation of an organic, indigenous culture within America, and they pointed to the work of artists and writers who were actually engaged in such a project. The basis of this culture, according to Emerson himself, was to be a radical, even mystical, individualism. The only source of true culture, he argued, was a virulent self-reliance, a turning of the individual (and the culture) inward toward the solid nucleus of the self. As we will see, both aspects of this program were to play a role in the later stages of Cowley's generational plot. By that time, however, the call for an organic culture would be transformed and subsumed by Cowley's turn to Marxism, and the individualism upon which that culture was to be based would suffer a serious reversal of fortunes. Instead of serving as a talisman against bourgeois philistinism, individualism would be exposed as the mortal sin underlying that mode of culture.

Neither constructive nor critical Emersonianism, however, formed a part of the Lost Generation's consciousness as they were growing up, partly because it played no part in the high school or university humanities curriculum under which Cowley and his peers were educated. As a result, Cowley's peers are doomed, in his narrative, to repeat the generational plot outlined in Emerson's Harvard address three quarters of a century earlier. Like their nineteenth-century predecessors, they must live out the alienation, frustration, and despair that Emerson predicted as the inevitable consequences of American cultural conditions. Some of Cowley's peers will even "turn drudges, or die of disgust"; some, like Hart Crane and Harry Crosby, will be "suicides." In response to their alienation, Cowley's generation, as everyone knows, initially rejected the America dominated by philistinism, puritanism, and pioneerism, and took themselves off to Europe to devote themselves to the pursuit of an increasingly individualistic notion of "pure art." Nor were these exiles, in Cowley's narrative, composed merely of artists and writers, though these groups were certainly the most visible. The exiled included a much larger section of society—"architects, doctors, painters, bond salesmen, professors and their wives, all the more studious and impressionable section of middle-class youth" (215).

Eventually, however, the idea that they could save themselves through exile would prove delusory. They would eventually return to America, repatriating themselves and, in the process, reconstructing their ideas about who they were and what their role in society should be. This story of repatriation is in part the story of their movement toward the rediscovery of Emersonianism and cultural nationalism, but only partly. It would require the mediation of another theory of culture to make it happen.

Generational Identity and Marxism

Cowley may have made use of the Emersonian tradition when he constructed his collective identity in *Exile's Return*, but his Emersonianism, like his generationalism, was only partially embraced. In 1934, Cowley could see in neither of these theories a means of saving his generation (or America) from the downward spiral of cultural decadence and economic exploitation that had culminated in the stock market crash of 1929 and the Great Depression that immediately followed. For this task, Cowley blended his Emersonian narrative with a Marxist one. In many respects, the two traditions mixed well. The Emersonian romanticization of the common laborer complemented the Marxist glorification of the proletariat; the Emersonian struggle against an "inorganic" culture stood shoulder to shoulder with the Marxist effort to expose capitalism's alienation of the worker from the products of his labor. The near interchangeability of Emersonian and Marxist language is apparent in all of these pairings, but the text clearly privileges the latter. In the midst of Cowley's Emersonian discussion of generational deracination, for example, he concludes that "our whole training was involuntarily directed . . . toward making us homeless citizens, not so much of the world as of international capitalism" (29).

In Cowley's recreation of the generational self, both traditions—the Marxist and the Emersonian—are used not only to explain the American past, but also to show how the generation's destiny and identity would unfold in the future. Emersonianism, as I have shown, espoused the development of a national consciousness that would recognize the "artisan knowing his tools and having the feel of his materials" as an example of true culture. Like Emersonians, the American Marxists found their examples of virtue and "real" culture in the ordinary man, the worker, the farmer in the field. In spite of its vulgarized appropriation by American entrepreneurial boosterism, true Emersonianism was critical of the materialistic, aggressive American businessman whose ideals were conquest and "millionairism." Marxism similarly criticized the social inequities resulting from the laissez-faire individualism of capitalism. Marxism may have been more concerned than Emersonianism with economic questions, and Marxism's European proponents may have been more convinced of the necessity of violent revolution to accomplish their aims, but Cowley and his fellow-traveling comrades in the League of Professional Groups (founded in 1932 to support the Communist Party ticket) clearly hoped that communism would establish a new culture based upon principles that were, in large part, Emersonian.[15] When Cowley finally makes his political stance clear in the book's epilogue, a perceptive reader can see that American philistinism, the bogeyman of Emersonianism, has become identified in Cowley's hybrid ideology with Bourgeois-Capitalist Culture, the bogeyman of Marxism; and the Organic Culture promoted by the Emersonians has somehow metamorphosed into the ascendant Proletarian Culture.

This is not to say that Cowley's conflation of Marxism and Emersonianism is entirely balanced. *Exile's Return* clearly sees Marxism as the stronger of the two theories vying for the generation's allegiance. Emersonianism had had its chance to revitalize America, and though it was largely right in its critique of mainstream culture, it would take the "scientific" formulas of Marxism to work the final transformation. As Cowley's chronicle argues, neither Emersonianism nor Marxism had much currency among his generation in the 1920s, but it was the economic collapse of 1929, more than Emersonian disgust, that brought the exiles home from Europe at the end of the decade. Intellectuals looking for an explanation of the situation turned to Marx rather than to the followers of the Boston transcendentalist. Still, the Emersonian struggle was in some ways revitalized by the social climate that followed in the wake of the economic collapse and the subsequent movement of intellectuals toward the left, for that movement entailed just what Emerson had called for, a closer look at the common and the near-at-hand.

At the same time, the Emersonian struggle that pitted the American writer against mainstream society began to look very different from the point of view of the revitalized left. At least in these early years, leftists were more aggressive, more certain of their own potential for success, less entrenched in a defensive posture than their Emersonian forebears. In the Emersonian tradition, the work of making the culture "organic" was dependent upon the efforts of a few crankish writers—men in the mold of Henry David Thoreau and Thorstein Veblen—to convince the public that an indigenous American culture was preferable to a borrowed European one. It was a forlorn task, and the arduous efforts to sustain faith in its eventual success led to that peculiar combination of croaking and crowing (or doomsaying and boosterism) so characteristic of the rhetoric of books like Whitman's *Democratic Vistas* and Brooks's *America's Coming-of-Age*.[16] Besides, Emersonians had a philosophical investment in the idea that the genius always lives in individualistic opposition to society; the actual success of their cultural program would have occasioned an embarrassing obviation of the very basis of their conception of the American writer. What the Marxist vision called for, by contrast, was an alliance between writers and society, or at least between writers and the working classes. Instead of sitting perennially on the outside, suffering from what Cowley characterizes as the "spectatorial attitude" (47), they would be invited to the dance, asked to participate in the construction of the new world.

Central to the Emersonian failure, from the Marxist point of view, was its radical individualism. It is central as well to the plot of Cowley's book, for the last seven of its eight sections trace the consequences of his generation's adherence to a philosophy of individualism, both in art and in life. Cowley's plot suggests, as I have shown, that the Lost Generation was "lost" in an Emersonian sense, because they were schooled away from their connection to America. But from his Marxist point of view, they were also lost precisely because of their Emersonianism, because Emerson's radical individualism, once stripped of its doctrine of commonality, was ultimately a philosophy of despair and isolation. The generational plot that takes Cowley's peers from the American heartland to Paris, Pamplona, Berlin, and Greenwich Village, or from realism to modernism, symbolism, dadaism, vorticism, and superrealism, is a plot that relentlessly pursues the generation's demand for free expression and the working out of individual personality. It is a plot of generational catastrophe, disintegration, decline.

In the thirties, however, Marxists like Cowley thought that things would change radically. They confidently believed that they could undo the Emersonian opposition of writer and public by reconstructing the worker as the voice of culture. Their optimism was also bolstered by the apparent success of a humanistic socialism in the Soviet Union, which swelled the ranks of American Marxists, not so much with new members for the Communist Party (though this was the period of the Party's greatest numerical strength), but with significant numbers of sympathizers. Besides, hadn't their historicist predictions already been largely confirmed by the stock market crash? Buoyed by these affirmations of their ideas, American Marxists confidently predicted an imminent victory for the proletarian class and its culture in America. The concurrence of the vogue of Marxism and these first historical signs of an apparent communist future gave writers like Cowley, who were writing in the "trough of the depression," an exhilarating optimism. Writing about the period during which he composed *Exile's Return*, Cowley later reminisced,

The casting out of old identities; communion with the workers; life in a future world that the workers would build in America as they were building it in Russia: all those religious elements were present in the dream of those years. It made everything else seem unimportant, including one's pride, one's comfort, one's personal success or failure, and one's private relations.[17]

What the Emersonians had failed to accomplish in one hundred years the Marxists and their worker allies would bring about in short order.

This sense that his generation was witness to the passing of a torch also infuses Cowley's construction of the idea of the Lost Generation. *Exile's Return* depicts the 1920s as the last years of capitalist culture. The bourgeois generation that came of age in those years was, according to Marxist prophecy, the last generation of an economic era that had lasted at least two hundred years. The social and moral degeneracy that characterized his generation's behavior in the 1920s, therefore, is partly intended to represent the final death throes of the bourgeois class. This Marxist vision of an epochal shift is reduced, of course, to a mere change of social mood in Cowley's 1951 revised edition, but readers of the first edition may also have difficulty appreciating its significance, given *our* historical perspective. Fully understanding *Exile's Return* depends upon recognizing the tremendous crack in history that Cowley perceived as having taken place between 1929 and 1931. This was the historical tremor during which, as Cowley then believed, capitalism, modernism, and individualism died. As he says in his prologue, "the story of the Lost Generation and its return from exile is something else besides: it is partly the story of a whole social class, how it became aware of itself and how it went marching toward the end of an era" (13).

In Cowley's narrative, however, being a member of the Lost Generation meant not only belonging to the last generation of the old bourgeois, individualist culture, but also, if one could but believe, belonging to the "found" generation, the first to see, and help to construct, the new proletarian age. His generation would be, in this vision, the first to realize the aspirations of the older Emersonian writers. During their years of exile, they had ignored the spirit of Emerson and had abandoned the task assigned to them by History. In exile, however, they learned to see themselves and America in a new light. Finally, the crash of 1929 forced them to return and "ally themselves with society." This return marked the end of their exile and the beginning of the recovery of what Cowley, in 1934, considered to be the real America.

The Structure of Generational Conversion

Generationalism, Emersonianism, and Marxism gave Cowley the historical and cultural paradigms with which to construct his generational plot and the identity that emerges from it, but they did not provide the over-all narrative structure of *Exile's Return*. There is some irony in this, since Cowley repeatedly lauded Marxism for its ability to offer the writer "a way to get hold both of distant events and those near at hand, and a solid framework on which to arrange them" (*Exile's Return*, 302). An explanation of the structure of his own book, however, is to be found not so much in Marxism as in Cowley's manner of embracing it, for he emplots his turn to Marxism as a conversion, and it is that older Christian plot, rather than Marxist dogma, that implicitly informs the book's structure, as well as its characterization techniques and tone. Cowley himself surely recognized this when he later acknowledged in *The Dream of the Golden Mountains* that his Marxism was, from the beginning, more religious than political in nature. Granted, his primary intention in making such an acknowledgment was not to describe the earlier book's structure, but to distance himself from a dogmatic Marxism that was, by the mid-1940s, threatening to ruin his career.[18] Still, the conversion plot is un-mistakably at the very center of the 1934 book, not because Cowley wants his readers to read his text as Christian but because he wants to borrow the familiar and powerfully affective religious structure to rein-force the impact of the Marxist narrative.

The first-person conversion plot typically narrates the self's passage through a series of stages on its way to redemption. Those stages include a descent into sin, an eventual dark night of the soul during which the self is convicted of its sinfulness, an infusion of redemptive grace and knowl-edge, repentance, and a final rebirth of a new self. I have expressed this plot in conventional Christian phrases (in Western literature, the form has most often been associated with Christianity), but in practice it mat-ters not whether the conversion is to Christianity, Marxism, militant fem-inism, or some other totalizing worldview. The Marxist and feminist will employ, of course, different terms from those used by Christians. "Sin-fulness" might be translated by the Marxist as "bourgeois decadence" and by the feminist as "patriarchy," and so forth. But if the convert is a true believer, the plot almost always follows the basic progression out-lined above.

The first-person conversion plot not only provides a series of stages through which the self progresses, it also provides a specific narrative stance with regard to these stages. Such a narrative is almost always re-lated by a converted self that excoriates the unconverted self as it degen-erates toward the converting illumination. The conversion plot requires that the stage during which the self descends into sin and the dark night of the soul be depicted as determined or brought about by superhuman forces, divine or historical, of which the unregenerate self is unaware. And finally, it requires that the narrating, converted self be portrayed as completely distinct from the earlier, unregenerate self. The unregenerate self does not *develop* into the regenerate self; the change is cataclysmic and radical. The old self is "shed"; it "dies," and the new self's emergence is conceived of as a "rebirth."

In Cowley's text, the conversion narrative is adumbrated by the inclusion of even older Christian plot patterns. One pattern that informs his narrative of generational development, for example, echoes typologically the Christian myth of expulsion from Eden and adds yet another layer of allusion to Cowley's use of the phrase "the Lost Generation." Thus, Cowley begins his narrative with a chapter entitled "Blue Juniata," which describes the generation's childhood. They grow up in various parts of the country, he writes, but whether it is the Schoharie Valley, the Appalachian Mountains, the Cumberland, middle Tennessee, northern Michigan, or the Wisconsin farmland, the locale is an Edenic one, a place "where they had once been part of the landscape and the life, part of a spectacle at which nobody looked on" (52). In their late teens, however, they are expelled from this site of childhood happiness, as we have seen, by the false knowledge proffered by American education and the irreversible forces of late capitalism. Thus begins the generation's long and unconscious decline into the 1920s, with its giddy flight to Europe and its social, artistic, and sexual excesses. In this period, Cowley and his writer friends adopt the "religion of art" and individual expression as a way of life. For Cowley, the "religion of art" is synonymous with modernism, both as a literary practice and as a way of viewing the world. It has a number of values or tendencies, which Cowley efficiently outlines as including the tendency toward aesthetic obscurity, the ideal of absolute art and pure poetry, individualism, relativism, disdain for the public, amoralism (but "animated by moral fervor"), adventurousness, and liberty (157–62). Above all else, the devotee of the religion of art must keep "moving on"; he must remain always on the cutting edge of aesthetic and moral experimentation. The religion also has "saints" such as Eliot, Joyce, and Proust, and "martyrs" such as Harry Crosby and Hart Crane, and every artist who subscribes to the principles of art for art's sake is a priest.

In Cowley's 1934 text, this rehearsal of the generation's journey through the 1920s is constructed with a clarity available only to the eye of the convert. It is a journey of decline. Once exiled, Cowley's generation becomes, as he wrote later, the "legion of the lost ones . . . the cohort of the damned."[19] His new Marxist faith allows him to see that to which he was once blind, that the religion of art, culminating in dadaism, is a false religion, wholly dependent upon the diseased individualism of the American political and economic system:

The system that made these dead things possible, that produced the War and the after-War, that created the mood by which the religion of art was nourished, that uprooted artists and workers from their homes and financed the

> middle-class migration to Europe—the capitalist system itself was sick, was
> convulsively dying. (287–88)

This focus on the younger self's seduction by a corrupt capitalist system
represents the main line of ideological attack in Cowley's collective autobiography, and the turning point of the downward-spiraling generational plot occurs, logically, in the conversion brought about by the 1929
stock market crash, which reveals that the "religion of art had failed
when it tried to become an ideology and an ethics: as a way of life it was
completely bankrupt" (286). The crash, according to Cowley, effectively
crippled that art and the economic system that produced it. It provided
the opportunity, also, for the members of the Lost Generation to find salvation in a new faith. They had come of age confident that salvation was
to be sought only in the gratification of individual desire. The stock market crash, like a blinding light from Moscow, reeducated them and compelled them "to recognize the importance to themselves of all the things
they had believed to be futile" (240–41).

In conversion narratives, the lives and experiences of acquaintances
and friends must be reconstructed as illustrations of various points of
doctrine in the writer's new faith. In *Exile's Return*, examples of this appear in almost every chapter. Cowley's dadaist friends exemplify, in both
their art and way of life, the logical outcome of a capitalist, individualist
ethic: "Dada, in art and life, was the extreme of individualism. It denied
that there was any psychic basis common to all humanity. There was no
emotion shared by all men, no law to which all were subject" (158). And
Cowley himself, in the sections entitled "Case Record" and "Significant
Gesture," is offered up as a kind of comic illustration of how these dadaist
attitudes might express themselves in the punching of a cafe proprietor.

In Cowley's plot, each stage of the conversion narrative is embodied
in particular representative figures. Throughout most of the text, as I
have already claimed, Cowley himself is the primary representative
figure. But the most dramatic instance of such representation is Cowley's
account in two sections of the book's final chapter (242–88) of Harry
Crosby, a minor poet whose life epitomizes the generational trajectory
Cowley traces throughout the narrative, and whose suicide becomes the
symbol of the generation's dark night and death of the soul. In Cowley's
words, Crosby's life had a "quality that gave it logic and made it resemble a clear syllogism" (265). Crosby's "brief and not particularly distinguished literary life of seven years," writes Cowley,

> included practically all of the themes I have been trying to develop—the sep-
> aration from home, the effects of service in the ambulance corps, the exile in
> France, then other themes, bohemianism, the religion of art, the escape from
> society, the effort to defend one's individuality even at the cost of sterility and
> madness, then the final period of demoralization when the whole philosoph-

ical structure crumbled from within, just at the moment when bourgeois society was beginning to crumble after its greatest outpouring of luxuries, its
longest debauch—all this is suggested in Harry Crosby's life. (243)

Crosby's suicide is portrayed, then, as a symbol of "the decay from within
and the suicide of a whole order with which he had been identified"
(284). Perhaps more important for the conversion plot, Crosby serves as
the sacrificial goat whose death is required by the narrative form before
the final Marxist rebirth of the generation can take place. Only through
such a death of its unregenerate self is the generation able to emerge in the
thirties with a new identity, regenerated and purified.

The way in which Crosby stands in for Cowley at this point exem-
plifies the way in which identity works generally in the narrative. What
interests Cowley in his reconstruction of collective identity is not individuality, but typicality, so that one character can easily substitute for another or for the entire generation. The narrated pattern of Crosby's life is
almost identical to Cowley's up to 1929. At this crucial turning point in
the narrative, just when the conversion plot demands a sacrificial offering, Cowley steps aside as generational representative and Crosby takes
his place.[20] Cowley later confessed (in the 1951 revision) that his account
of Crosby's suicide allowed him unconsciously to avoid dealing with the
suicide of another "HC," Hart Crane, a man to whom Cowley was very
closely attached.[21] But it seems much more likely that if an "unconscious" substitution occurred, it was one that was much closer to home.
Besides the "themes" just quoted, Crosby and Cowley also had in common the same birth year, 1898; and surely the alliteration and assonance
of their names would not have been lost on the poetically inclined Cowley. We will see in the next few chapters that authorial proxies, particularly proxies whose sacrificial deaths facilitate generational rejuvenation,
are a common feature of this subgenre of autobiography.

By means of the spiritual death symbolized in the Crosby suicide,
Cowley's generation would be the first, in his view, to experience a rebirth into the proletarian future. The primary exemplar of this collective
conversion, however, is Cowley himself, who, in the book's "Epilogue:
Yesterday and Tomorrow," renounces his identity as a devotee of the religion of art to become a proselyte for tendentious literature and proletarian culture. After the Crosby substitution, the epilogue regrounds the
generational narrative in Cowley's own experience and delivers the message of his conversion to his readers. "Before ending this book," he says,
"I ought to explain, at least in bare outline, the beliefs that underlie or
emerge from my own story" (294). What follows is, indeed, an outline of
Cowley's new program for an ideologically sound art. In a series of questions and answers, Cowley deals with the value and function of propa-
gandistic art, the role of the artist in the class struggle, and the future of

art and society. Now that the proletarian age has arrived, he says, bourgeois artists ought to abandon their natural class allegiance and throw in
their lot with the workers. Such an alliance, Cowley claims,

> can offer . . . a sense of comradeship and participation in a historical process
> vastly bigger than the individual. It can offer an audience, not trained to ap-
> preciate the finer points of style or execution—that will come later—but
> larger and immeasurably more eager than the capitalist audience and quicker
> to grasp essentials. It can offer the strength of a new class. (302)

The apparent historic task of this newly born generational self is to help
construct the promised land of the proletarian age, but it will also realize
the older Emersonian ideal of an art that is the true "outgrowth of a situation." As a prophet of the new era, Cowley offers his own text as an
example of how Marxism can provide an autobiographer with the tools
to clarify and organize life, to explain the collective chaos that was the
twenties, and to judge the religion of art that was the peculiar heresy of
that age.

Readers familiar with the socialist realist aesthetic that enjoyed a certain vogue in the 1930s will immediately recognize the tendency of these
suggestions. They are written in the accents of a convert, a man from
whose eyes the capitalist scales have fallen, a man who can finally make
plain the path of salvation to others.

The autobiographical accomplishment of *Exile's Return* has been made
more visible, I think, in the light of recent feminist and African American
rejections of the notion that the individualized self is the sine qua non of
autobiography. In the context of these critical stances, Cowley's first edition of *Exile's Return* offers an interesting case study. Cowley and his
friends, a group of primarily white male writers, perceived themselves as
members of a generation at odds with the dominant culture. As members
of a new literary coterie within that generation, they also saw themselves
as outside of the literary establishment. Cowley's project in *Exile's Return*, therefore, is threefold: to assert that his group is more representative of the generation than are other groups, to assert control over the discourse within which the generational plot is constructed, and to assure
the group's access to the literary canon. Although his book also contains
an explicit political intention (to facilitate the advent of a proletarian revolution), this intention seems to me secondary to his desire to gain access
to cultural power for his own group. If the revolution is successful, Cowley wants his group to have power within it; if it is not, he wants his group
to be positioned to vie for a place within the bourgeois literary tradition.

Because the generational autobiographer's own story is meant to
serve synecdochically as the narrative that will ultimately define the collective identity of the author's peers, contemporary readers almost in-

evitably perceive such works as attempts to manipulate the discourse concerning which people and which issues are central to a culture's meaning. This holds true whether the autobiographer opts to represent the generation as a member of an elite vanguard or as a member of the typical mass. In either case, generational autobiographers claim that the significant issues and events of the age are those in which they and their group have been involved. Such works are, therefore, almost inevitably engaged in generational polemics, either explicitly or implicitly, from their very conception.

In Cowley's case, the political implications of his collective autobiography became apparent in its first reviews. Cowley later recalled that most of his original reviewers "said that [*Exile's Return*] was a trivial story, intermittently amusing, that dealt with unimportant persons. They deplored and derided my political enthusiasms, as might have been anticipated, but they objected at greater length to my notion that the men of the 1920's had special characteristics and that their adventures in Paris were a story worth telling."[22] Bernard de Voto, in a review entitled "Exiles from Reality,"[23] vehemently attacked Cowley's assumption that he and his friends were representative of the times. "*Exile's Return*," he expostulated, is not a "history of a generation" but "the apologia of a coterie." Given readers' expectations of conventional autobiography, such a reaction was not very surprising. Traditionally, an autobiographer claiming to be "representative of his age" was expected to have had some influence on the course of history. De Voto offered as the "determinants of the actual generation" those "laboratory scientists and politicians [who were] . . . the engineers of economic and social pressures." Besides, he said, most of Cowley's generation—he was himself only a year older than Cowley—did not share the feelings of alienation that characterized the Paris exiles: Cowley's account of the twenties "is altogether subjective and he continually mistakes the emotions of his friends as the structure of society."

De Voto's major problem with Cowley's book arose over their different ideas about how a person can be "representative." As de Voto's counterexamples indicate, he was employing the term according to nineteenth-century usage: one was representative if one stood out from the multitude, if one was a leader, if one influenced the course of history. His usage of the term reflects traditional autobiographical theory, whose founder, Georg Misch, claimed in *A History of Autobiography in Antiquity* (1907) that the "supreme example of the representative autobiographer is the eminent person who has himself played a part in the forming of the spirit of his time."[24] Such representativeness is, according to Doris Sommer, metaphoric: it "assumes an identity by substituting one (superior) signifier for another (I for we, leader for follower, Christ for faithful)."[25] Of course, by this standard Cowley and his friends were not even remotely representative. But Cowley's usage of the term is radically different from that of traditional autobiographical theory. He did not see himself or his expatriate cronies as "movers and shakers," or even as people who had a very clear grasp of the issues and problems of their times. They were, as Cowley said in his prologue, distinguished only by a "barometric" (13) sensitivity to social change that was reflected in their behavior, attitudes, styles, and, occasionally, art. His representatives of the age are shaped by historical trends, which they inadvertently and unself-consciously express. As he explains, "the ideas that concern me here are the ones that half-unconsciously guided people's actions" (12). Like later generational autobiographers, Cowley attempts to depict the underlying historical forces that shape personality, rather than the outstanding personalities who shape history. Cowley's ideas about representativeness, in short, sprang from a notion that was essentially synecdochic and generational rather than metaphoric and individualist. He is the part that stands for the whole; his friends are the species that stands for the genus.[26]

Inevitably, Cowley's severest critics were either established men like de Voto who viewed him as an upstart, or men from the working class who felt that his bid for representativeness was based on class privilege. An example of the second group of critics was Karl Pretshold, a "Pittsburgh Socialist" who wrote an angry response to a chapter of *Exile's Return* that appeared in the *New Republic* prior to the publication of the book. Undoubtedly stung by this attack from the very group with which he was trying to forge an alliance, Cowley responded to Pretshold in the book itself. In a chapter entitled "The Other Side of the Tracks," Cowley answered the claim that Pretshold's experience as a worker was as representative of the twenties as Cowley's experience as a young middle-class writer. Cowley quotes at length from Pretshold's version of the period and grants that the workers' experiences did, in fact, represent "the sound beginning of a [proletarian] culture during the decade before the War." But while Cowley is willing to give Pretshold's class a voice in his narrative, he denies that voice any claim to representative status. Pretshold's article is "interesting in itself," says Cowley, and "it bears on my narrative," but "it describes an almost forgotten phase of American life." This phase was "shattered by the War and the anti-labor crusade that followed." Afterward, the working class, "except in statistics . . . had ceased to exist. . . . It was a class without a nervous system, a voice, a brain, almost without a purpose, except possibly to rise to the class above" (42–44). Presumably, the proletarian future would offer the Pretsholds of America, or their children, the representative status they presently lacked.

The assertion of a counteridentity by the groups represented by de Voto and Pretshold was, of course, unavoidable given the premises upon which the book was constructed. Unlike the individualist autobiographer who draws upon material to which he or she may have sole access, Cowley had depended upon material that was largely drawn from the public memory and was thus open to his contemporaries' scrutiny. And unlike an autobiographer who reconstructs an individuated past, the generational autobiographer challenges his contemporaries by claiming to define their identities as well as his or her own. It is not surprising, therefore, that persons with a generational or class perspective different from Cowley's would object to his claim to represent the age.[27] Recognizing this, Cowley often qualifies his portrait, particularly in his last chapter where he attempts to rectify his "partly distorted impression" (293) of the twenties by listing those aspects of the age that he has not included in his narrative.

In the traditional individualized autobiography that evolved out of the Romantic tradition, the self is conceived of as a unique essence that exists prior to language. Insofar as that self interacts with society, it does so to its own peril. Society corrupts the Romantic self, pries it away from its original relationship with nature and feelings, confuses it with social obligations and forms. The Romantic autobiographer, therefore, envisions his task as a very personal quest, doomed to at least partial failure, to rediscover and capture the original self in words. In such works, the type of negotiation Cowley undertakes with Pretshold about identity is unthinkable. A major characteristic of the collective generational autobiography, therefore, is that it highlights the negotiation process as an inherent part of self construction and undermines the Romantic notion that the individual alone has access to and authority over identity.

In spite of his willingness to negotiate, however, Cowley's book was premised on an audacious bid for representative status. That bid was authorized by Cowley's construction of himself and his peers as possessing a unique identity and role in history: they would be spectators at the death throes of capitalism, and they would usher in a new proletarian age. Since that age still lay in the future, Cowley's narrative was offered not only as a reconstruction of history, but also as a political tract designed to bring about a desired social reality: if enough people could see themselves in the version of the collective self he had created, perhaps they would adopt the whole narrative, including its upbeat prophetic finale.

That not everyone was willing to adopt Cowley's 1934 version of the collective self, even after his accommodation of Pretshold, was reflected in the book's initial unpopularity with both critics and the public. It sold only 983 copies during the first year after its publication.[28] The public's reluctance to endorse the book arose partly from Cowley's enthusiastic Marxism. The later history of the book—its revision, republication, and favorable reception in 1951—attests to the susceptibility of Cowley's collective self to political and psychological pressures. Although the revised version seems less compelling to me as personal narrative, it remains of interest to autobiographical theorists because its expurgation of the author's former self construction highlights both the textuality and the negotiability of identity. Like Benjamin Franklin's vision of the autobiographical self as a revised edition of an already published text, Cowley's later edition of *Exile's Return* took advantage of the author's right "in a second edition to correct some faults of the first" and to "change some sinister Accidents and Events of it for others more favourable."[29] Freud long ago compared the ego's repressions of unpleasant truths to the revision of a text that contains offensive passages.[30] Cowley's revision of his generational narrative to make it more acceptable to himself and to his anticommunist readers is an excellent example of this analogy in literal operation for a collective self. It was the first edition, however, that established the principal narrative strategies of generational autobiography.[31]

3
Generational Autobiography as Annunciatory Narrative

The uniqueness of Malcolm Cowley's position among American writers as the practitioner of a new form of autobiography continued unchallenged as succeeding generations appeared on the literary scene. For autobiographers who came of age in the 1930s, 1940s, and 1950's, the generational metaphor for the self was much less important than others that offered themselves. In fact, Cowley's approach to the self did not appear again until the emergence of the generation that came of age between 1960 and 1975. Among autobiographers of that self-conscious generation, Cowley's perspective tended to be the rule rather than the exception. Together with Cowley's book, the works of these later writers constitute a tradition of generational autobiography. What Cowley began in *Exile's Return*, the later writers have taken in a number of new directions, employing in their construction of generational identity a rather bewildering array of forms and styles. There is, however, one salient characteristic they all have in common with Cowley's book: a tendency to engage openly in identity politics. I mean by this that each of them is engaged in a struggle to assert the representative status of his or her own experience and to fix the meaning of generational experience in a plot that has a more or less specific political content.

In the following chapters, my discussion of select sixties-generation autobiographies will be arranged primarily according to when each of them was written in relation to the coming-of-age experience. In so presenting these works, I intend to pay some attention to formal questions and to discuss each work in the light of the problems I have raised in previous chapters—in particular, the relationship between autobiographical form, collective self-construction and assertion, and conceptions of history. A roughly chronological arrangement, however, will demonstrate how the dialogue between these texts contributes to a rich intertextual identity, even when the richness of an individual work may be lacking. We have already seen how Cowley directly addresses other generational voices in his book. Something similar to his dialogue with Karl Pretshold over the nature of generational experience is repeated in sixties-generation texts.

Sometimes that dialogue is explicit, as it was in *Exile's Return*, but more often the presence of those voices—the voices of former selves, parents, rivals, political foes, the other gender, the media, and so on—is apparent only in what Mikhail Bakhtin has called "hidden polemic": they are voices whose presence one must infer in order for the texts to make sense.[1] Unlike purely formalist or taxonomical approaches, this approach will reveal how each generational autobiography is called into existence by prior generational autobiographies, and that in order to understand them properly, one must read them in conjunction with each other, positioning each voice in the competing chorus of voices struggling to construct and control generational identity.[2] Consequently, not only are these autobiographies characterized by a peculiar insistence on the author's collective identity, but that identity itself is the object of a collective negotiation, debate, and construction. A clear by-product of this examination, therefore, should be the demonstration that the conventional definition of autobiography as a form dependent upon the individualized self, isolated either in its essence (as autobiographers in the Romantic tradition would have it) or in a supreme act of self-invention (as autobiographers in the rationalist tradition assume), falls far short of describing the range of self-conceptions available to writers who choose the genre. An examination of generational texts should also clarify, in a way that is only rarely glimpsed in individualistic autobiographies, the complex and highly political process of identity construction and negotiation.

By now, of course, it is a truism that the 1960s was a period during which American culture was politicized along generational lines. It was a time when many members of the young generation felt that the institutions they were about to inherit from their "fathers" were outmoded, inadequate, or immoral. This phenomenon manifested itself in almost all aspects of cultural life, including autobiography, which was perceived and used by members of this generation as a form within which they could experiment with new narratives of identity. That experimentation seemed to develop around certain common lines. When they asked themselves the question "Who am I?" the answers they provided were often formulated in stories that were recognizably public in their orientation. In that respect they differed little from earlier writers who, having lived through social or political crises, had shaped their personal narratives in the form of memoirs bearing witness to their times. Unlike conventional memoirists, however, these autobiographers recognized little, if any, distinction between the private and the public realms of life. One's sex life, grooming habits, and personal relationships were as meaningful as one's participation in actions and events that were, as Michael Rossman said, in the "growing bud of the historical tree,"[3] and those same "historical" actions and events were themselves scrutinized in terms of their impact on the self's most private relations and attitudes. Perhaps an even more significant difference between these works and the traditional memoir is that the self these autobiographers construct is markedly collective. They provide not an individual's account of history in the making, but a collective self's account of its own making in history.

The narrative of the self in these books is, therefore, also the history of those events which the writer sees as specifically generational in scope and significance. As Joyce Maynard wrote: "It was not a time when we could separate our own lives from the outside world."[4] All the generational writers of this period cite specific public incidents that shaped their sense of the collective self. The selection of those incidents, of course, is never an innocent one, for invariably they are chosen as illustrations of a generational plot that confirms specific political assumptions and ideas. Once the events are selected, they are themselves narrated in ways that conform to those assumptions. These political assumptions and the shape of the larger generational plot vary from author to author, but the same public events tend to appear in all the narratives, regardless of the author's politics. It is perhaps worthwhile to list them here, partly to alert readers to their existence, but also because they suggest the historical backdrop against which all of these books were written. They include:

- demonstrations against the House Un-American Activities Committee (HUAC) in San Francisco (1960)
- the major events of the early civil rights movement, particularly the Freedom Rides (1961) and the Mississippi Summer (1964)
- the assassination of John F. Kennedy (November 1963)
- the Free Speech Movement, Berkeley campus of the University of California (1964)
- the expansion of the Vietnam War and the first Vietnam teach-ins at the University of Michigan in Ann Arbor (1965)
- the "Summer of Love" in the Haight-Ashbury district of San Francisco (1967)
- the assassination of Martin Luther King (April 1968)
- the Columbia University strike (April 1968)
- the assassination of Robert Kennedy (June 1968)
- the Democratic Convention in Chicago (August 1968)
- the breakup of Liberation News Service (fall 1968)
- "Woodstock Nation" (August 1969)
- the Weathermen's "Days of Rage" campaign (October 1969)
- the murder at the Rolling Stones concert at Altamont raceway (December 1969)
- the invasion of Cambodia and the subsequent killing of four students by National Guardsmen at Kent State University in Ohio (spring 1970)
- the implementation of a lottery system by the Selective Service System (1970)

- the White House-sponsored break-in at the Democratic National Headquarters in the Watergate Apartments complex (June 1972)
- the fall of Saigon and the return of the last American soldiers from Vietnam (1975)

The autobiographies that emerge alongside of and in response to these events constitute a story of their own. It is the story of the generation's dialogue about who they are and what their place in the world will be. Occasionally, the participants in the conversation support one another, but that is not always, or even usually, the case. More common are writers jockeying for superiority, clashing over representative status, arguing over public narratives as they engage in the process of co-constructing the meaning of their times and their shared experience. The reality that emerges from the din of their opposed voices, however, can only be described as a communal product. For the sixties generation, this dialogue divides roughly into three overlapping phases, each with its characteristic autobiographical forms. The first phase of this dialogue is initiated by autobiographical works written in an "annunciatory" mode. Annunciatory works have what young people today would call an "attitude." Typically, they are manifestos that aggressively announce the existence of the new group, celebrate its character, chart its coming of age, bruit its rejection of the parental past, vaunt its solidarity, articulate its myths, justify its demands, and offer up a vision of the future it intends to build. During the late 1960s, their plots were simple, apocalyptic in tone and melodramatic in style. Some of their authors borrow heavily from the advertising techniques of Madison Avenue, and, indeed, one could argue that they try to sell an identity as much as they describe one. Unlike conventional autobiography, they focus more on simply letting the world know that the writer's group exists than on detailing how it came to be. They are, in short, more oriented toward the present and the future than toward the past.

Annunciatory Narrative as Manifesto: Students for a Democratic Society and *The Port Huron Statement*

The first voice in the generational dialogue, *The Port Huron Statement* (1962), was a manifesto composed by fifty-nine young people who came together in June of 1962 in the small Michigan town that gave the document its name.[5] They had congregated there at an AFL-CIO camp to draft a statement of the goals of their new leftist organization, the Students for a Democratic Society (SDS). According to the accounts of those who participated, the group imagined their undertaking to be a momentous one from the outset. They were convinced that their generation was coming of age under circumstances that made it unique, and they believed that history was providing them with the opportunity to bring about significant changes in American life. The document they wished to write would perform four functions: it would formulate and announce the generational identity (both by distinguishing SDS from older socialists and by distinguishing the entire youth generation from the older generation); it would provide an analysis of the major social, economic, and political problems confronting America; it would provide a "vision" that would lead to the solution of those problems; and it would provide what the writers ambitiously referred to as the "agenda for a generation"—an articulation of the role that SDS and the young generation would "play as a social force" (367) in the carrying out of that agenda.

The sixty-page work that resulted from the meeting devotes sections to each of these issues and is still worth reading both for its historical interest and for the specific positions it outlines.[6] What stands out about the manifesto, however, is the narrative of generational identity that underlies its political positions and lends them whatever affective power they have. By beginning with a narrative of their own "growing up in America," the writers imply that the angle of vision provided by their position in history has crucially influenced their attitudes toward various issues. Perhaps more important, the writers of the document, like most generational autobiographers who follow them, see the narrative as a justificatory myth—a story that calls forth a particular kind of behavior or supports a particular course of political action. One can find examples of this sort of narrative in almost all generational autobiographies. Sometimes they are used alone to explain generational behavior; at other times they are used in conjunction with specific political or strategic rationales for action. As one of the earliest articulations of generational identity, the Port Huron manifesto establishes the general outlines of a narrative that one can see repeated in later generational works, though it is often modified or given new interpretations as different writers reconstruct it for their own political ends.

In the first section of the *Statement,* "Introduction: Agenda for a Generation," the outline of that narrative as it was conceived up to 1962 is already quite clear, and it consists of the following conspicuous elements: The generation enjoyed a childhood that was innocent and privileged. They were given a thorough education in moral and political idealism and in the national myths that depicted America as an almost all-powerful embodiment of altruistic democracy. They were then exposed to the "paradoxes in our surrounding America" (330), the realities that flagrantly contradicted that education and those myths. The two central "paradoxes" were racism and "the bomb." The first of these paradoxes disillusioned them and awakened them to "the hypocrisy of American ideals" (330) that asserted the equality of all people, regardless of race. The second gave them an apocalyptic sense that they might "be the last generation in the experiment with living" (330). And, finally, they were presently "housed in universities" (329) and confronted with the alternatives of a paralyzed acquiescence or a constructive activism.

The governing event in this narrative is betrayal—the young generation's conviction that the mythic world their elders had constructed for them in their earliest childhoods was a sham. In the *Statement*, this betrayal is only sketched in the most general terms, and it is somewhat mollified by language suggesting that all comfortable Americans—including the young—participated in the self-deception. Ultimately, however, the young were able to see through the deception, and what they saw, they responded to:

> we began to see complicated and disturbing paradoxes in our surrounding America. The declaration "all men are created equal. . ." rang hollow before the facts of Negro life in the South and the big cities of the North. The proclaimed peaceful intentions of the United States contradicted its economic and military investments in the Cold War status quo. (330)

Besides their failure to construct an accurate image of America, the older generation had also failed to give the young generation an essential part of its birthright: adequate fathers, professors, "prophets" who asked fundamental questions—"what is really important? can we live in a different and better way? if we wanted to change society, how would we do it?" (331). As this characterization of the manifesto's implicitly Freudian plot suggests, the language of the narrative is conspicuously gendered. The generational betrayal has been perpetrated by fathers on sons, who in announcing themselves and their plight must forcefully reassert their own potency as men. "We regard *men*," the manifesto complains,

> as infinitely precious and possessed of unfulfilled capacities for reason, freedom, and love. In affirming these principles we are aware of countering perhaps the dominant conceptions of man in the twentieth century: that he is a thing to be manipulated, and that he is inherently incapable of directing his own affairs. . . . (332, emphasis in original)

As we will see, the construction of the generational plot in almost exclusively masculine terms is a characteristic shared by many later generational works. The dual betrayal depicted here, however, has left the young with two alternatives: to accept disillusionment as a rite of passage, acknowledging that "there simply are no alternatives, that our times have witnessed the exhaustion not only of Utopias, but of any new departures as well," or to denounce their elders and insist by means of an ardent activism that America be remade to conform to the ideal image that the weak older generation had hypocritically insisted was a reality.[7] The first choice leads to cynicism and a self-centered materialism; the second to moral heroism and values worth living for.

Within this scenario, SDS saw itself as a generational vanguard on a crusade. "We are a minority," they wrote, whereas the great mass of their contemporaries "regard the temporary equilibriums of our society and world as eternally functional parts." That majority, having "closed their minds to the future," suffers from a fear "that at any moment things might be thrust out of control. They fear change itself" (330). The problem in part is again the older generation's failure to provide moral leadership. Even the "liberal and socialist preachments" of the previous generational vanguard, the older leftists, "seem inadequate to the forms of the present." Beneath the feelings of hopelessness, however, the writers were convinced there existed a "yearning to believe there *is* an alternative to the present" (331). It is to that yearning that the "appeal" of the *Statement* is directed, and it is as the bearers of this appeal that members of SDS saw themselves. The group was appealing, however, not only *to* their generation, it was also speaking *for* them, as is made clear in the manifesto's opening words: "We are the people of this generation, bred in at least modest comfort, housed now in universities, looking uncomfortably to the world we inherit" (329).

Perhaps the most important aspect of the "new vision" called for by the document is its claim that both the old left and its major collaborator, labor, had forfeited their role as agents of significant social change. To replace them (or at least to supplement them), the *Statement* argues that those hoping for change must, therefore, turn to the young in universities. Only the universities possessed all of the characteristics required of a viable agent of social change. The universities were committed to the intellectual task of grappling with social problems, they were sufficiently dispersed throughout the country to effect change on a society-wide basis, and they were populated by people born in the post–world war era, moral agents whose historical vantage was untainted by the paralyzing anticommunism that affected almost all of their elders. The vanguard of the future, the authors argued, would be the young, middle-class university students who took their lessons in social and political reform from the civil rights movement, which had recently made such honorable gains for African Americans. They would have the necessary moral fiber to reform the Democratic Party, expelling its primary cancer, the "Dixiecrats," and making it truly responsive to a liberal and radical coalition that would inaugurate a genuine "participatory democracy" in America.

The Port Huron Statement thus begins with a very conventional autobiographical strategy: it names itself and proceeds directly to a narration of its origins, its experience, and its education. Its methods of constructing a collective identity—like those of all generational autobiographies written in the annunciatory mode—are at least initially the methods by which a conventional autobiography constructs an individual identity. Since most of the autobiographies to be treated in this chapter share some of the characteristics of *The Port Huron Statement*, perhaps it would be useful now to discuss those characteristics in order to establish the manifesto's relationship to conventional autobiography. There are, of course, obvious differences between the two modes, but they are more often of degree than of kind, since they arise from the manifesto's tendency to make explicit that which remains implicit in conventional autobiography. A consideration of this generational manifesto's autobiographical features, therefore, can highlight tendencies that are frequently ignored in examinations of more individualistic autobiographies—especially the tendency of life narratives to serve as justificatory myths for consciously and unconsciously held political positions. It can also prepare us for our consideration of later generational autobiographies in which the generational protagonist is more often—as in Cowley's case—the overt projection of an individual writer's life history.

A primary characteristic of the *Statement* is that the collective identity it announces is called into existence by specific subjects who then speak on its behalf. They constitute themselves as an entity, and they name that entity the "generation." The collective self in such a work is the project of particular individuals, the members of SDS. In this sense, it is an arbitrary construct. One might argue, of course, that biological generations exist in nature as surely as do biological individuals, and in fact there are biological generations within families and specific bloodlines. This natural phenomenon, however, hardly translates into objective social collectives made up of large masses of youth. Generations could exist in that sense only if all parents of a particular age group produced all of their offspring simultaneously or if the offspring produced over a given period of time were all of the same physical type (as are, for example, "generations" of computers, tanks, or space shuttles). Human reproduction, by contrast, is continuous and lacks the temporal interruptions that would create naturally occurring age cohorts. Particular groups construct generational identity, therefore, for specific purposes such as the institutionalization of collective memory (of, say, the lessons of the Great Depression or the war in Vietnam) or the achievement of particular political goals.[8] When those purposes do not exist, the concept of the generation is highly unlikely to emerge, and autobiographers will focus on other kinds of identity.[9]

It might seem intuitively that this characteristic would distinguish the manifesto from the modern individualized autobiography, but the artifactual construction of the self is a characteristic of both modes. In individualistic autobiographies, however, the social production of subjectivity is disguised by the ideologies of capitalism, which attempt to naturalize the individual self. This naturalization becomes apparent when we consider the ways in which other cultures envision the self, particularly those in which the concept of the individual does not exist as it does in modern Western societies.[10] Of course, it is easy to point to the human body as evidence of the existence of the individual self, but it would be as misleading as pointing to a large group of twenty-year-olds as evidence of the generation's existence. Both the concept of the individual self and the concept of the generational self are culturally determined interpretations of physical facts that have been construed by different societies in different ways, many of which are incompatible with those concepts.

Another conspicuous characteristic of a generational manifesto such as the *Statement* is that it constructs an identity for overtly political reasons. In American politics, the voice of the individual, contrary to popular myth, counts for very little; but the voice that speaks on behalf of a block of voters, consumers, or campaign contributors counts for much. In politics, therefore, the creation of a viable group identity is all-important. Aware of that reality, the writers of the *Statement* create a collective self in order that they might then make claims for it, state its desires, articulate its intentions, and declare its particular view of the world—all fundamentally political acts. The creation of that collective identity, therefore, initially serves at least one political purpose. It places direct political pressure on those who currently hold power and set policy. In principle, "the people of this generation" constitute no small threat in terms of apparent voting strength, or, if they are disillusioned with electoral politics, they constitute no small threat in "their potential," as Tom Hayden says in a later work, "to disrupt the vital institutions containing them (the universities), to break the link between generations, to threaten the future stability of the country."[11] In order to remain in power, governing bodies must successfully dismiss, absorb, pacify, or meet the demands of potentially powerful groups such as those who declare themselves in manifestos. Works like *The Port Huron Statement*, in other words, are written upon the assumption that the autobiographical act itself—that is, the creation of a self through the written word—is a necessary prerequisite of any political act.

Again, it might seem that such a characteristic would distinguish the manifesto from individualized autobiography. Taxonomists of autobiography claim that conventional practitioners of the genre narrate the history of the self from a variety of motives (to confess, to provide an example, to vindicate, to boast, etc.),[12] but a good many of these may also be seen as inherently political; certainly they almost all represent the author's effort to position him or herself in a more powerful relation to readers and rivals. If there is a difference between the manifesto and conventional autobiography on this score, it is that the politics of the latter are usually unstated whereas those of the former are almost always explicit.

The manifesto also serves a function that has been wholly identified with consumer capitalism: it advertises. *The Port Huron Statement* is directed not only at those in power; it is also directed at youth who are only *potentially* identified by the document's characterization of the generation and its narrative. Specific portions of the *Statement*'s rhetoric are pure assertion of generational unity, particularly the opening paragraphs in which the writers proclaim, "we are the people of this generation." The hope behind this advertising ploy is that the group identity asserted will prove attractive to youth—or even that it will *create* the need for those to whom the need has not occurred. The *Statement*'s writers, like the writers of the soft drink commercial who also use generational rhetoric ("It's the Pepsi generation!"), want to sell their product; in their case, the product is a political agenda.

To the writers' chagrin, not everybody in the targeted market is buying, which leads us to the third characteristic of a manifesto such as the *Statement*: the autobiographical self it depicts is a problematic representative "we." It is problematic first of all because America's highly privileged and individualistic culture confers legitimacy on any collective self only with great reluctance. The ideology of capitalism and the myth of individualism in America have it that the successful fulfillment of human destiny is accomplished only when one realizes the uniqueness of one's individual potential; self-conscious identification of self with a collective, particularly if that collective is a race, class, or gender, is frequently perceived as a kind of weakness, a tacit confession that one could not make it on one's own. Indeed, the mere acknowledgment of such identities is perceived as a denial of the central tenet of capitalist faith: that success is equally available to all individuals who, acting with sufficient self-reliance, can seize the opportunities that capitalist societies offer. Of course, within this faith, stigma is attached only to some collective identities, not to all. National identity is acceptable because the capitalist myth maintains that we are a nation of *individuals*. This also holds true for other group affiliations that do not imply a criticism of the individualist myth. Avowal of membership in a class, race, or ethnicity, however, seems to cast an aspersion on the individualist myth, suggesting that such group identities play a dominant role in the distribution of power and ought, therefore, to be acknowledged as politically important aspects of one's self. So when a group announces its collective identity and attempts to speak in its name for specific political goals, dominant groups within the culture are very likely to invoke the myth of individualism in order to delegitimize the upstart group's ambitions. Short of such delegitimizing, they will deny that those who presume to speak on behalf of the collective have any truly representative status. Its spokespersons will be stigmatized as "fringe elements," "extremists," or, in a recent formulation, "perpetrators of the politics of division."

The representative status of the generational "we" is also problematic because even those who apparently belong among its ranks inevitably struggle with one another over the characterization of the collective self. In other words, the collective "we" of generational autobiographies is always a political presumption, advanced in competition with characterizations offered by other groups or individuals who have a stake in the way in which that collective identity is formulated. The *Statement* acknowledges a difference between its composers and what it refers to as the "vast majority of our people" (330). The former consider themselves a generational elite, whose role in history was outlined by writers such as Bourne and Ortega.[13] They are those who perform the analysis of the times and perceive the real issues that the rising generation inherits from its elders. The latter are the generational mass, who see, according to the *Statement*, no alternatives to life as it is, who "have no real conception of personal identity except one manufactured in the image of others," and who aspire only "to be almost as successful as the very successful people" (334). The writers see themselves as speaking on behalf of this unthinking mass, to whom they openly offer a "real conception" of identity. Even if the mass is not actively seeking to change history, it has at least the potential to do so with the proper leadership.

The SDS conception of the relationship between individual writer, social vanguard, and generational mass becomes clear in James Miller's account of the composition of the *Statement*. Miller reveals that Tom Hayden was the principal author of the document, composing the first draft almost entirely on his own. Afterward he submitted it to the group assembled at Port Huron, and they came up collectively with "general instructions for revising the document" (109) which were then turned over to a "styles committee" consisting of Hayden, Al Haber, and Robert Ross. That committee, again led by Hayden, put together the final document. Much of its language, of course, might be read to refer to SDS alone, but its opening announcement that "we are the people of this generation" and the group's belief that it was an intellectual and political vanguard indicate that the document's authors intended to construct not only an "agenda" but also an identity for the entire age cohort. In an interview with Miller, Richard Flacks, one of SDS's leading lights at the time of the Port Huron conference, says that Tom Hayden "was really trying to write a manifesto for a generation. You had to make it broadly understandable, realizable, and he was very willing to play that role" (123). Obviously, SDS's account of the past was debatable. Still, in the absence of other forceful attempts to "name" a generation, the narrative offered by SDS (and, later, by the New Left in general) became the narrative with reference to which all people of that particular age group were compelled to define themselves. The generational autobiographers who followed *The Port Huron Statement*, even those who wrote to repudiate it, are all indebted to it for having provided the first definition of the collective self.[14]

Again, one might suppose that this struggle over collective identity is a characteristic that singularly distinguishes the generational manifesto from conventional, individualized autobiography, but analogies between the two modes hold. Modern studies of the self have amply demonstrated that one of the characteristics of experienced individual identity is its multiplicity. Such multiplicity is accentuated in certain pathologies, such as multiple personality syndrome, where distinct personalities within a single individual vie with one another for dominance. But the existence of multiplicity (or "contending identity elements," as Erik Erikson would have it) in a more attenuated form is accepted as "normal" by modern psychology. In conventional individualized autobiographies, what we witness is the attempt on the part of an "author" (itself a kind of ad hoc construction) to create a unified self that stands in as a substitute or representative for a subjectivity that is experienced as multiple. Individualized autobiographies, in other words, might usefully be considered by theorists as literary strategies by which a person attempts to "control" the chaos and multiplicity of experienced life. There is a striking similarity between this process and Tom Hayden and SDS's (or earlier, Malcolm Cowley's) attempt to represent the generation, with its multiple subgroups, as a unified identity.[15]

Finally, the *Statement* is future-oriented to a degree uncommon among conventional autobiographies. This is hardly surprising given its political intentions. A significant portion of the *Statement* is devoted to what its authors called the "agenda for a generation," an analysis of recent American history and a call for the reformation of American political and social life through the activism of its youth. The announced self of the manifesto is, therefore, much more *prospective* than it is *retrospective*. It is a self newly constructed, so even while the manifesto is partly concerned with the historical roots of the generational self as well as with the effect of specific past events, it is even more concerned with that self's future.

This, too, is an observation that one might usefully apply to the study of more individualized autobiographies. The consideration that such works are always more revelatory of the present (or writing) selves of their authors than they are of those authors' earlier, reconstructed selves is by now almost commonplace among students of the genre. It is taking this consideration but one step further to say that the genre has always been used to construct blueprints for the future. This is as true of Saint Augustine's *Confessions* as it is of any of the works I will discuss here. One cannot live a life devoted to God without first constructing an identity that allows such devotion. Augustine's book self-consciously reflects that conviction in its structure: the first nine books concern themselves with the author's past and his conversion; book 10 is devoted to a consideration of the author's present moment; the last three treat the implications of conversion for the author's future and go on to a consideration of cosmic, divine history. Neither can one reform the United States of America without first constructing a collective identity that desires such reform. The construction of past selves in autobiography serves always as the necessary groundwork for that prospective intention. It is a function that dominates the version of autobiography under consideration here—the generational manifesto or annunciatory autobiography.

The Port Huron Statement was written at a time when the Movement—that catchall term denoting all youth who were sympathetic with left-wing and counterculture ideals in the 1960s—was just beginning to develop its identity. Later writers, attempting to construct a coherent identity for themselves and the "people of this generation," shared with *The Port Huron Statement* a sense of the preeminence of public acts and events. Their works are usually more conventionally individualized, at least insofar as they present a single identifiable author, but the identity of that author is almost always advanced as a synecdoche for the generation. Insofar as each of them also represents a modification of the generational identity as defined in Port Huron, they are very much in keeping with the spirit of generational self-construction and revision that the *Statement* called for in its opening paragraph. The *Statement*, the authors write there, is "a living document open to change with our times and experiences. It is a beginning: in our own debate and education, in our dialogue with society" (329).

Annunciatory Narrative as Myth: Abbie Hoffman's *Revolution for the Hell of It*

Between 1962 and the appearance in 1968 of Abbie Hoffman's *Revolution for the Hell of It*,[16] the United States went through a transformation that polarized Americans along generational lines. That six-year period was also charged with events that changed the way in which the generational self was conceived by spokespersons for youth. The assassination of John F. Kennedy ended the optimism that his administration had inspired among the young. The Berkeley Free Speech Movement initiated the era of large-scale campus protests and focused the attention of the young on the meaning and means of their education. Lyndon Johnson's escalation of American involvement in the Vietnam War triggered what would become the mass disaffection of the young from their political leaders. The San Francisco Summer of Love in 1967 was one of the first widely publicized media events focused on the counterculture and its rebellion against middle-class values. The Robert Kennedy and Martin Luther King assassinations hardened many of the disaffected in their belief that substantial change in America's policy toward third world countries and the poor would come about only through violent means. And, finally, the confrontation between demonstrators and police at the Chicago Democratic National Convention in August of 1968 highlighted for many the futility of trying to work "within the system." This last event—organized by the Yippies (followers of Jerry Rubin and Hoffman's

Youth International Party), the National Mobilization Committee to End the War in Vietnam ("Mobe" or "MOB," organized by Dave Dellinger and Rennie Davis), and various other New Left and black liberation organizations—took on the greatest symbolic meaning for the next group of autobiographers.

Just as generational autobiographers use themselves synecdochically to represent generational identity, they also often use key historical events as synecdoches representing larger historical trends crucial to generational identity formation. Albert Stone notes that one function of individualist autobiographies is to "convert historical event and psychological experience into personal identity."[17] That is precisely what Abbie Hoffman, Tom Hayden, and Jerry Rubin attempt to do for collective identity in their treatment of the Chicago events. The Chicago demonstrations and the conspiracy trial that followed them represent for each of these writers a quintessential moment in which generational identities confronted each other and revealed themselves. That confrontation becomes, in their works, an opportunity for autobiographical self-discovery.

In general, the events that culminated in the Chicago police riots provoked two responses among generational writers: the first, characteristic of the New Left, was a sense that politically active youth and their elders were becoming so polarized that violent confrontation was inevitable; the second, characteristic of those who identified with the counterculture, was the conviction that only a complete withdrawal from established American society could free the young from its corruption. The counterculture's stance was that the young should construct, through imitation of other cultures and through their own creative improvisation, an alternative society, one that highlighted the spiritual, the tribal, the sexual, the expressive, and the free.[18]

Elements of both of these responses can be seen in Hoffman's book. *Revolution for the Hell of It* is the least conventionally autobiographical of the several self-narratives Hoffman (b. 1936) wrote during his life, but it conforms more completely to the sense of collective autobiography I have been examining here than does its sequel, *Soon To Be a Major Motion Picture* (1980).[19] In *Revolution*, Hoffman seeks to establish as central to the generational plot an event he calls the "Myth of Chicago," reconstructed from the confrontation between police and demonstrators during the 1968 Democratic National Convention. To do that, Hoffman assembles an autobiographical narrative in which the Chicago myth is actually the culmination of a series of what he calls diary "snapshots" or "flashbacks," numbered and arranged chronologically, that narrate other potentially mythical events. Each of these flashbacks is an anecdote of the "revolution" narrated in the present tense. Hoffman re-presents them here as fables of action or "images" (203) that confound parental truths, demonstrate the how-to of generational revolt, manifest the superiority of youth, and "show a development and . . . emphasize the point that for me, and I know for many others, Chicago didn't begin on August 25th" (203). In form, then, the book is a diary of Hoffman's movements and of the Movement from the early months of 1967 to August 1968, interrupted by meditations written in late 1968 on the meaning of the revolution, economics, language, myth, rumor, public theater, runaways and youth as "white niggers," and mass media.

The book also contains an introductory, and presumably fictional, letter to "Free" (Hoffman's nom de guerre) from his "Mom" which highlights ironically the gap between this American Jewish mother and her revolutionary son, as well as separate concluding sections devoted to Hoffman's revolutionary aphorisms (presented as "advice to the brothers"), "props" used for the Chicago myth (various posters, lists of Movement demands, maps of delegate hotels, etc.), aphorisms by venerated writers such as Albert Camus, Che Guevara and Theodore Maslow (to "lend a certain respectability to the book"), "ego-tripping" (Hoffman's boasts about himself), an epilogue, and a complete copy of his earlier booklet "Fuck the System," which catalogues various ways to get things for free.

The key word in Hoffman's book, however, is "myth." As he generally uses the term, a myth is a particular interpretation of an event or series of events that allows the holder of the myth to feel comfortable with his or her place in the world. Myths, in other words, are explanatory and justificatory fictions constructed from the materials of what people take to be actual events. There are major myths that seek to justify collective history, and minor myths that seek merely to make a particular event conform to a larger mythic understanding of history. There are also good myths, held by youth and Yippies, that further self-realization and freedom, and bad myths, held by the establishment, that are used to manipulate others and maintain power structures. Myths are, by their nature, irrational oversimplifications and distortions of actual events and facts. This very irrationality, however, is the source of a myth's strength, for it is through such distortion that myths empower people to act collectively. And however much they may falsify reality, myths, Hoffman would argue, never lie at their deepest levels, for they reveal basic truths about the collectives that hold them. The primary myth to which Hoffman's book is devoted resembles in many ways Cowley's narrative of inevitable proletarian revolution. They are both historicist and revolutionary; that is, they both see the future as the result of an inevitable process that will bring about the displacement of the present social/political arrangement by a better, freer, and more equitable one.

Perhaps more important for the purposes of autobiography, Hoffman also uses the term "myth" to describe individual and group identities. The hippies, for example, are described by Hoffman as a "myth created by media," just as the Diggers (a San Francisco-based activist/an-archist group) were a "grass-roots myth created from within" (26). Celebrity and leadership, both forms of individual identity, are also en-joyed (or suffered) by "mythic" persons, people whose public personae are incarnations of collective aspirations and worldviews. Abbie Hoff-man himself is "a myth" (15), and the publication of *Revolution* will en-hance that status. The media pay attention, according to Hoffman, only to myth, and the media are the major manufacturers of myth in America. Nonmythic persons and events, therefore, are simply invisible. As a mythic generational representative, Hoffman is in a position to use the media to further his own reading of generational aspirations, such as bringing about the end of the war, or revealing the hollowness of elec-toral politics, or exposing the sham of middle-class values. His mythic persona is also the embodiment of all the positive elements of what he hopes will become the new generational self: joy (even "revolution" is carried out simply for the "hell of it"), communalism ("property is the enemy" [35]), instant gratification (all social arrangements are judged according to the degree to which they allow people to do what they want to do), and vigorous heterosexuality. It is noteworthy here that in spite of these values, Hoffman writes in terms that are rabidly homophobic and often sexist. Later historians of the period have frequently pointed out that the New Left's male chauvinism was a catalyst for the feminist movement that emerged in the early 1970s, but one hears a good deal less about such things as Hoffman's attacks on members of the Hudson Institute as "fags" (38) and the peace movement as "fag-ridden" (39). On this score, at any rate, Hoffman seems to have something in common with the older generation and its sexual mythology. His prosecutor at the Chicago Seven trial, Tom Foran, also characterized the Movement as a "fag-revolution."[20]

As a part of this self-mythification, the cover of *Revolution* sports a photo of Hoffman leaping for joy with a rifle in one outstretched hand. Between his legs is a superimposed photo of a campaign button with the book title printed on it. The word "free" is printed in block letters on Hoffman's forehead. (The word the author had actually written on his forehead was "FUCK." According to Hoffman, the publisher changed the word without his permission.)[21] Another photo of Hoffman being ar-rested adorns the back cover. Both photos are meant to convey aspects of the generational myth. The cover photo is not merely Hoffman, but the generational persona he constructs in his book and offers to his peers. It is a Whitmanian gesture, and the Whitmanian strain—with its self-glorification and self-mockery, its emphasis on myth, its identification of persona and reader, its rejection of history—is pervasive in Hoffman's work. The photo here, mimicking the frontispiece of the first edition of *Leaves of Grass*, is qualified by the inevitable response of the American powers-that-be, captured in the photo image on the rear cover—Hoffman being led away by two policemen.

Both photos are also meant to serve as counters to other images that are offered on behalf of the myth. Although Hoffman defines his generational self in opposition to a wide range of other generational spokespersons (Mobe, SDS, and hippies, for example), his closest competitor for control of intragenerational rhetoric is Jerry Rubin. SDS and Mobe are dismissed by Hoffman as out-of-date, overly intellectual, and "boring"; the hippies are politically timid even when they are culturally advanced. But regarding Rubin, Hoffman claims: "Ours might be the greatest debate in the Movement. Jerry wants to show the clenched fist. I want to show the clenched fist and the smile. He wants the gun. I want the gun and the flower" (123–24). An amalgam of that image—gun and smile— is the one we see on the cover of the book.[22]

Hoffman the writer is never, however, quite comfortable with Hoffman the myth. He complains, as do later generational autobiographers, that individual identity myths (or celebrity/leadership status) can trap those who hold them into positions that limit mobility, both spiritual and physical. In a self-interview he conducts early in the book, Hoffman complains that his celebrity status cramps his personal freedom and contradicts his commitment to a collective, democratic self:

> Imagine this scene: You are trying to steal some groceries and some old lady comes up and says how much she likes what you're doing. That's why I use disguises, so I can keep in shape by having to hustle without the myth. The day I can't shoplift, panhandle, or pass out leaflets on my own is the day I'll retire. The myth, like everything else, is free. Anybody can claim he is it and use it to hustle. (63)

Hoffman's desire to escape the almost inevitable attachment of the collective myth to his own name and person partly explains why he uses the pseudonym "Free" on the title page and throughout the book. He also distances his person from the myth by including a generic autobiographical photo section that contains pictures of various demonstrations and hippie groups; "Free" is identified in each of these photographs as a different person, including some African Americans and women. Using the pseudonym and the photos furthers his penchant for disguise at the same time that it makes one of his most important Whitmanian points: the myth (the persona who speaks this book) is available for appropriation by any member of the generation.

The section actually devoted to what happened in Chicago begins significantly with a blank page under the heading "THIS IS WHAT HAPPENED"; a note at the bottom states that "the reader should write or draw in the space above HIS CHICAGO. More paper can be stolen at any stationery store. The rest [of this section of the book] is my trip. It is by no means everything that happened or that I learned" (113). What happened in Chicago, according to Hoffman, was nothing and everything. It was an empty space whose blankness was filled in by everyone who participated in it in any form. In any case, all of the constructions of the Chicago Myth, including his own, are parts of, or variations on, the Myth of "the Second American Revolution" (85), the great struggle between good and evil (as perceived from either and all sides) that was taking place in the latter half of the 1960s. The Yippie reading of the myth saw America as a nation divided into two fundamentally opposed camps: those who served the evil forces of competition, capitalism, and private property (conservatives, liberals, cops, military and Corporate America, or anyone over thirty), and those who believed in the beneficent forces of cooperation, some form of socialism, and the concept of "Free" (hippies, Diggers, Yippies, left-wing radical groups, and of course anyone under thirty). Those two forces came into direct conflict in Chicago. While both (or all) sides accepted the myth, everyone naturally interpreted it according to his or her own predilections and affiliations. At the end of a section entitled "The New York Times Enters the Myth," Hoffman describes the mental routes by which various American personages "enter" the myth. The list is too lengthy to quote entirely, but it distinguishes between those who construct their own myths, and those who borrow from others: "The road to Chicago begins and ends in your own head. [Mayor] Daley and the FBI will enter by finding a conspiracy. Jack Newfield will enter through his friend Tom Hayden. Richard Goldstein through me. Marvin Garson and the West Coast through Jerry Rubin . . ." (122). As partisans, each of them engages in distortion, in attempts to reconstruct events in a manner that is flattering to his or her own self and party.[23]

While Hoffman's endorsement of the Yippie reading of the myth is obvious enough, his own role in the mythmaking process remains somewhat ambiguous. There are moments in his text when he vaunts his ability to create and shape the myth. The idea of the "Yippies," as is well known, was dreamed up by Hoffman, Rubin, and some of their friends in December of 1967 as an intentional collective identity myth, a tool to get people to come to Chicago for the demonstrations. In the self-interview mentioned above, undated but apparently written before Chicago, Hoffman answers a question about why the "Yippies were created":

> We are faced with this task of getting huge numbers of people to come to Chicago along with hundreds of performers, artists, theatre groups, engineers. Essentially, people involved in trying to work out a new society. How do you do this starting from scratch, with no organization, no money, nothing? Well, the answer is that you create a myth. Something that people can play a role in, can relate to. (64)

Hoffman exhibits here a self-consciousness about the arbitrariness of self-proclaimed collective identities that is much less evident in the earlier *Port Huron Statement* (as well as in other New Left documents). In fact, it is one of Hoffman's refreshing qualities (not, unfortunately, consistently maintained) that he foregrounds the rhetorical tools by which the left allows itself to speak on behalf of the collective and in its name. Anecdotes such as this one underline that strain in Hoffman's thinking that emphasizes his ability to manipulate the myth for his own ends.

Often in *Revolution*, however, the myth (or "History," to use an earlier generation's term) is clearly larger than any one person; it has an autonomous existence, and members of the vanguard, such as Hoffman, are there simply to serve as its conduits, or, perhaps more appropriately, as its stagehands. He claims, for example, that his task in the Chicago myth was "to design its symbols and gather up the props"; Jerry Rubin's role "was chief ideologist or scenario designer" (123). Legally, of course, this posture has the advantage of allowing Hoffman to avoid taking responsibility for the consequences of his actions. Considering that he was awaiting trial for conspiracy to cross state lines "to organize, promote, or encourage a riot" when he was writing *Revolution*, this attitude was only practical. He is, he insists, merely the revolution's adman, PR consultant, observer, and celebrant: "I'm no leader. Nobody is under my command. I haven't any idea how to stop a demonstration, say, except to go home. I'm really not interested in stopping anything, so I'm not a leader" (63). The best example of such evasion is Hoffman's account of the police riot at the Yippies' Spring Equinox Celebration on March 22, 1968. On that occasion, Hoffman used the media to invite "five to eight thousand people to a party at midnight" at Grand Central Station in New York City (89–91). The celebrants took over the station and were violently beaten by the police. Accused of manipulating his "followers" into a bloody confrontation, Hoffman writes that "nobody was under orders to come. (Only people in business really manipulate people because they have money-power and, as everyone knows, money is power in America)" (91). Since much of Hoffman's book is devoted to the principle that anyone can exploit the media's ability to manipulate people, his evasion here is particularly transparent.

Consistent with his belief in the myth's autonomous existence, Hoffman even cites rare occasions when he has performed an action that does not "fit" the myth. For example, one press conference in which he participated prior to the Chicago demonstration received little national media attention because they never, according to Hoffman, "lie when you relate to them in a non-linear mythical manner" (92), however much they might distort the way in which events actually occur. What he means is that the media are interested only in the large melodramatic plots featuring struggles between good and evil characters who represent what Hoffman perceives to be the true forces underlying historical movement.[24] The media neglected the press conference

> precisely because it wasn't right. It didn't fit the truth of what would happen in Chicago. . . . In similar fashion, the YIP-out on Easter Sunday, with over 40,000 people in Central Park and fifteen rock groups and flowers from the sky, didn't fit the myth (as well as being a lousy spectator event) and was soon forgotten. (92)

The myth, which was the narrative-in-the-making of a violent confrontation between two generational identities, worked in strange symbiosis with the media and the government, as well as with elements within the generation over which Hoffman and his friends ultimately had little or no control. On a collective level, those three large groups recognized and perhaps even helped to determine the clumsy melodrama of violence that would be enacted in Chicago. According to Hoffman, it was his task merely to embody the generational reading of the myth.

This emphasis on myth in Hoffman's first autobiographical venture is at least in part a response to the major psychosocial element of the generational plot outlined in the *Port Huron Statement*. That element was the perceived betrayal of the younger generation by their parents, and, specifically, youth's discovery that the older generation's image of America was an illusion constructed to produce complacency and submission to the status quo. It is not that the *Statement* was the source of Hoffman's ideas about myth, advertising, and media, but rather that his autobiographical manifesto, like that of SDS, revolves around the gap between social realities and parental representations of America. That gap had led SDS to devise a political program and an identity based, in part, on a hostility to the mythmaking machinery of the powerful classes. It irked them that media propaganda had duped Americans into believing that the myth was the same as the actuality. They responded by trying to expose the actual condition of American society (with its poverty, racism, and militarism) as well as the machinery by which these conditions were hidden from view.

For Hoffman, however, the discovery of the gulf between actuality and myth paradoxically served as a kind of liberation. The problem, according to Hoffman, was not that the older generation had created an illusion, for reality is always, in his phrase, an immense "put-on," a Wizard of Oz contraption. Indeed, it is just such contraptions, if viewed properly, that make life worth living. It is no accident that Hoffman's first chapter includes an extended allusion to the MGM film musical. Hoffman describes how he began writing his book by taking LSD and hallucinating that a tornado strikes, "and before I knew it the house had become unfastened and was spinning wildly in the air like a scene from

The Wizard of Oz" (9). The film, watched annually on television by large numbers of Hoffman's age group, contained in its climactic scene a powerful image of the disillusionment in store for those who seek salvation in parental figures. Hoffman's anger, however, was aroused not because the American myth turned out to be a contraption, but because the parental generation, hypocritically pretending to believe in it, had abandoned the contraption:

> America is a mythic land. Dreamed up by European beatniks, religious fanatics, draft dodgers, assorted hippie kooks, and runaways from servitude off to the New World of milk and honey. . . . The myths of America are strong and good but the institutional machine is a trap of death. (84–85)

SDS too, of course, believed in the ideal images of American myth, but they believed that one should keep a careful eye on the precise distance between those images and reality. The job of the media was simply to record and transmit actuality, not to dress it up or present it in a way that fosters complacency. When it did otherwise, it violated a code of objectivity it shared, at least implicitly, with the SDS of the *Statement*. (Critics are quick to point out that SDS were anything but objective when evaluating third world revolutionaries.) Hoffman, however, was fascinated by the inevitable mythmaking role of media and paradoxically convinced by writers like Benjamin Whorf and Marshall McLuhan both to doubt the existence of any objective reality and to believe that powerful myths could by themselves bring about real change in social life. The best means of constructing those myths were those made available by mass media.[25]

The differences between Hoffman and the SDS of Port Huron over political methods and autobiographical strategies, therefore, stem in part from their differences on the issues of myth and language. Where the language of the *Statement* seeks to mask the arbitrariness of the collective self it constructs behind an objective, social scientific rhetoric, Hoffman's *Revolution* straightforwardly makes an advertisement for it, claims that it is invented, and invites his contemporaries to "buy" it. Likewise, if America is merely an invented myth, then the political organizing either at the community level or on behalf of other oppressed peoples called for by the early SDS (and the early Hoffman, for that matter) was also completely beside the point. Such organizing ignored the way in which American power structures perpetuated themselves, which was not primarily by exercising raw power at a local level, but rather by controlling the national media and other institutions that formed and perpetuated American myth. As Jerry Rubin argued in *We Are Everywhere*, "Thanks to the technology of media, *nothing is local any more*."[26] A truly effective political response, therefore, would begin by studying how the "put-ons" worked so that one could construct effective countermyths that allowed one to "actualize [one's] full potential" and have "fun" at the same time (62). The best way to construct those myths was by using the very weapons that the American establishment had long employed to maintain power—the news media, mythmaking "theatre," "pure information" actions, Madison Avenue advertising techniques, and books that incorporate aspects of all of these such as *Revolution for the Hell of It*.

Annunciatory Narrative as Advertisement: Jerry Rubin's *Do It!* and *We Are Everywhere*

Hoffman's co-defendant in the Chicago conspiracy trial and his co-partner in the founding of the Yippie Party was Jerry Rubin (b. 1938), whose first two books, *Do It! Scenarios for the Revolution* (1970) and *We Are Everywhere* (1971), are also generational autobiographies cum manifestos. Both books seek to construct the generational narrative and identity I have begun to trace in other works. *We Are Everywhere* is a journal Rubin smuggled out to his lawyer while serving a sixty-day prison sentence. Thirty days of the sentence were served in Virginia concurrently with a sentence growing out of the 1967 Pentagon demonstration; the other thirty were served in Chicago's Cook County Jail for rioting charges brought against him by the State of Illinois. The book, written just after the Chicago Seven conspiracy trial, is a running commentary on the identity of the new generation, an account of the trial and its meaning, and a handbook for the "second American revolution."

Of the two books, however, *Do It!* more clearly illustrates the general themes I have been examining.[27] In form, it resembles other annunciatory works of the period. Written within two months after a federal grand jury indicted Rubin for crossing state lines to incite to riot in Chicago, the book, like Hoffman's *Revolution*, provides an account of the Chicago demonstrations as its climax. But Rubin's book reaches further back into the generation's (and his own) history in order to provide a narrative explanation of those events. His book also provides more historical detail about the Movement's growth, so that the importance of the Chicago events is diminished somewhat; in his narrative Chicago appears to be simply the latest, rather than the central, incident in an escalating war between the generations.

Its many short chapters are easily divided into four sections. The first section, chapters 1 through 13, provides the basic narrative of Rubin's coming of age in America. The central events include an account of his hypertypical childhood, echoing the generalized childhood sketched by *The Port Huron Statement* and prefiguring that shown in later generational pieces. A first-chapter photograph shows Rubin in what appears to be his high school senior portrait; it conveys a sense of his conformity to a generational model in the late 1950s: short haircut, neatly dressed in a suit, clean shaven. To emphasize his typicality, Rubin refers to himself in this section as a "child of Amerika," citing as evidence of his all-Americanness his love of hamburgers, french fries, cokes, sports pages and gossip columns, radio and color TV, and Hollywood movies ("even bad ones") (12). This childhood, however, is given only one and a half pages; its main characteristics are a fondness for pop culture icons and complacence about America and himself. The events of importance here, as in all generational autobiographies, are the historical events that dominated his coming of age and contributed to his and his generation's public identity. In chapters that resemble Hoffman's narrative "flashbacks," Rubin recounts his liberation from middle-class rigidity by rock 'n' roll, his early experiences with the New Left, the Berkeley counterculture, antiwar protests, leftist factionalism, and, finally, the creation of Yippie.

The second section, chapters 14 through 26, consists of mini-essays, again echoing Hoffman's meditative chapters, on various aspects of the youth revolution and its culture. These include sermons on countercultural rebirth; explanations of youth identity as expressed in long hair, drugs, new language; invectives against Western civilization, ideology, and money; reflections on mass media, the tactics of revolution, street theater, right-wing myths; and harangues against liberals, American prisons, and the justice system.

The third section, chapters 28 through 38, returns to the narrative, but focuses on the Chicago events. It includes narrative accounts of the initial planning sessions for the Chicago demonstrations, the battle with police and national guardsmen, the purchasing and use of a pig ("Pigasus") as the Yippie candidate for Democratic presidential nominee, police and military spies within the Yippie camp, definitions of the conspiracy, and Rubin's official acceptance speech after being "awarded" the grand jury indictment. The section concludes with accounts of revolutionary highjinks following the Chicago indictment, including an account of the Peace and Freedom presidential campaign in which Rubin briefly served as vice-presidential candidate, a second HUAC hearing, an incident of guerrilla theater in the schools, a return to his hometown high school in Cincinnati, Ohio, and the violent confrontations between youth and police over People's Park in Berkeley.

The fourth and final section, chapters 39 through 43, imitates other manifestos in its prospective envoi. In it, Rubin makes final exhortations to the generation, warning the "brothers" against false prophets of the new age (particularly capitalist prophets) and calling for collective thought and action. He reminds his peers that their movement is larger than the individuals who compose it: "We are all under the influence of a collective historical unconscious. . . . This generational movement cuts across class and race lines. The generational revolt is not explained by Freud or Marx. It is a war between historical generations" (250–51). The future that is being constructed by youth, he concludes in the final chapter, "Scenario for the Future/Yippieland," will bring a utopia free of money:

> The world will become one big commune with free food and housing, everything shared. . . . People will farm in the morning, make music in the afternoon and fuck wherever and whenever they want to.
>
> The United States of America will become a tiny yippie island in a vast sea of Yippieland love. (256)

Hoffman, as we have already seen, called his intragenerational debate with Rubin "the greatest in the movement," but in fact, as the above outline of the book shows, their ideological and stylistic similarities far outweigh their differences. Hoffman characterized their debate as one that centered on the identity of the Movement and, ultimately, of the generation. Hoffman's image of generational identity in 1968 comprised a clenched fist, a gun, a flower, and a smile; Rubin, according to Hoffman, preferred simply the fist and the gun. Little in Rubin's published posturing, however, indicates that that difference was a very strong one in 1970 or 1971 since he, too, calls for hilarity and flowers along with the death of policemen, liberals, and the American way of life. And even though there is more stridency in Rubin than in Hoffman, the reader of a book announcing on its copyright page that "Rubin is the leader of 850 million Yippies" might be excused for supposing the author's advocacy of violent revolution is more hyperbolic than serious.

There are, however, differences both of form and of emphasis between Rubin's and Hoffman's first generational autobiographies. Rubin, for example, makes more extensive use of the lessons on rhetoric that pepper Hoffman's *Revolution* than Hoffman does himself. The key chapters of *Revolution* dealing with rhetorical method are "Blank Space as Communication" and "Figure and Ground." As Hoffman explains it, ground/figure theory suggests that most people watching electronic media respond to the dynamic relationship they unconsciously perceive between the unengaging noise that makes up the medium's rhetorical "ground" (its text, words, logic, debate) and the always active, colorful, engaging "figure" that this rhetoric offsets. Television, for example, abounds with examples of "talking-head" shows featuring intellectuals discussing the merits of various political or social postures. This, says Hoffman, is "ground." The "figure" that this ground highlights can be found in commercials, which do not waste their time arguing; they present pure information. Juxtaposed in this way, the images present a choice to viewers that makes it more likely they will embrace the message of the commercial. Another example can be found in the way that television news commentary frames a news video on a Yippie "happening." "It's only when you establish a figure-ground relationship that you can convey information" that engages the spectators (133). It doesn't matter what is said in the commentary; unbiased viewers will respond positively to the happening's action. In 1968, television gave major time to the Democratic National Convention events, and only ten minutes to the demonstrations, but the demonstrations were the commercials; they were, as Hoffman sees it, "an advertisement for the revolution" (134).

The principal insight of such theory for Hoffman and Rubin, of course, is that American audiences, and particularly the young generation, do not listen to words, pay attention to speeches, or read books; they respond to "action." The lesson for those rhetoricians who still work with media that use words, therefore, is to turn those media into verbal equivalents of action, and the principal models for such transformations are advertisements (for writers) and TV commercials (for speakers). Advertisements employ action rhetoric by aggressively capturing reader attention and, more important, by involving readers in the construction of the advertiser's message. Reader attention is obtained by the use of color, graphics, and varied typography. Reader involvement is insured by means of evocative pictures and blank spaces, both of which force readers to supply their own meanings or "myths." In his efforts to use autobiography as an advertisement for generational identity, however, Hoffman is almost conservative, employing his own theory rather sparingly.

By contrast, Rubin makes extensive use of Hoffman's advice on rhetoric in *Do It!* The book is replete with photographs underscoring the text (unflattering shots of California governor Reagan and Chicago mayor Daley, the corpse of Che Guevara, the Marx Brothers, pertinent images from old Hollywood films, exultant and naked hippies, etc.); its use of attention-getting typography is extensive; it contains comic strip illustrations and graphics, as well as photograph-and-comics collages. In all, over 100 of the book's 256 pages contain photographs or graphics of some sort. (*We Are Everywhere* similarly contains more than 155 photographs on its 256 pages.) The purpose, clearly, is to transform autobiography as manifesto into autobiography as advertisement. Rather than simply cite Marshall McLuhan as a formative influence on his thinking about communications theory as Hoffman does, Rubin actually employed McLuhan's assistant, Quentin Fiore, to "design" and package the book. The message, so aggressively packaged by its medium, conveys itself with the subtlety of a commercial for cigarettes: adopt this identity and you too can be a sexy revolutionary.

Rubin's and Hoffman's use of advertising techniques was not unique to Movement writers. It was completely consistent with the intellectual trends in the culture criticism of the middle sixties. By the time Rubin began writing, studies of American consumer capitalism had thoroughly paved the way for a generation conscious of the relationship between media, advertising, politics, and the construction of social realities. The growth of television technology and ownership in the 1950s and 1960s had brought about a complete "revolution" in American consumer habits. Advertising had been, of course, an integral part of consumer capitalism since its emergence in the late nineteenth century, but it did not so thoroughly permeate the lives of Americans until television brought it into their living rooms. Vance Packard's *The Hidden Persuaders*, a popular analysis of the use of subliminal advertising techniques in America, was a best-seller in the 1960s. Analyses of the use of advertising in political campaigns had been introduced in Theodore White's *The Making of the President* series in 1961, and it became the central thesis of Joe McGinniss' *The Selling of the President* series, initiated with the 1968 election.[28] Hoffman's and Rubin's Madison Avenue approach to radical politics, including their vision of public life as "spectacular," as composed of images more or less self-consciously constructed, was simply the application of contemporary culture theory to their own field of work.

One might reasonably wonder how these advertisement-type techniques figure in the construction of an autobiographical self, either individual or collective. One answer is that Rubin, like Hoffman, sees his autobiographical task as the creation of a literal, as well as a narrative, portrait of the generational persona. So like Hoffman, Rubin provides, among other pictures, a cover photograph of himself speaking into a microphone. Bushy beard, psychedelic face paint, and long unruly hair unsuccessfully contained by a colorfully beaded headband fill all of the available space. This persona differs somewhat from Hoffman's, whose full-body photograph on the cover of *Revolution* diminishes facial features and depersonalizes the image, leaving the impression of a generic joyful revolutionary. Rubin's cover photo, by contrast, appears to have been taken by someone standing among the audience at a rally, so that the angle of the photo forces the reader to look up into Rubin's face. Although the facial photo emphasizes the individual character of the author, the facial decor and the angle of the shot obscure Rubin's individuality and accentuate the hybrid quality of his generational persona. The facial ornaments are clearly part of the costume of the counterculture. The conspicuous presence of a microphone, however, is more suggestive of the New Left, with its deeply held conviction that youth must involve themselves in the issues of their times. The persona, in short, is precisely that amalgam of counterculture and New Left that both Hoffman and Rubin were seeking to construct as *the* collective identity of their peers.

Rubin, however, uses photographs of himself for more than the static depiction of the generational persona. He also uses them to accentuate aspects of the generational narrative. The controlling metaphor of the first few chapters of the narrative is the conversion, which, as we saw in the discussion of Cowley's book, posits two authorial characterizations—one of the author's earlier, fallen self, and another of the author's present, reborn self. To underscore this metaphor, Rubin departs from the conventional autobiography's developmental narrative and its complementary photographic section displaying the author as he or she progresses through life accumulating experience and maturity. Instead, he employs a photographic strategy that highlights the gulf between two selves separated by a conversion. Complementing the narrative's pre- and postconversion selves, the photographs display but two selves in an ironic variation on the familiar "before and after" motif of American cosmetic advertisements.

A key element in the rhetorical strategy of Rubin's book, and one that provides a good deal of the humor, is his reversal of fundamentalist conversion stereotypes: the preconversion self is stereotypically depicted by fundamentalism as a hedonistic degenerate, the postconversion self as a clean-cut and smiling gospel (and business) success. By contrast, Rubin's preconversion self, which appears in two photos in the chapter "Child of Amerika," reverses this convention. The first photo features a young man in a suit and bow tie shaking hands with his political hero, Adlai Stevenson; the second appears to be a high school graduation photo of the same young man. Both are smiling broadly, conveying the wholesome geniality Americans associate with successful sales. His postconversion, born-again self, on the other hand, is the hirsute one I have already described on the book's cover. It also appears in a photo on the back cover in which Rubin, bearing a generic resemblance to convicted celebrity murderer Charles Manson, is being led by police to one of the several HUAC hearings he attended as a hostile witness. In this photo (which echoes Hoffman's rear cover photo on *Revolution*), Rubin is shirtless, he has numerous beads strung around his neck, and he carries an assault rifle (a toy one as it turns out). More significantly, neither of the photos of the postconversion Rubin could be mistaken for the same character, preconversion, in the book's first chapter. The transformation is startling and complete: from smiling American uprightness to angry, dope-smoking, degenerate radical.[29]

In spite of Rubin's use of the conversion narrative as a strategy here, that form is not particularly typical of the first phase of generational writing. The logic of generationalism argues that identity is the result of experiences one accumulates during the period in which one comes of age. It is not consistent with this theory that identity is achieved in a single moment of illumination, as is the case in a conversion narrative. Rubin, in spite of this logic, uses the form for two reasons. First, the conversion narrative is a powerful literary tool for winning converts. It has the one advantage every advertising agency employs when it tries to sell a product: it offers all of the answers to life quickly and without major expenditure of effort on the part of the buyer ("All this can be yours in a flash!"). That quality alone would have made the conversion narrative attractive to a salesman like Rubin. Second, Rubin's first "self," the one that his conversion narrative rejects, was the "false" one imposed on his generation by its parents. In a sense, Rubin's text argues that its narrator was not a true member of his own generation until his conversion in Berkeley, when he suddenly assumed all of the experiences and values that others in his age group had been accumulating over time.

According to Rubin's own rhetorical theory, the photographic version of the conversion would serve as a more effective advertisement for generational identity than the verbal narrative of the conversion underlying the book's general presentation. As an extension of Hoffman's theory about blank space as communication within verbal texts, Rubin argues that youth need simply see the visual image; they can fill in the details for themselves. "The secret to the yippie myth," he writes, "is that it's nonsense. Its basic informational statement is a blank sheet of paper" (83). For that reason, Rubin eschews making an ideological pitch for the new identity in the manner of *The Port Huron Statement* and emulates instead the immediate nonverbal impact of television news and advertising. That medium, he believes, communicates primarily and most effectively with images that transcend their accompanying commentary. "The first 'student demonstration,'" Rubin argues, "flashed across the TV tubes of the nation as a myth in 1964. That year the first generation being raised from birth on TV was 9, 10 and 11 years old. 'First chance I get,' they thought, 'I wanna do that too'" (106). The television commentary on these demonstrations, of course, was generally negative, but the words had minimal impact: "The way to understand TV is to shut off the sound. No one remembers the words they hear; the mind is a technicolor movie of images, not words. I've never seen 'bad' coverage of a demonstration. It makes no difference what they *say* about us. The pictures are the story" (108). Rubin is quick to apply the idea to his book: he uses photographs, not only of himself but also of other embodiments of the generational myth, to provide visual advertisements for the collective self, as a rhetorical strategy for winning converts to the new identity. The young are always displayed in flashy, romantic, and sexy images; their negative counterparts in the older generation are shown to be overweight, sexually rigid, sadistically antipleasure, and phony.

In addition to blank space, typographical anomalies, comic strip, collage, and photographs, Rubin also employs an advertising technique I have already discussed in connection with *The Port Huron Statement* and Hoffman's *Revolution*: asserting that a "we" exists in the hope that young people, enticed by the "bandwagon effect," will join up. That technique is readily apparent in the title of Rubin's second book, *We Are Everywhere*. In that book, however, a change occurs in the New Left's earlier assumption that it spoke as a vanguard on behalf of the people.

Rubin no longer feels the need for a vanguard; the revolution has become a mass generational movement. It is everywhere.

> The 1968 election and demonstration were a Historical Theater for thousands to change from. The crowds at radical rallies went from 500 to 3000, 4000, 10,000. Everybody saw it: "Last year in my law school I knew all the radicals, I could count them. But this year there are so many, I can't count them."
> The same in business schools, medical, everywhere.
> The number of stoned freaks quadrupled: from a mere handful to hundreds, thousands. And among young kids, the straight left was dead, everyone was a freak.
> You didn't have to go to Berkeley any more—Berkeley came to you, Berkeley was everywhere. (102–3)

In short, Rubin (and other generationalists in the late sixties) began to believe their own "myths"; it was a belief that proved catastrophic to some of them.

With all of these strategies and with Rubin's emphasis on the instantaneous nature of his own conversion, *Do It!* rewrites the generational narrative we have already seen in *The Port Huron Statement.* Rubin depicts the generation leaping directly from middle-class conformity to heavy-lidded epicureanism and revolutionary radicalism not as a result of disillusionment with the parental world, but as a result of youth's intuitive discovery of pleasures the older generation is too frightened of to experience. There is, therefore, no reasoned process by which the generation moves from an innocent acceptance of the status quo to a troubled skepticism about and eventual rejection of it. Rubin's narrative features abrupt discontinuities. "Radicalism," he asserts, "does not proceed step by step, logically or rationally: radicalism is an insight, a historical explosion with body and mind, an Apocalypse, in which individuals change themselves overnight" (*We Are Everywhere,* 101). In Rubin's rendering of the generational story, therefore, youth do not achieve their revolutionary stance by means of a gradual escalation of intergenerational negotiations. They simply wake up to the discovery that the status quo has been designed to suppress pleasure. They have discovered that "sin" is a parental code word for "fun."

This discovery also provides Rubin with the solution to a central problem facing generational autobiographers. For Rubin, as for Hoffman and Hayden, one of the most serious obstacles to the construction of a collective identity for white middle-class youth was its dependence upon a theory of identity politics acquired from the civil rights movement. According to that theory, collective identity is shaped by a group's shared experience of oppression and by their desire to create a collective identity distinct from the one imposed upon them by a dominant social group.

They also possess some outward "badge" of the oppression they experience; in the case of the African Americans, that badge was race. Because white youth could articulate no such obvious oppression or badges in their own experience, they often identified themselves vicariously with oppressed minorities within the United States or with third world peoples abroad. After several groups within the civil rights movement expelled their white allies in the late 1960s, Hoffman, Rubin, Hayden, and others in the New Left sought to construct a generational identity built specifically upon white youth's alienation. What they needed, however, was a "shared oppression" as well as an easily identified "badge" of that oppression. They found a name for their shared oppression in new Marxist and Freudian theories that emphasized the suppression of pleasure in the middle classes.[30] Youth, who desired and fought for those pleasures, were necessarily oppressed. And the badge . . . well, the badge could be grown. Generationally identified youth signaled their rejection of middle-class sexual repression by not cutting their hair.

In a chapter on this subject entitled "Long Hair, Aunt Sadie, Is a Communist Plot," Rubin articulates the generationalists' construction of youth identity within the framework of identity politics. Reminiscent of Hoffman's letter from his "Mom" in *Revolution*, the chapter takes shape as a dialogue (presumably largely fictional) between Rubin and his Aunt Sadie, an older-generation communist and, like her nephew, a "black sheep" in the family. Rubin tells his aunt that

> long hair is a commie plot! Long hair gets people uptight—more uptight than ideology, cause long hair is communication. We are a new minority group, a nationwide community of longhairs, a new identity, new loyalties. We longhairs recognize each other as brothers. . . . Young people identify short hair with authority, discipline, unhappiness, boredom, rigidity, hatred of life—and long hair with letting go, letting your hair down, being free, being open . . . *long hair is our black skin*. Long hair turns white middle-class youth into niggers. (93–94)

Aunt Sadie's problem in this dialogue is that, as an old leftist, she sees "only two classes in the world, the bourgeoisie and the working class" (97); she fails to see that present-day social divisions are between generations. Besides long hair, youth identity is built upon other "badges," including every outward sign of youth culture—its sexuality, its drugs, its music, its dancing, its language—and Rubin provides chapters to sell each of them. But the badges all have one thing in common: they represent youth's rejection of American puritanism and fear of sex (96), and they have all been either outlawed or demonized by the older generation. Young people have also been "colonized" like a third world country. Their communities (Berkeley, Isla Vista, Haight-Ashbury) and universities have been invaded and exploited by "external" forces: "Students, nonstudents, hippies, women, Weatherpeople, gays, yippies—young people—are an oppressed people living within Imperialism, living on campuses controlled from the outside. . . . In riots, in battles with police, in overthrowing unrepresentative, foreign control, we are writing the history of our generation in the streets and becoming liberated men and women" (*We Are Everywhere*, 98). The strategy is one that Hoffman also uses in *Revolution*, which contains chapters entitled "The New Niggers," "The White Niggers," and "Runaways: The Slave Revolt." In short, the condition of youth can best be described by analogy with the oppression of blacks, minorities, and third world peoples. Young people must begin to think of themselves as an oppressed group, and they must use as a weapon in their struggle against that oppression the creation of a generational identity. Rubin, using all the persuasive arts invented to serve the economic system of the oppressor, will make sure that that identity is a seductive one.

Annunciatory Narrative as Melodrama: Tom Hayden's *Trial*

Tom Hayden's *Trial* (1970), like Hoffman's *Revolution* and Rubin's first two books, is an annunciatory autobiography/manifesto that focuses on the Chicago demonstrations and the ensuing trial of the Chicago Seven as "a watershed experience for an entire generation of alienated white youth" (9). Together with Hoffman, Rubin, and five other leaders of the antiwar and youth movements, Hayden (b. 1939) was charged by the federal government with conspiracy to cross state lines in order to incite to riot at the Chicago Convention. At the trial's conclusion, Hayden, Rubin, Hoffman, David Dellinger, and Rennie Davis were found guilty of crossing state lines to riot (but not of conspiracy) and of numerous contempt-of-court charges that arose during the trial.[31]

Less experimental than either Hoffman's or Rubin's book, Hayden's second essay in collective autobiography is tightly organized into four sections of several chapters each. The first and last sections comprise narratives that frame the Chicago events and the trial. The first section, "From Protest to Resistance," like the first part of Hoffman's *Revolution*, recounts the increasing repression of American youth politics leading up to and including the Chicago violence, and pays particular attention to the enactment of the 1968 Interstate Riot Act, which had the effect of making what Hayden calls the "Southern Way of Life, generally regarded in 1960 as immoral and archaic . . . synonymous with the American way of life" (13). This section's apocalyptic rhetoric updates the generational narrative underlying *The Port Huron Statement*, arguing that "the paranoid wrath of the older, entrenched generation" and the hardening of "America's famous democratic pragmatism . . . into an inflexible fascist core" (9) had forced the young to move away from the politics of protest and reform and to embrace revolution. The older generation had responded to the reformist activism of the early SDS not with cooptation, as the framers of the *Statement* had expected, but with harassment, illegal domestic espionage, police violence, and, finally, the enactment of federal statutes outlawing, in effect, a "defiant and rebellious 'state of mind'" (25). In short, the underlying justificatory narrative of the generation had ceased being one of disillusionment leading to protest, and had become instead one of oppression leading to war.[32]

It is, however, the two middle sections of the book, "A Generation on Trial" and "The Trial in Perspective," that make most explicit the generationalism that was largely implicit in *The Port Huron Statement*. Both of these sections reveal the sociological and political assumptions underlying many of the generational autobiographies of the late sixties, and provide as well the clearest explanations (or rationalizations) for the behavior of those who acted on behalf of a generational constituency ostensibly comprising "millions." One reason for Hayden's explicitness clearly arises from his greater confidence in the Chicago Seven's representative status. While the writers of the *Statement* issued their generational manifesto largely on the strength of the conventional left-wing belief in themselves as a historical vanguard, Hayden in *Trial* attempts to provide evidence that he represents more than a small group of historically prescient radicals. During the trial the defendants would, Hayden relates, travel around the country speaking at youth rallies where they discovered the real "jury of their peers." They met, he says, "thousands of young people who felt themselves to be part of the ordeal" (90). Thousands more waited patiently outside the Chicago courthouse each day in the hope of obtaining a seat in "solidarity" with the accused. After the announcement of the guilty verdicts, TDA ("the day after") demonstrations were called all over the country, and young people again turned out in the thousands "with a spontaneity flowing from legitimate outrage because their collective identity had been violated" (95). Accordingly, Hayden claims (echoing Hoffman),

> we were not leaders in command of legions of youth; we were a myth in
> which millions could participate. We were symbols of what millions were
> going through themselves. . . . We were moved and shaped by the collective
> rising anger of these thousands of others. (91)

The Chicago Seven were, in short, "representative people, acting out many of the impulses of our generation. It was like riding the crest of a great wave, a wave made by the power of the people" (96).[33]

Based on his belief that the Chicago Seven were generational representatives, Hayden devotes his second section, "A Generation on Trial," to the core meaning of Chicago: the case, he argues, was not about specific criminal acts or individuals, but about the identity of an "entire generation of alienated white youth" (9). Accordingly, the Chicago events in Hayden's reading represent a theatrical melodrama, a confrontation of generations first in the streets of Chicago, and later in the federal courthouse. "A Generation on Trial" contains an extended dramatis personae section in which Hayden defines first the generational identity of youth and then the generational identity of the "dinosaurs." Both groups are represented by those who enact the drama within the trial. On the one side are the defendants, their legal staff, and their constituency in the streets; on the other are the prosecutors, the judge, the police, the informants (including military, police, FBI, and civilians), the jury, and the older generation that identified with them. However much sixties writers may have ordinarily disagreed with each other, they could occasionally manifest a remarkable accord. Rubin, for instance, saw the trial's dramatic cast in almost precisely the same terms as Hayden. In *We Are Everywhere*, he wrote: "Each defendant had a myth which was on trial— and collectively we stood for the rebellion of young people." He goes on to describe the confrontation as an "international theatrical drama" with characters who were "symbolic figures . . . caricatures, comic book characters. TV made the trial a worldwide soap opera, every night another chapter, kids versus parents, students versus teachers, prisoners versus the court system. Everyone had someone to identify with. It was impossible to be neutral" (14).

The first chapter of the section offers a portrait of the generation as a young collective, together with a theory of the politics of collective identity. The main components of the new generation's identity include its internationalism, its unique culture, its new sexuality, and its language.

Its internationalism was evidenced in its rejection of the racism that affected both domestic and foreign policy in the United States, and in its identification with "peoples whom the U.S. government defines as enemies" such as North Vietnam, Cuba, and American black nationalists (33). That identification, as Todd Gitlin later wrote, was one of the essential elements of leftist identity in the late sixties; it "preserved the drama of black hats and white hats by reversing them. It confirmed that we were worthy of being the enemies of the American state."[34] The generation's culture was most clearly expressed in its music, rock and roll. In allowing the lyrics, but not the music, of Arlo Guthrie, Judy Collins, Phil Ochs, and others to be used as evidence for the defense, the court missed the point that "there has grown up a generation of young whites with a new, less repressed attitude toward sex and pleasure, and music has been the medium of their liberation" (36). The trial also revealed the new and less repressed sexuality of the young. The defendants, Hayden claimed, "for all our male chauvinist tendencies, represented a gentler, less aggressive type of human being" (36) epitomized by the pan-sexuality of Walt Whitman and Allen Ginsberg (38). And finally, because new words

are "vital for the identity of people seeking to remake themselves and society" (39), the young generation had rejected the hypocritical euphe-
misms "of the Establishment" (39) in order to create their own language,
which included words that "cannot be spoken in the 'legitimate' world:
fuck, motherfucker, shit," as well as neologisms: "right on, cool, outta
sight, freaky" (39).

To his credit, Hayden was not wholly lacking in perspective on the
shortcomings of his generational representatives. He admits in another
chapter, entitled "Limits of the Conspiracy," that atavism still exists
among the defendants, but he insists that it is the result of the older generation's manipulation of the means by which youth leaders are chosen:
"Our male chauvinism, elitism, and egoism were merely symptoms of the
original problem—the Movement did not choose us to be its symbols; the
press and government did. The entire process by which known leaders
become known is almost fatally corrupting" (109). The Yippies in particular, he says, are good examples of the corrupting influence of media-
created leadership, and he singles out Jerry Rubin's book *Do It!* (109–10)
as an illustration of the way in which apparently revolutionary rhetoric
can be coopted by the capitalist system. As a result of such corruption,
Hayden finally calls upon the other members of the conspiracy to give up
leadership of the Movement to radical feminists and younger revolutionaries such as the White Panthers (112).

Once Hayden has completed his collective self-portrait, he turns to
the older generation. Their primary representative, of course, is federal
judge Julius Hoffman himself:

> Julius Hoffman is symbolic, then, of an entire class. He is not an accident,
> not a vestige of the past, but a perfect representative of a class of dinosaurs
> that is vengefully striking out against the future. Hoffman's vanity, arro-
> gance, racism, paternalism, indifference to official violence, and blindness
> are the primary features of that class. (52)

Likewise, the prosecuting attorney, who characterized the Movement as
a "freaking fag revolution . . . , represented imperialist, aggressive man"
(36), as well as "the conventional image of manhood . . .—a fighter, a father of six, earthly but intelligent, still vaguely handsome, knowledgeable
in the ways of the world, but struggling as a Catholic to retain purity. He
was the sort of man whose apparent politeness conceals a vulgar rage"
(53). Finally, the jury itself comprised people chosen from voter registra-
tion polls that "systematically exclude racial minorities, the young, the
mobile, and those who are alienated from the American political
process." It would have been impossible, Hayden writes, for the defendants, "critics of the political system," to be judged fairly "by people who
were registered in it" (78). The drama of the trial was, therefore, a ritual
guaranteed to reveal identity even as it suppressed justice.

The theory of identity underlying this dramatis personae is one with which we are by now familiar. Though most often considered leftists or Marxists, Hayden, Hoffman, and Rubin were actually more closely linked to earlier generationalists, such as Bourne and Ortega, than to Marxism (in *Revolution*, Hoffman mentions Ortega y Gasset's theory of continuous generational renewal, but points out, like all generationalists before him, that "young people today are very different from previous generations" [58]). They were aided in their generationalism by many New Left theorists, who were beginning in the late sixties to argue for a generational orientation from two points of view: first, that the real center of conflict within capitalism now resided not between the workers and the owners, but between the young and the old;[35] and second, that young white radicals had, in their identification with third world liberation movements, mistakenly overlooked their own oppression. Following these writers, Hayden revises his own Marxism:

> "[Y]outh" is more important than "economic class" in analyzing the American struggle. A generation ago it was the industrial working class that felt the shock of industrial change most severely. But since the war, young people of all classes have been the chief victims bearing the burden of the expanding empire. . . .
> With the passage of time, with the further decay of the American empire, the discontent now felt most by youth will spread with them wherever they go to work or live. In the long run, then, the alienation of youth may become an alienation of *the whole people*. (154–55)

Combined with this generational orientation in Hayden's book is an analysis of the new youth identity consistent with the identity politics of any oppressed collective. Exaggerating somewhat the amount of time that the new identity has been in the making, Hayden argues that

> One of the first tasks of those creating a new society is that of creating a new and distinct identity. This identity cannot be fully conscious at first, but as a movement grows, through years and generations, it contains its own body of experience, its styles and habits, and a common language becomes a part of the new identity. (40)

The last section of *Trial*, "From Resistance to Liberation," like the conclusions of the other manifestos we have seen, provides a political agenda for the future action of the generation; it is a narrative map, a prospectus for generational warfare and the construction of a society based on the values and characteristics Hayden believes are central to the new generation's identity. His primary intention, it would seem, is to escalate the level of revolutionary rhetoric. It calls for the abolition of a system of private property that benefits only a few; self-determination for America's internal colonies (made up of black, Puerto Rican, Chicano, Asian, and Indian ghettos); the creation of "Free Territories in the

Mother Country" for alternative lifestyles "more in harmony with the interests of the world's peoples" in places like "Berkeley, Haight-Ashbury, Isla Vista, Ann Arbor, Madison, rural Vermont, the East Village, the Upper West Side" (158–59). Those Free Territories would be centers of new cultural experimentation, internationalism, confrontation with the Mother Country, survival, self-defense, and the abolition of individualism:

> Certainly the excessive individualism and egoism, which dominate the culture of young people, must be overcome if we are going to survive, much less make a revolution. But the organizational form must be consistent with the kind of revolution we are trying to make. For that reason *the collective* in some form should be the basis of revolutionary organization. (163)

In its apocalyptic tone, Hayden's book reflected the mood of left-wing radicals between late 1968 and the middle of 1970. And whatever Hayden's differences from writers like Hoffman, Rubin, and (as we will shortly see) Rossman, he shares with them this apocalyptic sense that America was about to enter a drama much more serious than the one performed in Chicago. As these writers portrayed it, the culture was on the brink of outright intergenerational war.

Annunciatory Narrative as Prophecy: Michael Rossman's *The Wedding within the War*

Michael Rossman, a Berkeley-based apologist for and historian of the Movement, is not as well known nationally as Hayden, Hoffman, or Rubin, but he was conspicuous in the Movement on the West Coast, where he still lives. Born in 1939, Rossman is about the same age as the other three writers, all of whom were born between 1936 and 1940. Unlike them, he is also a "red-diaper baby" (the child of parents who were active leftists during the 1930s) and so grew up in a politically charged atmosphere. That background led him to an early interest in radical protest, and he joined others to demonstrate against the witch-hunting activities of the House Un-American Activities Committee in 1960. Rossman was a prolific writer of political/cultural commentary throughout the 1960s for a wide variety of journals, both mainstream and underground. His three books, *The Wedding within the War* (1971), *On Learning and Social Change* (1972), and *New Age Blues: On the Politics of Consciousness* (1979),[36] are all concerned with personal witness and historical change, leftist politics, educational reform, and the human potential movement.

The Wedding within the War shares with other generational works written in the late sixties an apocalyptic tone that is sometimes off-putting, but in spite of this, it serves as an excellent recapitulation of the themes important to this group of autobiographers. Like Hoffman,

Rubin, and Hayden, Rossman sees autobiography as an instrument of identity politics, but unlike them, he places a specific emphasis on the autobiographer's prophetic role. The difference may be accounted for by his other emphases—the notions that generational identity grows dynamically and only those who can successfully predict its direction will remain abreast of History.

For Rossman, the most important event in the coming of age of his generation was the emergence of the counterculture in the mid-1960s. That culture offered, he thought, a new model of identity for a collective self that would merge with and transmute the political identity already established for the generation by New Left manifestos such as *The Port Huron Statement*. The counterculture offered an identity that called for a radical change of consciousness, with an emphasis on communalism, alternative lifestyles, altered (drug-induced) realities, New Age therapies, and sexual liberation; it was utopian, mythic, and visionary where the New Left was socialist, historical, and pragmatic.[37] Like Hoffman and Rubin, Rossman imagined a merging of these two identities, and during the Free Speech Movement (FSM) at Berkeley, he thought he saw this merging beginning to take place; for Rossman, FSM constituted a generational experience that sharply distinguished his own age group from earlier generations of radicals. The revolution of the sixties would occur both within society and within the minds of revolutionaries. In dating his own rebirth from the FSM, he echoes Rubin, who writes in *Do It!* that "we're born twice. It's your second birth—your revolutionary birth—which is the important one. I was born in the FSM in Berkeley in 1964" (90).

Despite Rossman's use of the rhetoric of conversion at this point, his narrative differs in significant ways from a conventional conversion narrative. While Rossman's FSM experience, which he refers to as "a heavy turning, a re-beginning. . . . an historical thunderbolt" [52]), is comparable to Rubin's "historical explosion with body and mind, an Apocalypse," Rossman's "turning" is to a process of becoming rather than to a wholly new self. For Rossman, FSM provided not so much a new self as a new means for constructing identity in the face of massive cultural dislocation. What Rossman found during FSM was not a new political or religious outlook, but a new understanding of his generation's potential for self-invention and growth. As a result, the primary model behind Rossman's understanding of collective identity, as he makes clear in *On Learning and Social Change*, is "radical education" rather than religious or quasi-religious belief, and, like the framers of *The Port Huron Statement* and other autobiographers in the first phase of generational writing, he places most of his emphasis on growth and change as a central feature of the generational self.[38]

To underscore this feature of generational identity, Rossman employs two techniques—one structural, the other verbal. Structurally, *The*

Wedding within the War is an attempt to re-present the various stages of generational growth from the point of view of the collective at significant points in the process. Building upon and extending a method already used by Hoffman in *Revolution*, Rossman arranges chronologically a collection of his essays, letters, poetry, and transcribed tape recordings produced between 1959 and 1970 in order to present "not a history of what came to be called the Movement, but a series of views from its perspective—windows into time, key moments as *they seemed at the time* to one young man growing up through them" (3–4). Those moments include the protests in 1960 against the execution of Caryl Chessman and the San Francisco HUAC hearings, the civil rights movement (especially the 1964 Mississippi Freedom Summer), the Berkeley Free Speech Movement in 1964, the Free School Movement between 1967 and 1970, the Chicago demonstrations in 1968, and the People's Park struggle in Berkeley in 1969. Between each selection, Rossman has included short retrospective analyses that place the selections in historical context and reveal his present—1971—perspective on them. His intention in "building" an autobiography from earlier essays is to provide a narrative of the most important generational events in a way that reveals, without retrospective mediation, the "limited consciousness" of the generational self as it *was* in the process of development.

Verbally, Rossman emphasizes the dynamic quality of the collective identity by transforming several of the catchphrases of his generational moment into metaphors for generational identity. For example, the various events that make up the narrative blocks of the autobiography are all "demonstrations." On one level, this term retains its usual reference to the mass protests that were so vital a part of the Movement's political style. For Rossman, however, the term denotes something more; these public occasions are also opportunities for the young generation to demonstrate *itself*, to announce its changing identity. Rossman calls them "our public theater . . . in which we came together to show ourselves to each other and the world" (4). The changes that took place in the style of these "demonstrations" reveal, according to Rossman, the development of the generation's identity over the course of the decade. The concept of "public theater," of course, is common to almost all early generational writers, as we have just seen in Hayden's casting of the Chicago trial as a melodrama of identity and as we earlier saw in Cowley's use of his fight with a cafe proprietor as an example of generational theater.

The same kind of verbal transformation takes place in Rossman's use of the phrase "the Movement." In usual parlance, this term referred to the broadly based groups that opposed America's Vietnam policy, its oppression of minorities, and its repressed middle-class culture. In Rossman's book, however, the term becomes a metaphor denoting what he takes to be the central feature of generational self-definition. "Always," he says, "the Movement was a process of redefining ourselves" (77). And later, he adds that "the Movement *is* a process of growth: for groups no less than individuals, a fixed identity is a death" (150). In *Wedding*, therefore, Rossman constructs a plot that simply traces the "movement" of generational "demonstrations" and ties them together. The book begins with accounts of old-left-style demonstrations against capital punishment and the House Un-American Activities Committee in 1960. The public identity that these demonstrations evinced is brought to an abrupt and dramatic turning point during the spontaneous 1964 FSM uprising with its radically democratic forms. Unlike the old-left demonstrations, which grew out of the careful planning of an ideologically oriented cadre of socialists, the FSM was a spontaneous expression of popular dissent. It was characterized by collective discussions in which hundreds of people, not simply an elite cadre, took part. The rest of the book records the way in which the collective self that emerged from the FSM experience eventually expressed itself in the frustrated rage and violent confrontations that characterized the 1968 demonstrations in Chicago, the People's Park protests in Berkeley in 1969, and the rise of the free school and educational reform movements in the late 1960s. The final chapters of the book are marked by the same two developments we have already noted in Hoffman, Rubin, and Hayden: an increasingly apocalyptic rhetoric, as the young generation readies itself for an inevitable civil war with official "Amerika," and a coming together of the youth culture's identity, which Rossman celebrates in his accounts of the counterculture ceremony marking his marriage to Karen McLellan in 1969 and his announced intentions concerning the education of their son, Lorca.

Consonant with his emphasis on growth as an element of collective identity, Rossman also stresses the notion of the collective autobiographer as prophet, the one who will predict the direction in which growth will occur. Given the prospective nature of annunciatory autobiographies, it is not surprising to find Cowley, Hoffman, Rubin, and Hayden making predictions about the direction of history. Those writers, however, reserved most of their predictions for the final chapter of their books. In Rossman's book, prophetic concerns dominate the entire narrative and are intimately related to his notion of his own generational role. Unlike Ortega who held that an intellectual elite heralds and conducts the generation's historical tasks, or Cowley who believed that artists provide a sensitive barometer of the generational spirit, Rossman and many other sixties generationalists subscribed to a belief in what I term "geographical vanguardism"—a conviction that specific locales almost automatically confer prophetic powers on those who live there. There was, in fact, a variation of the common sixties question "What's happening, man?" that went "Where's it happening?" Colloquially, the "it" in this phrase simply meant "fun" or "good times." But for serious

Movement members, the "it" clearly refers to "the cutting edge of history." In a typical pronouncement of the period, Raymond Mungo described Jerry Rubin as a "thirty-year old self-conscious theoretician of the movement, anxious to be at the forefront of What's Happening."[39] One manifestation of the breakup of the Movement after 1968 was the intragenerational argument over where "it was happening." Mungo and the counterculture "communards," as we shall see, thought "it" was happening in places such as Vermont, Taos, Mendocino, and British Columbia where a withdrawal from leftist politics and a backto-the-land movement were taking place. More politically minded generationalists continued to believe that "it" was happening only in major urban centers. Rossman held up the special virtues of Berkeley, which he called, in a phrase recalling Cowley's artists, "Barometer City." Berkeley was a kind of middle ground, neither too urban nor too rural; it was known both for its radical politics and its alternative lifestyles. "The wavelengths of our common transformations flow strongly through Berkeley," Rossman claimed. "For twelve years now what happens here and across the Bay happens a year or two later in concentric circles spreading out across Amerika" (12). One function of the generational prophet, therefore, was to remain in such centers to serve as "an active conduit for the common sea of our Energy," and to hang "on the tip of the rushing wave" (12). Rubin, as we have seen, finally dissolved the problem of geographical vanguardism by one-upping Rossman's predilection for Berkeley. After 1968, he argued in *We Are Everywhere*, "You didn't have to go to Berkeley any more—Berkeley came to you, Berkeley was everywhere" (103).

Rossman, however, remained true to his belief in Berkeley's special character, so one of his intentions in *Wedding* is to establish his credentials as a prophet from the city where all those who "stay open and are transmuted" (12) are, by dint of geographical placement, gifted with foresight. Given that intention, his "windows-into-time" approach to autobiography provides a form that allows him to make the strongest case for his prophetic powers. Because his readers can see the actual texts of the predictions he was making in 1963, they can form their own judgment about his prescience and his ability to formulate the identity adaptations the generation would have to make to accommodate historical change.

It would be unfair, however, to say that Rossman chose his "windows-into-time" form only with the intention of establishing his identity as a seer. More important to Rossman was his sense that this approach would be the most appropriate way to convey a story of their past that would both empower the generation and enlighten it politically. It was an extension of the identity politics we have already seen in the three earlier writers. Addressing the younger members of the generation in his opening comments, Rossman explained:

these tales are scraps of our common history. You will recognize their experience, archaic as some of its aspects may seem. You are not alone, least of all in Time. You share a heritage of developing struggle which stretches back continuously through these events, and through earlier roots we have all but forgotten—we who were born in the landscape the glaciers scoured clean. (31–32)

The form Rossman chose was one that he believed would effectively provide the developing generation with a sense of its political identity, and the characteristic of that identity that most concerned him was its ability to adapt to the changing conditions of history. Describing his intentions in a formulation remarkably similar to Cowley's claim that *Exile's Return* is "not so much a record of events as a narrative of . . . the ideas . . . that half-unconsciously guided people's actions," Rossman writes that his book is "not so much [a history] of events as of the perceptions and consciousness that attended them" (77).[40]

In order to convey this history of consciousness, Rossman, like other generational autobiographers, uses himself as a representative figure who stands in for the collective consciousness: "My accounts are typical," Rossman claims, "of the consciousness of the white Movement at the time" (31). At the same time that he speaks for the Movement, Rossman insists that the Movement was representative of the whole generation: "the Movement itself had become a presence, forcing all the young to begin in some way to define themselves with respect to it" (76). Even for those young people who disagreed with the politics of the Movement, the central issues of identity it raised remained the issues against which everyone had to define him or herself. That Rossman was not alone in this sort of thinking is clear from the many others who echoed his sentiments. In a formulation very similar to Rossman's, Rubin wrote in *We Are Everywhere*: "No individual can escape the mood of his or her generation. We live in one of those periods of history, including rapid change [*sic*], where the history of the movement is the history of each individual" (98). According to such writers, one is typical if one is present at the great, symbolic rites of one's times (for Rossman, these events included the FSM, the Chicago demonstrations, and People's Park), but one could *become* representative by assuming a "voice," by explaining to the generation what their "demonstration" had, in fact, demonstrated about them and their world. Rossman's autobiography adopts the "we" from this position. He saw himself as someone who was (as he said of Jerry Rubin) "helping to articulate a myth of central significance to us" (267). That myth was meant not only to capture the emerging political identity of the young, but also to construct and direct it.

Like other writers examined in this chapter, Rossman fixes on a specific mythic event that epitomizes the identity themes characteristic of the new generational self. In the chapter "Barefoot in a Marshmallow

World," he examines the meaning of the early days of the FSM, and particularly the spontaneous sit-down on Berkeley's Sproul Plaza in response to the arrest of Jack Weinberg for passing out political pamphlets. Students protesting the arrest encircled the police car to which Weinberg had been taken and remained there for two days. According to Rossman, "every theme later developed [in the Movement] was huddled with us around that car" (128). In the course of the sit-down, which grew to include about three thousand people, students climbed barefoot on top of the car to argue and debate with each other:

> we used 4,000,000 sheets of paper to expand those barefoot thoughts (and *only* those) . . . in the first true dialogue I have heard in America. It was all there: the "non-negotiable" issues; the unexpected intensity of our commitment and community; our strange honest humor; the absent estrangement of the faculty; the Administration's refusal to speak to us save via 500 cops, or even to see us, encamped under its nose; our desperate spontaneous democracy; and the total loneliness. . . . You'd never know this from the books, never know that no single new element—psychological, tactical, dialectical, compositional—entered the controversy from then till its climax: all that we were, all that we faced, were there full-fledged around the car, in every sense. (128)

Though many of these "elements" were similar to the ones developed by other writers, Rossman's particular emphases made for differences between him and other generational autobiographers, all of whom may be said to be writing the same collective work. Reading Rossman in the context of their works, one becomes aware of an intragenerational and intertextual dialogue about the identity of the young that is reminiscent of Cowley's conversation with Karl Pretshold. That dialogue is most significantly present on an implicit level, in the selection of the specific "mythic" events each author uses as the center of his narrative. Rossman chooses the FSM partly in response to Hoffman, Rubin, and Hayden's choice of Chicago. The dialogue also takes place explicitly, as for example in an open letter to Jerry Rubin in which Rossman discusses the way in which the "mythic unconsciousness of the young" (263) ought to be addressed before the upcoming 1968 Chicago demonstrations. Taking issue with Rubin's plan to attract large numbers of youth with promises of rock music and peaceful street demonstrations, Rossman says that the organizers should warn people about the possibility of a violent confrontation with police. Ultimately, Rossman's arguments with Yippies on the one hand and hard-core leftists on the other arises from his belief that, in formulating generational identity and imperatives, the two wings of the Movement are "seeking too easy an alternative. The joy [of Yippie] and the politics [of the New Left] must be fused, as they began to be in FSM" (269). We can see another side of this dialogue in Hoffman's *Revolution*. In a chapter entitled "A Response to the Doubting Thomases,"

Hoffman answers those who suspect that the Yippies are knowingly leading their followers into a violent confrontation in Chicago and who suggest that America's youth ought to abandon "politics" for the counterculture. Hoffman insists that one cannot limit the definition of "politics"
to electoral demonstrations and claims that "doing your thing"—the
counterculture idea of right living—is just as political as marching. As for
the threat of violence, Hoffman asserts that those who want violence will
naturally find it and enjoy themselves; those who want to come to
Chicago for other kinds of "politics," such as visiting the zoo, selling
newspapers, debating ideology, dancing, smoking dope, or giving flowers
to cops, will also have an opportunity to practice their politics (111). For
Rossman and the other participants in this dialogue, the issue is clearly
not a matter of political strategy alone, but a matter of who it is, ultimately, that the generation will *be*.

There also exists an intergenerational dialogue in each of these
works. In Rossman's book, it can again be seen most clearly in "Barefoot
in a Marshmallow World," which is largely a response to the older generation's efforts to explain FSM. Summing up several books on the subject, Rossman says that "plowing through this telephone book" of data,
"one doesn't notice that the face above it is featureless: there's no sense of
identity. . . . [H]undreds of articles have been written on and around
FSM, but only a bare handful by us. Everyone's quick to speak for us, but
no one asks us to speak" (127). What is missing, he says, "besides poetry,
is our face; and with it any real understanding of what the whole affair
meant" (126). In response, Rossman offers this chapter as a collective
self-portrait of FSM, a preliminary sketch of that "face," both for the
older generation and for his own peers. It is shorter and more tentative
than either Rubin's or Hayden's portrait, both of which tend to catalogue
the conspicuous aspects of the new identity: its music, language, and
recreational interests. Rossman's portrait, like theirs, is informed by the
belief that "few not branded from childhood by post-1948 America could
view the world with our eyes" (135) and by the conviction that the young
generation had its own style of humor and poetry. More important, however, is Rossman's sense that the young are creating, without benefit of an
articulated ideology, a new form of community founded on a passionate
belief in democracy, pragmatism, and the humanization of learning.

However, even as Rossman concludes his description of the new
generation's culture, he confesses the inadequacy of his portrait; the outsiders' false "frameworks," he says, are also his own (129). "Barefoot in
a Marshmallow World" was written in 1967, and it marks only one stage
in Rossman's dawning awareness that new "vocabularies" (251) had to
be invented to express the generation's changing sense of itself. The
means for finding those vocabularies are developed in the essays that
make up the final chapters of the book, most of which treat Rossman's

growing involvement with educational reform, a major focus of Movement energies in the late sixties and early seventies. The central theme of those chapters is Rossman's belief that one must be open to chaos and to mental and spiritual states that language has not yet been able to define. Only out of such chaos, he believes, can real learning and growth occur. This distrust of orthodox language, together with his insistence on the creation of new frameworks, is yet one more reason why Rossman refuses to impose a conventional generic structure on his autobiography. In his search for a language that would adequately articulate the new generation's concerns, Rossman borrowed from the work of the newly emerging feminism, with its insistence on the collapsing of "personal" or "sexual" politics and state politics, and from the writing of maverick anthropologist Carlos Castaneda, who made the disruption of cultural preconceptions a prerequisite for any sound moral education.

What Rossman believed about his own need for "re-education" he also applied to the political reform of society in general:

> it is not surprising that the skills of the learner are essentially the skills of the society that is able to learn; that the problems involved in changing private behavior mirror those involved in changing public behavior; or that the processes whereby individuals and cultures reconstruct their identities are closely similar. (*On Learning*, 46)

As we have seen everywhere in this chapter, many sixties-generation autobiographers believed that individual experience may be used to interpret and provide direction for collective behavior. It is not surprising, therefore, that Rossman should see in his development as an individual the solution to the difficulties facing the generation as a whole. In his own development, he sought the integration of the two major themes of the Movement—the desire for political justice and psychological wholeness—and he saw in that integration the potential source of his generation's uniqueness. The failure of the generation to adapt his vision became one of the chief reasons for dissent and argument among various generational groups. By the end of the 1960s, the argument over how one can negotiate the division between the public and the private aspects of the self, between the demands for social justice on the one hand and psychological health on the other, came to characterize the split within the Movement between the New Left and the New Age. As we shall see more clearly in the next chapter, other writers from this generation, even when they agreed with Rossman, found themselves in circumstances that forced them into polarized attitudes with regard to these issues.

The other autobiographers we have seen in this chapter employ strategies similar to the ones used by Rossman in order to make clear the various audiences and voices they are addressing. Because they were writing early in the generational experience, they tended to direct themselves at the imagined voices of parents and at those peers who had already assumed a competing generational identity: civil rights worker, Black Power activist, SDSer, New Leftist, hippie, Digger, Yippie, and early feminist. *The Port Huron Statement* refers to itself as "a beginning: in our debate and education, in our dialogue with society." Hoffman's *Revolution* is replete with attempts to engage the other voices contending for the right to define the new generation. It begins with a "letter" from Hoffman's mother that represents, comically, the older generation's voice as well as its perception of the young. Hoffman also includes accounts of encounters between himself and other contenders for generational status such as the Diggers and SDS. In all of these accounts, of course, Hoffman emerges as superior to his rivals. He also includes an open letter to Stokely Carmichael (written in the deferential tone that almost all of his white peers employed when speaking to or about Black Nationalists), a self-interview that posits as the questioner someone who is not a member of the new generation, a chapter of "advice to the brothers," another chapter of "advice to my black brothers" (composed of blank space), and a chapter addressed to members of the Movement who do not agree with his Chicago strategy. Rubin's *Do It!* contains an imaginary dialogue with his Aunt Sadie, which stands in as a symbolic conversation between the new generation of radicals and the older thirties-style leftists, with their bourgeois concerns: Sadie is more worried about the length of "Jerry's" hair than with real social change. Rubin's second book, *We Are Everywhere*, even contains a section devoted to a critique of the Rubin who wrote *Do It!* (109).

Enumerating these passages of explicit intragenerational dialogue will mislead, however, if one assumes that they represent the primary way in which this autobiographical dialogue takes place. The truth is that all of these works are necessarily engaged with each other even when they are not doing it overtly. The generational plot outlined in *The Port Huron Statement* is a plot picked up by other writers who respond by modifying, adumbrating, revising, or rejecting it. In addition to plot, these books also share common issues, characters, and events. Each of their versions of these narrative elements constitutes an implicit contribution to the argument over the precise meaning and form of generational identity and experience. Dialogue, therefore, is integral to each book's fundamental purpose and content, not a mere addition to be included from time to time.

One of the things that this dialogue makes clear is this group's conviction that identity and politics are inextricably connected and the corollary belief that autobiography is an essentially political act. Rossman, like the authors of other annunciatory autobiographies, narrates the collective's past principally as a means of directing its future political behavior. It comes as no surprise, then, that Rossman, like Rubin and Hayden, ends his book with a chapter that offers a prospectus of generational action. In "Toward the Future," Rossman announces the secession of youth from the state, declares their "independence from its essential instrument, the System of Education," calls upon the young "to come together, to share their powers in critical mass and intimacy," and advises them that they must prepare "to fight for the cradle of the future" (395–97). Like his fellow writers, Rossman is finally concerned not so much with the politics of socialism as with the politics of identity. This phase of generational writing seeks to envision a society in which those who have adopted the new identity can "be themselves." It is the primary goal of the annunciatory autobiographer to discover and reveal the precise nature of that identity.

4

Generational Autobiography as Reactive Narrative

By 1970, even as Rubin and Rossman were publishing their first books, other autobiographers were already entering the second phase of generationalist writing. This new phase continued to be dominated by Movement and ex-Movement writers, but new voices began to enter the dialogue, some of them quite self-consciously distinct from those we listened to in the last chapter. Their emergence was accompanied by a dramatic change in America's political climate. By 1969, as we have seen, Movement writers were predicting a civil war between the generations in America. Encouraged in part by right-wing reaction, in part by the illusion of overwhelming generational solidarity, and in part by their own apocalyptic fantasies, some of them went so far as to advocate violent confrontation as the only solution to the political and social conditions against which they were struggling. It was probably no coincidence that even as they made such announcements their crusade was falling into disarray and confusion. The demise of the Movement after 1970 put a decisive end to certain illusions about generational unity on social and political strategy, but generational thinking continued. For autobiographers, the fall of the Movement became simply one more episode in the story; each writer of the second phase of generational writing looks to the years between 1968 and 1970 to find the specific event that signified the end of the era during which they had come of age.

The reasons for the disintegration of the Movement were several, and they are made clearer as one looks at the events that have taken on symbolic or mythic stature in generational autobiographies of the period. Internecine arguments over political strategy and lifestyles were becoming increasingly common after 1967. They caused the breakup in 1968 of the collective that formed Liberation News Service—a major source of underground, counterculture, and Movement news. In 1969, SDS itself fragmented during its national convention as hard-core Marxist-Leninist factions called for greater ideological purity and other factions insisted upon a more revolutionary—that is to say, violent—response to government policies and state repression. By that time, the old guard, comprising the moderate activists who had written *The Port Huron Statement,* had been replaced by, and was largely ineffectual in responding to, the new, more radical members of the organization. The older members felt that they were themselves under attack by a "new generation" of radicals who were less aware of, or totally unconcerned about, the history of left-ist struggles in the United States.[1]

Another factor contributing to the Movement's fall was the increas-ing violence in the world at large. The assassinations of Robert Kennedy and Martin Luther King in 1968 seemed to herald a period of social chaos. Rubin, Hoffman, and Hayden all saw the Chicago police riots and the trial that followed as events that solidified generational unity and made revolution a possibility, but the violence of these events actually frightened away large numbers of youth and gave many of their leaders pause. Few of them wanted to take responsibility for what the media was calling the "war at home." In spite of the numerical success of several an-tiwar rallies after the Chicago events (particularly the National Morato-rium of November 15, 1969), the most visible activists were increasingly committed to violence, and it became evident to more discerning ob-servers that any apparent unity within the Movement (not to mention the generation as a whole) was largely illusory. The SDS split in 1969 spawned the Weathermen, a faction that declared war on the state while preparing to go "underground." That intention was put into effect in October of 1969 as the group took to the Chicago streets for a vandalism campaign it called the "Days of Rage." Other groups around the country, such as the Mad Dogs in New York, imitated them. In March of 1970, three members of the Weathermen were killed in an accidental explosion as they prepared pipe bombs in a Manhattan townhouse. In August of 1970, a similar-minded group in Madison, Wisconsin, accidentally killed a graduate student when it set off a bomb next to a University of Wiscon-sin building housing U.S. Army research laboratories.

In addition, the counterculture's belief that it was ushering in an al-ternative world of peace, freer sexual relations, mind-altering drugs, and rock music was dealt a large blow in 1968 when its Mecca—the Haight-Ashbury district of San Francisco—was invaded by the media, rip-off artists, bad drugs, and thousands of runaway adolescents. It was dealt an-other setback just two months after the great counterculture rock concert celebrated at Woodstock, New York, in August of 1969. Four hundred thousand persons had attended that drug, music, and sexual happening, and many youth leaders had claimed that its relative peacefulness proved the viability of the new generation's cultural and political identity. Other rock concerts followed Woodstock, but the one that assumed the great-est generational significance was held at Altamont racetrack south of San Francisco in October of 1969. The Rolling Stones, always fascinated by the dark side of the epoch, hired the Hell's Angels to act as their bodyguards during a performance marred by fights in the crowd and "bad vibrations." In the end, one of the Hell's Angels stabbed and killed a member of the audience; the event was captured, and its significance as a generational event dramatized, in the film documentary *Gimme Shelter.*[2]

The fragmentation of the Movement and its increasing domination by fringe elements were not the only evidence that the Woodstock dreams were hopelessly deluded. In 1970, the war in Vietnam, in spite of everything the antiwar movement had accomplished, was suddenly escalated once again as Richard Nixon, who had announced a secret formula to end the war in his election campaign, began sending bombers into Cambodia to attack North Vietnamese supply lines. The violation of Cambodia's borders was met by demonstrations on campuses all around the country. At Kent State University in Ohio, National Guardsmen responded to the local demonstration by firing on students and bystanders with live ammunition, killing four of them. The Cambodia bombing demonstrations in the spring of 1970 were among the era's last mass demonstrations. At the same time that the war's violence seemed to be escalating, American ground troops were being gradually withdrawn as Nixon implemented his "Vietnamization" policy. That policy shifted more responsibility for the ground war onto South Vietnamese troops, who would be backed up by American technology and bombs. The policy somewhat calmed Middle Americans' fears that their own sons would die in the war, even as it maintained the American presence in Southeast Asia. By 1970 Nixon had also reduced the threat of the draft by instituting a lottery system. Without the immediate threat of mandatory military service and possible duty in Vietnam, many young men whose lottery numbers were unlikely to be called suddenly lost interest in the war and in their fervently held political activism.

After 1972, the infamous Watergate scandal also took the fight against Nixon's domestic policies out of the hands of the already debilitated Movement and placed it in the hands of senators and legislative committees. The same young people who months before had flocked to the streets in order to bring about social change now sat passively in front of their television sets as they watched history being made in the usual corridors of power. One had the sense that the generational moment had passed, that the country and many young people wanted nothing more than the return of social stability. The move away from politics was heightened by the defection of a number of significant Movement leaders to the "New Age" therapies that were the vogue of the early and middle 1970s. Rennie Davis, one of the Chicago Seven, gave up mass organizing to become a disciple of Maharaj Ji. Jerry Rubin also began his movement away from radical politics toward New Age consciousness during the early 1970s under the guidance of Swami Raj-ji. In fact, the leaders themselves began to disappear from public view as their names were displaced in the mass media by "human potential" gurus such as Baba Ram Dass, Alan Watts, Fritz Perls, Werner Erhart, and Arthur Janov. The sheer variety of therapies available during this period is itself testimony to the changing direction of the cultural tide. The Esalen Institute and EST are two of the best-known institutions that marketed therapies for this generation, but others devoted to bioenergetics, yoga, consciousness-raising, transactional analysis, orgone therapy, Rolfing, primal screaming, and transcendental meditation—to mention just a few—offered alternatives that effectively replaced political involvement in the lives of many young people.

Many autobiographies written during and after this period of political and generational disillusionment became forums within which their authors renounced earlier versions of the generational self or described their conversions to some new identity. In doing so, they adopted the narrative plot form by which writers have long accounted for—or facilitated—radical breaks with the past. The conversion plot, as we have already seen, forms the implicit basis of the narrative structure of Cowley's *Exile's Return.* In the 1970s, Dotson Rader, Raymond Mungo, Jerry Rubin, Jane Alpert, and later Peter Collier and David Horowitz all undertook autobiography in order to reestablish themselves with new identities when the "sixties ended." While each of these writers interpreted generational developments in his or her own way, they all responded to the demise of the Movement and the frustration of their own expectations by producing an *autobiography of conversion* or an *autobiography of renunciation,* two reactive literary forms that allow an author to destroy an earlier identity.

Although Chapter 3 demonstrated that the annunciatory mode dominated the first phase of generational writing, both Rubin and Rossman, as we saw, use conversion rhetoric in their annunciatory works. There are, however, differences between such rhetoric and the conversion narratives written in the second phase of the generational dialogue. The narratives in the first phase describe rejections of an identity constructed for youth by the parental generation. In Rubin's *Do It!* for example, the narrator rejects the model of the successful American businessman. Rossman's narrator in *Wedding* similarly rejects the type of activism his parents' generation offered as a model of leftist behavior. In both cases, the casting off of the first identity serves the primary purpose of distinguishing the young from their elders, and the narratives remain focused on the annunciation of the new self. Among the books we will now examine, the authors reject an identity constructed by their own peers. These rejections are often the autobiographical equivalents of intragenerational purges, and they will prove far more traumatic than the earlier casting off of parental values. Perhaps for that reason they assume a much more central role in the overall structure of the narratives in which they occur.

The autobiography of conversion and the autobiography of renunciation are both secularized variants of the much older Christian conversion narrative. The paradigmatic conversion, of course, is provided in Saint Paul's account of his dramatic transformation on the road to Damascus in the twenty-second chapter of the Acts of the Apostles. Paul's preconversion identity and name, "Saul," are discarded after he is struck down by a blinding light from heaven; what emerges from the conversion experience is a new identity from whose point of view the narrative is told. Paul's conversion from persecutor of Christians to apostle of Jesus Christ is more, however, than a simple change of vocation; the Christian convert, he claims in his letter to the Romans (chapters 5–8), is like Christ: the old self of fleshly desires has been crucified; the new self, "resurrected in Christ," is governed by the spirit of holiness. The converted self is new in its very essence.

Modern forms of the conversion narrative, as we have seen in the case of Cowley's book, have preserved the major plot outline of the older form while doing away with the Christian doctrines that inform it. At the center of the modern conversion autobiography, just as in the older form, is a crisis in the narrator's life, a moment or period when he or she undergoes a complete change in worldview. This change splits the narrator into two radically distinct selves: the old self (the Old Adam or sinful self of the Christian narrative) and the new self (the reborn and sanctified New Adam of the Christian form) which is also the present self of the narrator. Like the earlier form, the modern conversion autobiography includes a narrator who renounces his old self by means of a newly embraced ideology that allows the errors of the old self to be perceived and judged.

The modern autobiography of renunciation is similar to the autobiography of conversion, but the new self's ideology is either unstated or so conventional that it cannot effectively displace the old ideology's dominant position in the writer's life plot. The author's present center of meaning, in short, does not make for a good story or serve as the basis for proselytizing. The focus of attention in such works, therefore, is not the narrator's present set of beliefs, but the old self and its faith. In the autobiography of renunciation, the final state of the authorial self is dominated by a sense of loss or diminishment: the Old Adam is indeed dead, the spirit and flesh have been mortified, but the New Adam has unfortunately either failed to arise from the grave, or is a mere ghost of the former self.[3]

Writers who undertake one or the other of these forms do so with rather different intentions. In the autobiography of conversion, the author constructs a life story in order to win readers over to a newly acquired faith. The narrator relates his or her "turning" in order to inspire a similar turning in the reader. The greatest worry is that recounting the sins of the former self might titillate or seduce that reader. The prudent author, therefore, makes sure that the narrative dealing with the sinful self remains subordinate to the new faith's vision of salvation. The autobiography of renunciation, on the other hand, is literally nonevangelical; it bears no good news. The new values of the narrator are merely an incidental (though necessary) facet of his or her present perspective, and the focus of the form remains fixed upon the renounced faith and the earlier sinful self. As former insiders, such authors lay claim to a uniquely privileged view of the renounced faith; they have special access not only to its tenets, but also, presumably, to the psychological mechanisms that motivate its followers. They tell their stories because they believe that readers need to be made aware of the dangers of the former faith; its errors (and frequently its agents) need to be exposed. Conversion narrators are typically *reformers*; renunciatory narrators, by contrast, are *informers*. Bella Dodd, for example, writes in her renunciatory autobiography, *School of Darkness* (1954), "I knew I had information that might be of help in protecting our people. I knew also that honest citizens of our country were uninformed about the nature of Marxism and I recognized now that in the best sense of the word to 'inform' means to educate. As avenues of education are blocked and twisted into propaganda by the agents of conspiracy, my country needed the information I had to give."[4]

Another aspect of these contemporary conversion and renunciation narratives that distinguishes them from the older form is their continued focus on collective identity. Like Cowley, these writers are usually not content to reject an earlier collective self by returning to a conventional individualistic autobiographical path. Their conversion or renunciation is shared, as they would have it, by the entire generation; it is a collective turning. So the reactive narratives written during the 1970s and afterward frequently retain the earlier writers' habit of speaking in the collective voice. However, since one of the articles of the faith they are renouncing is often the belief in generational consensus, their claims of representativeness are routinely qualified. The narrators of these works may even explicitly renounce the collective voice, but as we will see in our examination of Dotson Rader's and Raymond Mungo's work, they usually employ it even as they renounce it.

Since the twentieth century has been an age abundant in lost and shaken faiths, particularly those that have attributed meaning to history, it is not surprising that autobiographies of renunciation have flourished in modern times. To take one well-known example: many Americans who identified themselves with communist historicism during the 1930s suffered a crisis of identity at the time of the Moscow trials in the mid-1930s, or later during the Hitler-Stalin Pact of 1939, or later yet after the Khrushchev revelations in 1956. Reacting to these events, some of the disenchanted wrote autobiographies renouncing the faith they had placed in

Marxist historicism. Richard Crossman's famous anthology of renunciation narratives *The God That Failed* (1950) and Whittaker Chambers' *Witness* (1952) are probably the best known of these works, but there are a number of others, such as J. B. Matthews' *Odyssey of a Fellow Traveler* (1938), Benjamin Gitlow's *I Confess* (1940), Louis Budenz's *This Is My Story* (1947), Hede Massing's *This Deception* (1951), Elizabeth Bentley's *Out of Bondage* (1951), and the aforementioned book by Bella Dodd, *School of Darkness* (1954).[5] Although some of these works—Chambers', Budenz's, and Dodd's—are written from the perspective of a new, and all-embracing, ideology (capitalism/Quakerism for Chambers and Catholicism for Budenz and Dodd), the real center of interest in all of them remains the communist faith that is being renounced rather than the new faith that has been embraced.

The 1960s constituted another period during which large numbers of people placed their faith in various forms of historicism whose claims were eventually undermined by the caprices of history. Consequently, one can see in the later period a roughly similar situation giving rise to similar reactive autobiographical forms. In spite of the New Left's repeated insistence on their differences from their predecessors in the old left, they shared with them many of the same tendencies. The most important of these, of course, was the tendency to reify history and to hold dogmatically to beliefs about the direction in which it was headed. In addition, both groups constructed at least part of their identity by associating themselves with another country. The older leftists identified themselves, to their later chagrin, with the Soviet Union. The New Left proved themselves largely exempt from that temptation, but they much too readily idealized third world struggles for national liberation in places such as North Vietnam and Cuba. Both groups also shared a penchant for revolutionary and apocalyptic fantasies; Cowley's ascendant working class and Rubin's generational war were probably about equidistant from American realities.

There are, however, differences between the two periods during which individual members of these generations began their renunciations. The most important of these is that the political climate that followed the collapse of historicist hopes in the 1940s and 1950s was determined in large part by fears of Soviet expansionism and actual events in Central and Eastern Europe. Fueled by those fears, the anticommunism of the period was characterized by an intense paranoia. The political climate of the 1970s and 1980s, on the other hand, while increasingly conservative in tone, never led to the kind of witch-hunts that happened sporadically in the 1940s and 1950s. The autobiographies that arose out of the frustration of the later generation's revolutionary hopes were, consequently, usually less violently self-renunciatory and Manichaean than those that arose out of the frustrations of the 1930s. Of course, this did not prevent individual writers from achieving impressive outbursts of antileftist denunciation in the later period, and some of them, as we shall see, actually borrow plots directly from the renunciation narratives written in the forties and fifties.

Generational Disfigurement: Dotson Rader's *I Ain't Marchin' Anymore!* and *Blood Dues*

Dotson Rader (b. 1942) was among the first writers of this era to treat the collapse of the Movement, and he did so, typically, by publishing two autobiographies. Although rather eccentric in their treatment of the generational narrative, and often bewilderingly self-contradictory in their analysis of collective psychology, Rader's two books establish the major themes of the conversion and renunciation narratives we will examine in this phase of the generational dialogue. In some ways, Rader is a transitional figure whose books straddle these two phases of the dialogue. For like the annunciatory writers in Chapter 3, Rader often seems to celebrate the Movement and generational solidarity. He even includes stories—as Rubin's early books did—of conversions away from parentally constructed identities. Like the reactive writers I will look at in this chapter, however, he constructs other narratives that suggest that psychic, sexual, and social pathologies lie at the very heart of the generational plot articulated in Rubin's and Hoffman's books.[6] These other narratives finally dominate the text and radically undercut any idealization of Rader and his contemporaries. At times as brazenly self-congratulatory as any of the annunciatory writers, Rader is also curiously—and perhaps only half consciously—self-critical, at times to the point of self-loathing. Finally, it is the two books' rejection of earlier generational plots and identities that most clearly qualifies them for inclusion in the reactive phase of generational writing.

The title of the first of Rader's two books, *I Ain't Marchin' Anymore!* (1969), suggests the author's rejection of earlier "demonstrations" of generational identity, but the extent of that rejection does not become entirely clear until the second book, *Blood Dues* (1973).[7] In *I Ain't Marchin'*, Rader charts the Movement's transition from protest to resistance as the reforms they sought to effect in American life were consistently ignored or denied by those in power. Like several of its predecessors, Rader's book focuses on a relatively limited period in the author's life (early 1967 to late 1968) and is divided into sections primarily devoted to the author's participation in significant generational demonstrations: a portrait of his friend Rachel and the author's childhood and Movement background (chapter 1); the New York City antiwar march in April 1967 (chapters 2–3); the march on the Pentagon in October 1967 (chapters 4–5); the SDS meeting on violence and political

action in November 1967 (chapter 6); a December 1967 protest at Whitehall Military Induction Center in Lower Manhattan (chapter 7); the Columbia University occupation and strike in the spring of 1968 (chapters
8–12); and finally, a protest at Madison Square Garden against George
Wallace in the fall of 1968 (chapter 13).

The demonstrations are used here as they are in annunciatory works
as a metaphor for generational identity. Unlike the works examined in
Chapter 3, however, Rader's book moves beyond the celebration of this
identity to provide another narrative that suggests the deeper reasons for
the Movement's transition from pacifist protest to violent resistance. This
secondary narrative focuses on the narrator's subjective response to the
frustration of the demands voiced in those demonstrations. The resulting
text is one that vacillates between stories that serve the openly justificatory aims of the annunciatory mode and other stories whose intent is not
always entirely clear. From the perspective of a later feminism, they look
like *counternarratives* that support the self-critical aims of the conversion
or renunciation mode, but in the context of Rader's occasional romanticization of sexual violence, they appear to be *complementary narratives*
that provide a psychosocial rationale—if not an outright justification—
for the narrative of generational change.

This ambiguous (and probably ambivalent) structure is noticeable
already in the first chapter, which offers both a hagiographic portrait of
the author's friend, "Rachel the Social Worker," and an introspective account of Rader's own background and Movement experience. The portrait of Rachel is embodied in a narrative that justifies the generational
trajectory from pacifism to violence; the self-portrait, on the other hand,
provides a complementary narrative that delves into the motivations underlying that trajectory. Rachel's story represents the Movement's journey from the idealistic but naive early days of *The Port Huron Statement*—significant paragraphs of that manifesto serve as the book's
preface—to the conviction of the late 1960s that only violence could
make America "what she had once imagined America to be" (2). Her
story is sketched in broad, sentimental strokes: schooled in the early
ideals of the Movement, she is now worn out "by daily facing the hopelessness of her job (she worked with the poor in block organizing, fought
to improve the schools, watched out for the sick, played Little Miss City
Hall to the wretched of the Lower East Side)" (2). In spite of living the
ideals of the Port Huron manifesto, Rachel discovers that nothing in
America really changes; the old power structures remain in place, and the
poor are systematically excluded from access to American opportunity.
She is a patriot who loves America, but America, she believes, has been
"ruined by the Americans." Finally, after years of grassroots work with
the poor, Rachel opts for violent revolution "since America was not a
democracy and . . . playing by 'democratic rules' was to play in a game

where the rules were made by your opponent, a game you could never win" (15).

The complementary narrative, which is framed by Rachel's story, provides a sketchy account of Rader's childhood in St. Paul, Minnesota, but it focuses in several flashback scenes on the innocence and unconscious arrogance of Rader's younger self. One of the more suggestive of these is a story Rader relates concerning his early experiences with African Americans. As an adolescent, Rader tells us, he was "jumped by four black high school students." "Scared pissless," he waited for the inevitable beating. To his surprise, however, one of the boys simply "crossed his arms over his chest and stood like an Indian chief scanning the horizon, his eyes looking beyond me. 'Shine them shoes,' he said in an even voice, as if he were ordering a meal." The young Rader did as he was told, but afterward he felt

> disappointed, for I had expected violence. I thought the living shit would be knocked out of me in the bushes by the blacks. I both feared and wanted it to happen, wanted violence that tested a man. . . . I was about fifteen and I suspected that part of the significance of the black in the white imagination was the potential of their violence. And violence was liberating. (6)

The juxtaposition of this story, in which violence is perceived as a liberating rite of male passage, with the Rachel story, in which violence is a reluctantly adopted political strategy, suggests that the generation's rationalization of revolution was unconsciously accompanied by a deeper, more primitive drive to test, prove, and discover one's manhood in violence. In other words, the Rachel story, with its emplotment of "official" Movement ideology concerning the transition from pacifism to violence, is given depth, as Rader sees it, by his own story, with its suggestion that the reasons for the generation's movement toward violence are to be found elsewhere than in arguments over political strategy.

The dual pattern discernible in the first chapter of the book becomes more dominant in later chapters. In them, Rader continues to intertwine exemplary narratives that provide political justification for the generational trajectory toward violence with personal narratives that rather repugnantly suggest that violence for its own sake was a necessary ritual through which generational identity—synonymous for Rader with "manhood"—could be established. Chapters 2 and 3 narrate a demonstration against the Vietnam War in April of 1967, but they focus on another of Rader's friends, Philip, who also serves as a representative generational figure. His narrative, like Rachel's, neatly confirms Movement rhetoric concerning the necessity of violent opposition. But where Rachel, as we have just seen, represents the early New Left pacifist who evolves slowly into a revolutionary, Philip represents the comfortable bourgeois who converts overnight to revolution. His narrative also emplots an important element of Movement ideology in the late 1960s—the idea that American society would not reform its basic institutions until the comfortable middle classes were confronted in their own bodies with the brutality and intransigence of American power structures. Philip's character is established in the first chapter, where, arguing with Rachel, he maintains that the only effective forms of opposition are those that work within democratic structures. In spite of her efforts to convince him that democracy in America is merely a bromide used to dupe the oppressed, he is unable to understand because, as a "frat boy from a cake-eater family," to choose revolution would be "to choose against his family and his past and his conception of his countrymen" (16).

In chapter 2, this portrait of Philip as "upper class WASP" (19) is filled out in more detail: "he believed in American decency because he believed himself to be decent and good. And because his future lay unbounded before him he could not believe the actuality of *millions* of Americans without a future who existed in wretchedness and poverty" (20). Faced with the actuality of poverty and ghetto life, he can think only of the need for "better police work. Moderate. Liberal. Unable finally to believe, he found the propaganda of the Left to be ridiculous" (20). Almost inadvertently, Philip decides to accompany Rader in the nonviolent, legal march against the war, leaving behind a group of his "equally cool, faintly superior" frat brothers. During the march, he and Philip are attracted to an illegal breakaway demonstration of about 20,000 people led by "young Trotskyite partisans" (26). Following it, they are swept up by "the illusion of power, absolutist, making the unreal, the wished-for, seem within reach" (30). This "mob," blocking traffic and threatening municipal chaos, is eventually trapped and attacked by mounted police whose indiscriminate clubbing includes both Philip and Rader as they desperately seek refuge.

The description of the immediate effects of the clubbing echoes the language of the two conversions we saw in the last chapter: Rossman's "heavy turning, a re-beginning. . . . Whap! an historical thunderbolt" and Rubin's "historical explosion with body and mind, an Apocalypse, in which individuals change themselves overnight." In Rader's story, there is an element of humor in the description of the clubs' effects: "*Whack!* The comic strip stars . . . pretty lights." The consequences for Philip, however, are anything but humorous. In chapter 3, he recovers from the beating in his apartment, "lying naked on the rug, his arms tucked between his thighs, his feet curled up under his bottom" (35). From this conspicuously fetal posture, he emerges a new person, awakening "to the darkly fierce tokens of repression which the poor and black and homosexual and angered and Leftist and nonconformist young know everyday. American all his life . . . and only today he woke to America" (35). Watching this new self emerge, Rader marvels at

Philip's remarkable anger and his ability in the shortest time to become other than what he was. He converted. What was improbable for him before . . . the whip on the head, became actual.

Of the many moderate students who chose against their past to side with us, Philip's conversion . . . was the first I witnessed. It was public and quick, completed in an afternoon. In the process of growing up in our country . . . he confronted the essential indecency of industrial capitalism and facing it *consciously* for the first time he either had to deny its existence . . . , destroying his manhood, or he had to choose to act in rebellion, placing himself consciously in opposition to the dominant values of American society. (38–39)

Philip's story is typical of the conversions that occurred in the annunciatory works. It revolves, like Rubin's, around the sudden realization that the legacy he has received from his parents is a sham. It takes only this one encounter with the police to overturn his vision of the world and convince him to embrace the views of the Movement.

Like the Rachel story, the Philip story also simplistically emplots the Movement's increasingly militant posture regarding the necessity of violent revolution. But intertwined with the politically correct narrative of Philip's conversion to radicalism is Rader's very different account of his own subjective response to the police violence. Instead of arousing Rader to the brutality of American power (he already possesses such awareness), the beating awakens in him a "sexual hunger" that reminds him of a character in André Gide's *The Immoralist* who, after beating up a coachman, is able "for the first time, to possess his wife. The violence was liberating" (35). Leaving Philip asleep and naked on the floor, Rader heads for the bars "to hustle up some action" (36). His first stop proves unsatisfactory because the women he finds are mostly "washouts from Barnard, the ugliest, hairiest, most desexed, over-intellectualized sluts on God's green earth" (37), but he eventually picks "up a piece in the Ninth Circle [another bar] and took it home. At last I got some mileage out of the cop's knock on the head" (47).

Although this account of the narrator's less than admirable search for a "piece" may seem at first glance a far cry from the orthodox tendentiousness of the Philip story, Rader clearly sees them as intimately related. The connection is Rader's nearly obsessive concern with "manhood," the term that links the justificatory narratives to Rader's complementary narratives detailing his sexual response to American political realities. For him, what is at stake in both is the feeling that one's actions count, that one is potent. Lacking that feeling, young white men who take on the Establishment to protest injustices perpetrated on others are also acting on behalf of themselves. In all of Rader's stories, the real oppression against which young men fight is the Establishment's denial of meaningful outlets for their idealism, and that denial is ultimately, for Rader, a denial of their manhood and their sexual virility. The country's failure to pay attention to its young men results in sexual dysfunction, forcing them, as Rader sees it, to seek violence as sexual stimulation and release. Like the first chapter, then, the second and third chapters intertwine the "official" Movement reading of the generational plot with another reading, which, as Rader understands it, is rooted in male sexuality. The first reading shows the overt political rationale for violence. The second demonstrates the deeper sociosexual reasons for it.

The climax of the book occurs in the final chapter, in which the narrator describes the fall 1968 demonstration against "the country's most honest, most *American* politician," George C. Wallace (neither of these adjectives is meant to be complimentary). Abandoning the earlier pattern of juxtaposition in order to focus entirely on the narrative of Rader's sexuality, the chapter depicts the author's response to fifteen-year-old Rosalie's rejection of his sexual advances just before the march. Although she explains that she prefers "chicks" (168), Rader believes she is contemptuous of him because he is unable to "act like a man!" and because, when the police beat demonstrators, he lets "those pigs get away with everything" (172). In his torment over this rejection, Rader realizes that he does "not know what to do. I had tried just about all of it across the country and I had come to believe that my generation's response to and judgment on the use of violence was the central issue of the age" (172). For young white men caught between women who demand that they "be the *man,* the one with the balls between the legs" (172), and a System that "emasculates young men," "street disorders, seizures of buildings, dislocation, confrontation, the tempting of violence had become rituals of manhood" (174). The final confrontation of the book, therefore, is one that lacks any political justification at all:

> As we attacked the bus [of Wallace supporters] I do not think we cared anymore whether the demonstrations of the Left were self-defeating or not . . . whether they would in effect swing the country right or left. . . . We simply did not exist politically anymore. Demonstrations had become a kind of theatre, a play through which we mollified our outrage. . . . Violence was wanted. I hungered for it. I wanted to fight in front of my chick. To prove myself. (174)

The abandonment of the exemplary narratives here announces that the generation is beyond invoking political strategy to justify violent resistance. All strategies are futile in America's powerful "police state." Rader's feeling that the white, middle-class males of his generation are emasculated by their culture serves as the basis for his understanding of their emerging collective identity. The same instincts that drove him into the bars of Manhattan in chapter 3 are those that drive the revolution. As generational autobiography, Rader's book bears witness to a civil war whose underlying cause is the adult generation's sexual oppression of the young.

Whatever its audience may have thought in 1969, present-day readers of *I Ain't Marchin'* will likely find Rader's treatment of young white men's problems an embarrassing apology for a sexist sociopathology. One might, however, make the case that Rader's text is sufficiently ambiguous to support a more generous reading. That reading would argue that the book's psychosexual narrative purposefully undermines the Movement's justification of violence by juxtaposing the hollow tendentiousness of the Rachel/Philip stories with the introspective chauvinism of the Rader plot. It would be a dubious interpretive maneuver, but there is some evidence in the text (and even more in its sequel) to support it. As we will shortly see, the narrative strategy upon which the reading is based—an author confesses a history of psychosis in order to demonstrate generational shortcomings—is actually standard fare in autobiographies of renunciation.

I wouldn't myself go quite so far, though Rader's book certainly contains almost all of the elements underlying later renunciation narratives. My own feeling is that the book's ambiguities stem from something else, from Rader's inability to decide between the plot of youthful reformism suggested by *The Port Huron Statement* and the plot of youthful rebellion with which he grew up in the 1950s. The latter plot derives from models of rebellion made popular in Hollywood movies like *The Wild One* (1953) and *Rebel without a Cause* (1955). Played by Marlon Brando and James Dean, respectively, these films' heroes are misfits alienated from "straight" American values and disillusioned by unreasonable or ineffectual authority figures. Certainly in the Dean film, and arguably in the Brando film, the antihero is looking for precisely what Rader says his generation is looking for— adequate and strong male adults who will pay attention to them. Lacking such authorities, they create their own subculture, where they seek integrity in a cool toughness, a macho sexuality, and a violent bravado. The basic assumption of such rebels, however, is that theirs is a lost cause and that no larger causes exist. Since the world cannot be changed, they will live in it only on their own, usually self-destructive, terms. Inevitably, such plots end violently or tragically, if not for the hero, then for those around him. Meanwhile, the uncomprehending adults stand stupidly about, wondering where they went wrong.

In the 1950s, alienated young people had access to subcultures depicted in the plot of such films. They were constructed by hipsters, beats, and juvenile delinquents. Norman Mailer, one of Rader's cultural heroes, describes the Hipster with theoretical eloquence in his contemporary essay "The White Negro."[8] Rebels in the mold of Dean's and Brando's characters are, in Mailer's sympathetic analysis, modern psychopaths or "hipsters." They are a breed of individual created by what Mailer considers the conditions of partial totalitarianism prevailing in America. In order "to be a man" under such conditions, the modern psychopath must live with a "disproportionate courage" (313) because his emotional survival depends upon a continuous rebellion against "square" culture. He is an outlaw, but he is also a kind of philosopher, someone "who extrapolates from his own condition, from the inner certainty that his rebellion is just, a radical vision of the universe" (317). Mailer is careful to distinguish this kind of rebel from the psychotic, who rarely has a clear sense of himself or what he is doing. "The psychotic," he writes

> is legally insane, the psychopath is not; the psychotic is almost always incapable of discharging in physical acts the rage of his frustration, while the psychopath at his extreme is virtually as incapable of restraining his violence. (317)

In fact, the modern psychopath's self-consciousness assures his membership in "an elite" whose "language most adolescents can understand instinctively, for the hipster's intense view of existence matches their experience and their desire to rebel" (317).

"The White Negro," as even this short synopsis should indicate, offers a rationale for the less savory aspects of Rader's self-portrait. His acting out of sexual needs and his use of "political" violence to assert his virility are, in Mailer's view, the courageous expression of "primitive" realities in the face of a repressive culture. Mailer admires the psychopath, for he is "better adapted to dominate those mutually contradictory inhibitions upon violence and love which civilization has exacted of us" (318). Nor was Mailer alone in offering a justification for such psychopathology. Paul Goodman, another writer whom Rader looked up to, also provided models of youthful rebellion for the plot of violence and sexual self-assertion in Rader's autobiography. Goodman's widely read books on the alienation of youth—*Growing Up Absurd* (1960) and *Compulsory Mis-education and The Community of Scholars* (1964)—offer, like Mailer's essay, an explanation, if not exactly a justification, of Rader's plot.[9] Like Mailer, Goodman was sensitive to the social roots of delinquent behavior and saw youthful rebellion, sexual dysfunction, and violence as the result of "the psychology of powerlessness" that characterized youth's reaction to a hypocritical and repressive society. In Goodman's writings, the central problem facing young men—the problem does not, he argues, affect young women—is that they are not "taken seriously" by the adult world.

The model of youthful rebellion that emerges from Mailer's and Goodman's work clearly clashes with the model provided by *The Port Huron Statement*. The former writers depict young men in conflict with a society whose repression is perceived as virtually invincible. The manifesto argues that young men can affect the quality of their lives by acting collectively in responsible political organizations. Mailer's and Good-man's youth are "rebels without a cause," youth trapped in an absurd and unmanly culture. The manifesto, by contrast, claims to represent a generation overcharged with causes to be fought and won. At least some of the ambiguities of Rader's book, then, stem from confusion over these two models of rebellion, for its narrative begins with the plot suggested by the Port Huron writers, only to regress to a plot available to unhappy and frustrated youth in the fifties. In so far as Rader's narrative accurately mirrors the extreme left's abandonment of collective political action in favor of purposeless violence during the late sixties, one might even argue that that period witnessed a regression (on a mass scale) to an earlier plot of generational rebellion. The late sixties Weathermen, like the fifties "Wild Ones," were acting out a romantic fascination with violence in their desire to become what Mailer referred to as "frontiersmen in the Wild West of American night life" (272). In my opinion, not enough attention has been given to the influence of fifties models of rebellion on the style of late sixties violence. Rader stands out because of his autobiographical candor, but he was not unique in his fascination with the fifties-style antihero; nor was he unique in his ambivalence. Tom Hayden, for example, said in a 1972 interview with *Rolling Stone* that even in 1960 he was "very divided between being what now you would call a radical and what then didn't have a name . . . it was mainly like trying to mimic the life of James Dean or something like that."[10]

Without fully abandoning the narrative arguments of *I Ain't Marchin' Anymore!* Rader's second autobiography, *Blood Dues* (1973), rejects one aspect of the generational self constructed in the earlier book and raises considerable doubt about another. In *Blood Dues,* Rader completely disavows the idea, embodied in the justificatory narratives of earlier characters like Rachel and Philip, that the generation was fully aligned with its historical moment and that it would realize its destiny by means of a mass revolution led by the New Left. And he reexamines, without completely discarding, the belief embodied in the first book's psychonarrative, that his own troubled sexuality was the direct expression of his generation's oppression and marginalization. In a confession that amounts to a retraction of the first book's entire thesis, Rader acknowledges that the attractiveness of violence and his insistence "on giving it a political content were based upon sexual disorder, feelings of sexual inadequacy and dysfunction" (8).

Addressing himself to the first of these revisions, Rader makes the unstable relationship between the generation and its historical moment the center of *Blood Dues'* narrative. This autobiography, which picks up where *I Ain't Marchin'* ends and continues through late 1972, tells the story of what happened to the author and his generation after "History" shifted away from them toward an undefined present and future. The narrative argument itself is divided into four parts. The first locates the historical shift away from a unified sixties radicalism and narrates the generational vanguard's initial refusal to believe that it had occurred; the second presents the alternatives that appeared to offer themselves to those who wished to continue in the historical vanguard; the third relates the failure of those alternatives; and the fourth tells of Rader's exile, spiritual death, and possible rebirth.

Part 1, "Bye, Bye Miss American Pie," focuses on the historical shift itself—both the actual moment at which it occurred and the response to it on the part of the generational vanguard. The shift is described in some detail in Rader's preface: he claims that it first became apparent at the July 1969 SDS convention in Chicago. At that meeting, SDS split into two factions: Progressive Labor (a Marxist-Leninist group) and the followers of the National Office (Rader refers to them as "leftist adventurists"). The split marked the culmination of a sectarian tendency that was by then widespread in the Movement—Black Nationalists, women's liberationists, third worlders, gay liberationists, and many other groups were already fighting with each other over political strategy. The split effectively signaled the *end* of the Movement's effectiveness in carrying out what youth leaders saw as generational tasks. For Rader, those tasks and the direction of History had been articulated, even if fuzzily, at the end of *I Ain't Marchin' Anymore!*: massive street demonstrations and the use of violent resistance would bring about the final revolution in American society. By 1969, however, even those tasks had lost their clarity amidst internecine arguments over their definition. The vanguard was, as Rader puts it, "continually embracing and then abandoning modes of belief in light of new evidence or new demands or new situations resulting from a change of consciousness on the part of one radical constituency or another. One was continually out of step" (107).

The immediate response of the Movement to the shift was one of denial. Rader, like others of his generation, suspected that something had changed, but he continued to act in accordance with the design of history outlined in *I Ain't Marchin'* because "so much of my identity and self-respect and sexual self-image was involved in street activities of the left that I could not, did not want to contemplate its end" (31). Since it portrays a self stuck in an outmoded historical vision, part 1 aptly employs the method of depicting that self that was characteristic of the autobiographies examined in the last chapter—the self as revealed in "demonstrations." Besides the SDS convention, these include the 1971 May Day demonstrations in Washington, D.C., a September 1971 Attica Prison massacre protest and a pro-gay demonstration in New York City, the October 1971 Eject Nixon demonstration in Washington, D.C., and, last, the December 1971 People's Coalition for Peace and Justice benefit in

New York City. But instead of depicting the demonstrations as a theater for the expression of generational identity (as in the earlier annunciatory works), Rader exploits them to display the generational vanguard making inappropriate gestures and speaking the wrong lines on a historical stage that has been assigned, without the actors' knowledge, a new script.

Moreover, although demonstrations form a part of the structural backbone of part 1, they remain secondary to another organizing principle. Unlike earlier generational autobiographies, the chapters in *Blood Dues* are devoted primarily to Rader's encounters with figures who represent different ways of responding to the collective identity crisis facing Rader. The best example is Gus Hall, the aging head of the Communist Party in America, who serves as a prophetic image of what Rader fears he will become in his middle age: an irrelevant has-been, "trapped in his role" and stuck in history (44). At the end of chapter 1, Rader relates a conversation he had in 1971 with Norman Mailer in which he first expressed the fear that Movement leaders were "going to end like Gus Hall," a caricature of a man who has lost touch with the times: "He still thinks it's 1946" (39). As evidence of that possibility, Rader recalls his service as an unthinking party functionary organizing the doomed benefit for the People's Coalition for Peace and Justice in 1971. What saved Rader from such a fate was his awareness that the benefit's failure was more than a single incident in Movement history:

> it forced me to contend with a change in my experience in America, something others in the movement also had to contend with. . . . It was not that my politics had changed; rather, the narrow corridor of history in which the movement played had bent away from me, leaving my sensibility inadequate to it, my responses untrue. (104)

More successful than Hall in dealing with historical change were Mailer and Tennessee Williams. Their generational heyday had also passed, but unlike Hall they were aware of it and of the need to maintain contact with History via the new generation. Williams, according to Rader, was completely out of touch, but unlike Hall he "desired to connect with radical youth, to catch up with history, for somewhere he had lost the sixties" (52). Mailer, he says, also had "a romantic conception of the young and of history itself, the sense that there was an imperative for direct, active participation in the struggles of the left if you were to maintain any credibility among the rising generations" (53–54).[11]

Once aware of the great shift in History, Rader and his generation have to decide how to realign themselves with their times, how to carry on in the future. Part 2, entitled "Alternatives," focuses on the options among which the generational elite had to choose. The two main alternatives, according to Rader, were writing and terrorism. As in part 1, Rader treats this problem by telling stories of his encounters during 1971 with men who served as exemplary figures for each of these options. Considering writing as one way to keep a hand "on the rump of History" (a phrase he applies to Mailer), he found models in dramatist Tennessee Williams (chapter 10) and Russian poet Yevgeny Yevtushenko (chapter 11). Yevtushenko serves here roughly the same purpose that Gus Hall served in part 1. He is someone who claims to act on behalf of History and the Revolution, but in fact he has "the heart of a Soviet functionary, and the degree to which it commanded him was the exact degree to which he was an enemy of socialism and human freedom" (131); in the end, Rader claims, "history has passed him. He was of the fifties, his poetry and his politics. He belonged in a room exchanging polite banter with Richard Nixon" (134). Williams, by contrast, is a writer with integrity, but he has already answered the questions that face Rader's generation in ways that are "unapplicable to my life" (122).

When he considers the terrorist option in 1972, Rader can find no real models except those provided by his own generation. Of these, the best is Jann Eller, "who represented, in its finest personification, the committed revolutionary" (136). Terrorism appealed to Rader both because it would have allowed him to continue exploiting his natural penchant for violence and because he believed it was politically justified. In his first autobiography, Rader confesses, he described himself as someone who undertook violence largely because it was able "to satisfy some psychological need in me (revenge, for instance)," but in 1971, he came to understand violence "in terms of its political utility" (108) as a tool "lush with humanity, moral and life-enhancing," intentionally chosen because of its ability to disrupt an overly rational, impersonal, and "therefore dehumanizing" order (109). In the end, however, Rader finds himself unable to take up terrorism because it requires that he convert his enemy into an abstraction. He keeps seeing "Richard Nixon, for example, not as a mass murderer (which he objectively was) but as a pathetic individual, however dangerous, worthy of pity" (110). But besides rejecting terrorism for contributing to the dehumanization it seeks to combat, Rader also provides a narrative reason for abandoning it: Jann Eller, his only model for the terrorist alternative, disappears from History in a drug-dazed descent into San Francisco's sordid underworld. The story, as Rader presents it, is the inevitable consequence of the terrorist's social and spiritual isolation.

The most interesting aspects of parts 1 and 2, however, are not their schematic treatment of the historical alternatives facing the generational vanguard, but the introduction, new to the subgenre, of an introspective skepticism. History's ungracious shock to Rader's generational vision gave rise to two doubts that serve as recurrent themes throughout the autobiography. One of these doubts concerns his use of himself as generational representative. The other, closely related to the first, is his suspicion that the collective self that dominates all of I Ain't Marchin' and much of *Blood Dues* is based on a misunderstanding of his own motives and nature.

Doubts about his representative status manifest themselves in qualifying statements throughout the book, but in spite of them, he steadfastly clings to the possibility of his representativeness. Feeling chastened by the failure of past projections of the self, Rader simply reduces the number of people for whom he claims to speak. In the preface, for example, Rader tempers his assertion of representative status by informing his readers that he makes "no claim to speak for the movement." But in the same paragraph he goes on to say, "I am immodest enough to believe that my reactions to the period in history, the close of it anyway, which I lived through, are representative of many others who, like me, came to a position of defiance and dissent within America in the early sixties and are now at a loss for what to do" (23). Part 2 begins with a similar claim: "If I alone had begun to break it would not have mattered much, but the hell of it was that I saw others of my generation experiencing the same difficulties in identity and sex and work, the same recourse to drugs, as if blind stupor were an answer to fear and purposelessness" (103–4). The shift in History, however, makes him doubt the validity of such claims, so he issues a caveat: "I am generalizing. Suffice it to say that a significant number of friends with whom I started out in the sixties and with whom I shared similar experience and politics began to fall apart in the first years of the seventies. . . . Since I cannot speak for them, I have to tell you how it was for me" (104). So if not for the generation, Rader speaks for the Movement; if not for the entire Movement, then for significant numbers of its members; if not for significant numbers of Movement members, then for quite a few of his friends. Well, anyway, he speaks for himself, and, by the way, he writes of himself only because he seems to be like a lot of other people. Detectable in this apparent double-talk is a shift away from a claim to representativeness based on membership in a historical vanguard toward one based on typicality. In the earlier work, he saw himself clearly as a member of a generational vanguard; in the later work, he begins to suspect that he is simply a typical member of the generational group, subject to historical forces beyond his understanding.

The source of his new modesty also lies, in part, in Rader's suspicion that the self he has been offering in public acts and in autobiography is a false one. That suspicion emerges in the course of narratives that reveal aspects of his character that are not entirely consistent with his former theories of generational identity. In an early chapter devoted to his relationship with Norman Mailer, for example, Rader tells how, in Mailer's presence, he acted more "scruffy and rugged" than he actually was, used language that was "fouler" than he ordinarily used, and had the urge to "talk about the number of pussy belts [*sic*] nailed to the wall." Commenting on this behavior, the narrator laments the adolescent ease with which he was able to "disavow the majority of my being and choose one aspect of my fantasy self and offer it to Mailer as myself" (37). Rader never says which part of his "being" he has disavowed, but in later communications with Mailer's biographer, Hilary Mills, he refers to himself as "the only homosexual who has become a close friend" of Mailer's.[12] One might forgivably imagine, therefore, that he refers in this passage to the disavowal of his homosexuality. That impression is strengthened by Rader's further comments:

> Christ, the mutilations we practice on ourselves short of violence. Maybe, in this regard, play-boxing with Mailer, what was at work there, muted, was the kind of need for transcendence which drove the Weatherman to enforce homosexuality in their heterosexual communes as a device for making subversives. In the United States, in a sex-repressive culture, somehow everything seemed to be purchased with the coin of sexual self-disfigurement. You became a caricature of yourself—Super Butch. (37)

The passage suggests an inversion of the Weatherman formula, so that his bragging of "pussy belts" to Mailer becomes a means of "enforcing" a heterosexuality on his homosexual self in a desperate attempt at "transcendence." But in spite of the implication of a repressed homosexual self, Rader never clarifies the precise nature of his "sexual self-disfigurement." And although in the remainder of the book, he repeatedly refers to his tendency to adopt a "false" self (37), he never overtly concludes that his "true self" is the reverse image of the obsessively heterosexual self that dominates the two texts. That reverse image is, however, embedded in the logic of the analogy he draws here between his self-enforced heterosexual bravado with Mailer and the "enforced homosexuality" in the Weatherman communes. If the analogy holds, then his behavior with Mailer is false, and his "true" self is homosexual. Rader's reluctance to voice the implications of the analogy and his insistence throughout the book on seeing homosexuals as "other" constitute the chief interpretive problem of his attempt to explore his own self-fictions.[13]

The method employed by Rader to carry out this exploration includes the telling of more stories in which he hovers around the homosexual issue, picking at his responses to it in an effort to alight upon its generational significance. As in the Mailer episode, the narrator in these later stories possesses a greater self-awareness than his former homophobic self, who is characteristically bewildered by his own emotions. In one chapter, for example, he tells of his reactions to a gay demonstration in New York City. As he watched the police brutally beating the marchers, he found himself sharing their contempt for the gays:

> I did not know how to explain that, whether it was because these homosexuals being up front . . . in some way were threatening to my sexuality . . . or because I held some secret bias against homosexuals arising from my early

days in New York when I was broke and often resorted to them as sources of money and in the payment received humiliation and abuse as gratuity. Perhaps it was deeper than that, a resentment coming from my belief that they cheapened life because they were antipathetic to creation. . . . Even my reaction to the [antigay] violence was bewilderment, for the event was unmapped. That is, I owned no key to my own feelings. (72)

The narrator in this scene distances himself from the homophobia of the former self he is describing, but the strategy he employs to do so maintains the distance between his present self and homosexuality. That strategy translates both his former homophobia and his own past as a homosexual hustler into experiences whose meaning is essentially nonhomosexual: he was homophobic because he had been abused by his former gay clients and, as he goes on to rationalize, because gays were responsible for the "murder of seed" (72); and he had been a hustler only because he "was broke." In short, he may have behaved like a homosexual, but that behavior does not define who he is.

The homophobia he describes in this passage recurs repeatedly in later scenes. In another chapter, Rader tells of his discovery of a young hustler in Tennessee Williams' hotel room. He repressed his first impulse to beat the hustler up because he knew that it "was born of a reality or fiction about myself, about my sexuality, which I could not then afford to abandon, something I had been defending in the streets every time I assumed the role of activist." Looking back on this incident, he writes that he is not sure "even now . . . of the final definition of that reality or fiction," but he realizes that it was fueled by a desire to extinguish something in himself that he "had left behind, paid for and abandoned." As in the police gay-bashing episode, however, his past homosexual activity here is given a nonhomosexual significance. Unable to accept sex between men without "exchange being involved—money, concern—of sufficient nonsexual value to justify the act," he explains his past hustling as simply a demeaning "matter of barter" he had been lucky enough to escape by turning to politics, by looking upon the men he admired as "fathers" and "the bleeding dirt, the punks," as "sons."[14] Politics, a generational "combat between fathers and sons," had rescued him from "the life" (homosexual prostitution) so that what he had hated in the hustler "was the memory of myself before politics and before manhood" (118–20). This reading of his sexuality as repeatedly threatened by a homosexuality he has escaped by means of political activism is a significant departure from the reading he gave it in *I Ain't Marchin'*, where his "manhood" (that is, his heterosexual virility) was threatened by the older generation's indifference to the political opinions of the young.

Significantly, however, Rader does not mention his homosexuality in the aggressively heterosexual *I Ain't Marchin'* either. On the contrary, he is at constant pains to assert his macho status. According to Rader himself, he suppressed this information in his books because the liberal classes (including his own editor) had not yet come to accept homosexuality, and besides, he couldn't see why anyone would be interested in what he did in bed.[15] The first of these reasons strikes me as likely enough, though a bit odd given that the premise of *I Ain't Marchin'* rests on a connection between sexuality and generational character. The second seems a bit disingenuous, or perhaps just forgetful. I would assume that since *I Ain't Marchin'* treats sexuality as an expression of cultural pathology, Rader suppresses his homosexuality in order to create what his readers might take to be a more representative generational persona.

But in spite of Rader's obsessive picking at this theme in *Blood Dues,* he was not able to convert its significance into anything that could redirect his historical footsteps in 1972. As a consequence, parts 3 and 4, which cover March to December of that year, abandon the historical trajectory of the generation to focus on the disintegration of Rader's "fictions" about his sexual self. Part 3 is largely devoted to the flight from New York Rader undertakes in order to resurrect his heterosexual self-confidence. But each stage of his journey only brings him further failures. In Los Angeles, he beds a hooker named Peg, who ends up robbing and insulting him. In San Francisco, he picks up a hippie girl, but finds himself impotent until he fantasizes about some boys he once saw in a shower. When he returns to New York, he attends a dinner during which Jim Morrison, recently dead, is being discussed. A gay "boy" in the group, who brags about how he made it with the singer, infuriates Rader because the story represents yet "another betrayal, taking from my world one more supportive myth that someone of my generation having been tempted went through it with his sexuality tough, hard, intact, straight, unspoiled, unconfused" (171). The section ends with a sordid scene in which hustlers, pimps, and friends of both genders attempt, unsuccessfully, to mount an orgy.

In the final section of the book, "Lafitte in Exile," Rader describes the deepening depression and physical breakdown that followed the moral collapse narrated in part 3. Leaving New York again, he goes to New Orleans where he picks up a male hustler. His intentions, he makes clear, are nonsexual. As he and his new friend sit in a French Quarter bar, he thinks back on his friendship with Paul Goodman, whose death he learns about from a newspaper headline. Goodman, an up-front homosexual like Williams, had alienated Rader with his incessant talk "about latent and unacknowledged homosexuality" (200) and his suggestion that Rader seek therapy. But although Rader rejected the older man's advice and advances, he realizes that they both had a powerful need for "the attentions of the young" and each of them "viewed young men, especially loners and rebels, as his adopted sons" (188). In some respects, Goodman appears to have been the ideal father figure Rader seeks. In Goodman, he could see a man who combined the roles of intellectual, writer, poet, and social activist. In addition, Rader's placement of Goodman at the end of the book suggests the culmination of his search for an apt father. Still, the figure remains ambiguous because the thing that concerns Rader the most—his sexuality—is the aspect of Goodman he *apparently* rejects out of hand. The dominant tone of the section, therefore, is not discovery but loss, as Rader realizes his own attempts to be a "father," a "Sugar Daddy," to the young men he idealizes have largely been failures (202).

In spite of the intense introspection of this book, Rader's descriptions of his journey into increasing isolation are not primarily meant to conduct us toward the construction of an individual self. Although the book clearly reacts against his earlier reading of his sexual dysfunctions as symptoms of generational oppression, he stops short of rejecting the generationalist project that underlay that reading. His serious meditation on his reactions to homosexuals, his turning to homosexuals as father figures, and his own homosexual activity never lead him to conclude that his confusions spring from his unique physical and psychological makeup. For Rader never defines his "sexual disfigurement," and its meaning is ultimately cast in entirely generational terms. What, after all, was the primary feature of the Movement's attempts to gain power "in the name of others" if not the requirement that "you choose against your past, the people and class from which you came, and thus against something that was indelibly part of your being" (105)? In its efforts to be true to its ideals, Rader claims, the Movement required its members to think of themselves in a way that was "mutilating. To reject overnight conventions and feelings which were your nature, to roughen up, to adopt a role, try so hard to learn it, be what your parents warned you against . . . the bill for it is now coming due" (106). The narrative argument of *I Ain't Marchin'* asserted that a generation of young men turned to violence to assert their manhood in a society that ignored them. *Blood Dues* revises that assessment and asserts that the same generation of men mutilated themselves to "transcend" their natural class and race affiliations and to atone for "tribal guilt." The price of such mutilation is the "dues" to which the book's title refers.

In the resigned tone characteristic of many renunciation narratives, Rader ends *Blood Dues* with an implicit judgment on his generation's self-destructive militancy and a claim to an insider's knowledge of the reasons for it:

I know it had something to do with sexual disfigurement and dysfunction, with transgressions against, and mutilation of, young manhood, of a male's self-esteem. I know that because . . . I lived through and was intimate with the conditions and events that spoke of male disfigurement and despair. I was changed by it, injured in some lasting measure, and I suppose what remains of my life will be lived as an acting out of a course determined irrevocably by being witness and participant in an extraordinary era. (209)

He also ends his narrative with another typical feature of the conversion and renunciation modes, a death-rebirth image. The final scenes of the book depict Rader's decline into suicidal depression, his ironic baptism by nasal hemorrhage, and his final recuperation under the care of his friend, Ruth Ford. The episode as a whole suggests, of course, spiritual crisis, symbolic death, and rebirth as a new creature (like Philip's plot in *I Ain't Marchin'*). But as in all renunciation narratives, the new Rader and his worldview are defined almost entirely in terms of what they are *not* rather than in terms of what they are.

Whatever one thinks of Rader's treatment of his sexuality, his implicit use of the "closet" metaphor to define the generational self sets a pattern of psychopathological exploration that later becomes a staple element in the intertextual dialogue we have been tracing. Because his portrait of the collective self is so thoroughly grounded in his own sexual confusion, Rader's autobiographical voice is situated in a unique and vulnerable position in the generational dialogue. As one who believes himself forced by social prejudice to repress his deepest desires (or his "true self," if one defines the self in terms of its desires), he is particularly sensitive to the elusiveness of identities constructed for public display. This is unsettling not simply because an awareness of it leads one to distrust what can be seen of the "other." The problem, Rader suggests, is that the public self can prevent even its "owners" from knowing who they really are. Rader's frustrated attempts to unlock the doors that hide the real thing, and his projection of his findings onto the generation, imply that whatever collective "face" his peers put before the world may well disguise a mutilated reality, locked away somewhere in a closet. Later writers such as Jane Alpert, Joseph Epstein, and Martha Bayles all take up this thread, but they will be, as we will see, much more certain of their ability to see through the generation's political facade and much less sympathetic to the self they discover behind it.

New Age Renunciation and the End of History: Raymond Mungo's *Famous Long Ago* and *Total Loss Farm*

Raymond Mungo's *Famous Long Ago: My Life and Hard Times with Liberation News Service* (1970) is the first fully self-conscious conversion narrative to engage in this generational dialogue, and it possesses all of the typical features of that literary form.[16] Most conspicuous is its born-again narrator, who largely disapproves of his former self and who feels compelled to intervene frequently in his own narrative to point out the errors of his, and his generational cronies', erstwhile pursuits. But he also frequently falls victim to an inherent danger of a form that forces the narration of the Old Adam's vices so that the author may condemn them. The danger lies in the possibility that in the process of describing the Old Adam's sinful, but nonetheless exciting, way of life, the narrator will be seduced by and resume his old patterns of thought. In Mungo's case, this danger is accentuated by the narrator's proximity to the lifestyle he is rejecting, a proximity that occasionally induces him to forget the distinct line that the form draws between the "me-then" and the "me-now." That proximity is, of course, the consequence of generationalist logic. The immediate value of generational works is determined in part by their ability to locate the cutting edge of history, which, as Rader points out, was perceived as constantly shifting in the late 1960s. So authors who identify such a shift are at pains to publish their claim as quickly as possible. One result is that in the frenetic shuffle to keep at the forefront of history, one easily forgets where one's feet are. Mungo (b. 1946) manifests his awareness of this danger late in the book when his language begins to betray his partisanship for the past self he is describing:

> I find myself embarrassed at telling the story. Perhaps it's because I'm telling it as I would have told it then, recalling how my mind worked in those troubled hours, all the conceit and hostility and resentment and uptightness. I feel very different now. It is as if many thousands of years have passed since these events occurred, I have seen such things and been such places and experienced such a succession of changes. . . . I mean no insult to any of the people herein described, but that we were possessed of dark spirits in those days. Some of us, alas, remain so, but many others have freed themselves. The dread presence may, however, return at any moment. I am speaking to you from beyond the world right now. Please tell my loved ones I am well and happy on the other side. (170)

Of course, Mungo is not writing "thousands of years" later; not even a year has passed since the events he is describing, but he has moved to the "other side" that characterizes all conversion narratives. In his case, he has entered the "New Age" that succeeded the by-then moribund "1960s" (a code term in Mungo's book for the ideals and generational image of the New Left).

The content of Mungo's narratives is based on his postconversion belief that generational identity is defined by the "lifestyle" the young have created for themselves. His books concentrate, therefore, on describing his peers' day-to-day lives more than on their mass "demonstrations" or inner psychic turmoil. He wants his readers "to understand *the way we lived*: because perhaps in retelling it I too will understand it better ('by-and-by')" (25). Since that lifestyle has undergone what Mungo perceives to be a cataclysmic change ("by-and-by," like "the New Age," is one of Mungo's terms for the reborn state), it requires two portraits, and Mungo devotes each of his autobiographies to one of them. The first of the two lifestyles, described in *Famous Long Ago*, is based on a conception of collective identity similar to that found in earlier works, and, like many of those works, it remains grounded in the world of "history-making" events. The second, described in *Total Loss Farm,* is based on a conception of a reborn generational self which, having emerged from the ashes of an earlier generational self, has ostensibly established itself in some temporal space outside of such events. Both books, however, are narrated from the postconversion perspective of the self described in *Total Loss Farm.*

In *Famous Long Ago,* Mungo describes his experience as co-founder, with Marshall Bloom, of Liberation News Service (LNS), which gained national prominence during the late 1960s by supplying news from a Movement perspective to underground presses. Mungo's story is devoted not only to the rise and fall of this organization, but also to the generation-shaping events that he was witness to during the same period. Though perhaps less well known, the events that make up its ten chapters are roughly analogous to those we have seen in works such as Rubin's *Do It!* Like that book's opening pages, Mungo's first chapter is an ironic attempt to discover "what went wrong." It sketches the author's working-class childhood until he graduates from college to become a "good-for-nothing dropout, probably a Communist dupe," living on a commune in the backwoods of Vermont (1). Narrated at a brisk clip, it employs the breezy language of someone showing a family film: "That's me on the Merritt Parkway, hauling my cat, her kittens, my friend Steve who turned me on, and all my worldly belongings" (4). But as with almost all generational works, childhood is given scant importance, and Mungo is quick to dismiss it by telling his readers that the little information he has offered about his first twenty years is "as much about me as you need to know. What follows is a story, by no means complete, of what happened to me during the few years after I started. Please don't try to learn anything from it, for there is no message."

Besides echoing Mark Twain's famous caveat to his readers at the beginning of *Huckleberry Finn,* Mungo's advice here stems from fears that writing for an establishment press might be perceived by his peers as evidence that he has "sold out." One way of avoiding that accusation is to pretend that his literary efforts are not serious and that their only intention is to "rip off" the "boogers" (his term for the bourgeoisie). In his second autobiography, he confesses that both of his books began as "burn schemes," i.e., strategies for obtaining support from the very people whose downfall he is actively seeking to bring about. In addition, an integral part of the lifestyle he sets out to describe is its insistence on freedom from tasks, such as serious writing, that require too much "ped-xing" (his term for routine, hard work). But in spite of his caveat, *Famous Long Ago* is heavy laden with "message," often delivered in the form of direct address to its readers.

The chapters following his brief account of childhood are devoted in turn to a meeting between antiwar people and Viet Cong leadership in Czechoslovakia in the spring of 1967, the first disastrously anarchic meeting of underground press editors during the Pentagon demonstrations in October 1967, the establishment of LNS in Washington, D.C., in 1967, the futile efforts to set up a free community in the same city, a debate between Eugene McCarthy and various leftists (with bad political fallout for both sides) in February 1968, the bloody aftermath of the murder of Martin Luther King in April 1968, a tour of America and its underground presses ending in California in the same month, the hard-line-left-inspired LNS move to New York City in the summer of 1968, the heist of the LNS press and its relocation to a Massachusetts farm by Mungo and his friends in August of 1968, their subsequent kidnapping and beating by their former political allies, and finally the demise of LNS-Massachusetts and the establishment of Mungo's New Age commune in Vermont in the fall of that year. Except for the experiences directly related to LNS, Mungo's list of "history-making" events does not differ greatly from those that comprise the generational works examined in the last chapter. What distinguishes this work from those, however, is the perspective from which these events are viewed. Whereas the last chapter's annunciatory works tended to celebrate such events as evidence of generational identity and a "coming together of youth," Mungo, like Rader, looks at them as evidence of a steady decline and an increasing sectarianism. In my examination of Mungo's book, therefore, I will focus on the born-again narrator's insistently intrusive view of these events more than on the view Mungo had of them at the time they were happening.

Mungo's treatment of these experiences invites comparison with Rader's first book because he deals with roughly the same period (1967–68) and with what both writers perceive as the demise of the Movement. Mungo's response to that collapse, however, is quite different from Rader's. Rader concludes from the Movement's demise that it had fallen out of alignment with History and could be resuscitated only through terrorism. Mungo agrees that the Movement had been on a steady path toward greater militancy, culminating symbolically in the riots that racked the capital after the death of Martin Luther King. But this event, which had "an air of finality about it for The Movement" (114), does not lead him to conclude that the generation must take up arms. Unlike Rader, Mungo is repelled by the mystique of violence and complains that "while it is now considered very good to be 'militant,' I could never associate 'militancy' with anything but the character disorder I stand *opposed* to" (150). As a result, Mungo draws two lessons from his "hard times" in the Movement: the first is that "ideals cannot be institutionalized" (69); the second is that the ideology and identity created by the New Left were really reflections of, rather than alternatives to, the corrupt bourgeois culture that it opposed. *Famous Long Ago,* therefore, is actually a critique as much of the New Left as of mainstream culture, and each of the events he narrates is used as an example of the left's inability to create a real alternative to American society: "What we called 'the movement' which started out as a peace-living [*sic*] opposition to slavery, racism and war, has become an enslaving, racist, civil war of its own" (69).

But while Mungo's born-again narrator has no tolerance for the option that Rader's first autobiography leans toward, neither does he long for a return to the early pacifist days when SDS still believed that the generational task was to gain greater access to existing American political structures. Looking back on the Washington Free Community (a Movement-identified coalition), Mungo concludes that all politics, including the participatory democracy advocated by *The Port Huron Statement,* are inherently wrongheaded. The Washington Free Community, he says, was "bound and limited from the start by its dead-wrong assumption that human beings seeking freedom can act as a group through a democratic meet-and-vote process, in short through the *same* system which the United States uses for placement of its rulers" (50).

The antidemocratic rhetoric that peppers both of Mungo's autobiographies is rooted in a very self-conscious Emersonianism. His contempt for the vote has its antecedent in Thoreau's "Essay on Civil Disobedience" (a kind of bible for certain elements within the Movement). For Mungo, who claims never to have voted, Americans in the mass are an unreliable lot who "may yet vote themselves dead and buried" (50), and he "would not submit the welfare and lives of anybody to a democratic vote by Americans!" (128). In any case, Mungo claims, "the vote has been shown to be worthless *everywhere,* but the mere fact of its availability is enough to convince many people that they are in control of their destinies" (15). The apparent nonchalance and aloofness of Mungo's rhetorical project also arise from his Emersonian belief that one cannot persuade others to adopt a position through argument; one either knows the truth intuitively or one doesn't. Mungo's style, as he puts it, "is to quietly avoid confrontations when I can; I seldom try to convince anybody of anything (except perhaps in print), 'cause if they don't already *know,* I figure I can't tell them. If it isn't happening to you right now, I can't save you, brother" (7). This reluctance to engage in expository argument is reinforced by Mungo's conception of his audience. Frequently addressed as "dear readers," these insiders are almost always conceived as hip people of his own generation who "know all about stuff like" the "harrowing Stephen Dedalus thing" (2) Mungo went through as a young Catholic or "the ideas which LNS published or . . . the contents of your average underground newspaper" (24–25) or "artsy-fartsy cinemas." Mungo contents himself with simply dropping the requisite buzzword and then tossing in, parenthetically, "you know the scene" (48). About most aspects of the world, he assumes his readers' agreement with his point of view. His proselytizing takes the gentle form of showing these generally sympathetic minds a better way.[17]

Despite this implicit appeal to a like-minded group, Mungo, like Rader, is suspicious of anyone who claims to speak for the generational collective. In *Blood Dues,* Rader drew back from his initial claims to represent his generation after coming to doubt the self he had projected onto the collective in his first book. In a similar mood, Mungo undertook *Famous Long Ago* to renounce the community envisioned by SDS, and he devotes much of his book to a depiction of the real in-fighting and factionalism that lay behind the media myth (which he had helped create) of the young generation as the monolithic conspiracy of like-minded youth. What the media didn't know, he claimed, was that "most of Our People really don't *like* each other, nor do they have anything in common" (49). In the crucial chapter on King, Mungo argues that although the response to his murder showed that "the future of the 'movement' was in coercion and violence, wars and propaganda" (107), middle-class white radicals were completely "irrelevant" to a revolution whose real protagonists were African Americans and the very poor. The assassination, in Mungo's reading, symbolized the death of the Movement and the collective it represented (114). But like Rader, Mungo renounces the collective self projected by SDS and the media only to construct a new and to his mind more viable one in a letter to sixty-five of his "dearest friends." This group is to constitute the core of Mungo's new "we": a collective that is not "a *granfalloon*—a gathering of people under some title which makes no sense . . . like America or the Boy Scouts or Harvard University or Students for a Democratic Society" (115). They are, in short, a "real" collective that Mungo is calling together to rediscover the "joy and purpose" that the Movement once held and "apply them toward a revolution in life, *my* life, *your* lives—not the lives of any silent constituency for which we speak" (114). In spite of Mungo's contention that he didn't trust "granfalloons," this letter is more than a personal document among friends. Like Cowley's 1934 conversion, Mungo's has a distinctly collective flavor. He is not turning away from the collective to an inner-directed salvation; the turning he relates is one that he fully expects his generation to share: "Everybody," Mungo says, "does everything in groups these days."[18] In that perceived social context and in the venue of a published book, the letter amounts to a new manifesto of the generation that produced *The Port Huron Statement.* And like the manifestos of Chapter 3, this conversion narrative is meant to serve as an advertisement for the new self, an invitation not only to one's "dearest friends," but also to one's "dear readers."

The nature of the "revolution" Mungo calls for at the end of *Famous Long Ago* was popularly known as the back-to-the-land movement. It demanded, in essence, a secession from America. His plan was to build a free agrarian communal nineteenth-century wide-open healthy clean farm in green lofty mountains! A place to get together again, free of the poisonous vibrations of Washington and the useless gadgetry of urban stinking boogerin' America! The Democratic Republic of Vermont! (108)

One shouldn't be misled, however, by the political sound of "Democratic Republic"; Mungo's sensibility was clearly much more religious and otherworldly than electoral. He was convinced that his generation's task was the creation of a completely new kind of man and woman in a completely new world. The history of the New Left and his own "hard times" with LNS were, for him, simply the purgatorial stage of the generational experience. The death of the Movement made possible the birth of what he called the "New Age":

Many of the people still active in the new movement are in reality dead men, killed off by bitterness and frustration and the unceasing attention of your television cameras. But many others have made the transition from the dying thing into a new living alternative which is trying once again to save the world . . . This New Age defies our attempts to put it down in print. . . . So you and I, dear friend, are pounding the streets of New Babylon for the last time [in these pages]. . . . We're closing the book on the 1950s, and good riddance to all that striving after wind. (69)

Mungo's second autobiography, *Total Loss Farm: A Year in the Life* (1970), was published the same year as *Famous Long Ago,* setting, one would guess, a speed record for autobiographical sequels. Mungo's primary aim in the second book is to "put down in print" the postconversion life "beyond this world"—that is, in his rural Vermont commune. Historically, *Total Loss Farm* is a continuation of the generational narrative *after* the political fall that is the theme of Rader's two books and Mungo's first autobiography. The opening pages of *Total Loss Farm* even echo the apocalyptic rhetoric of the end of *I Ain't Marchin' Anymore!*

Then Johnson resigned, yes, and the universities began to fall, the best and the oldest ones first, and by God every 13-year-old in the suburbs was smoking dope and our members were multiplying into the millions. But I woke up in the spring of 1968 and said, "this is not what I had in mind," because the movement had become an enemy; the movement was not flowers and doves and spontaneity, but another vicious system, the seed of a heartless bureaucracy, a minority Party vying for power rather than peace. (16–17)

In spite of its continuation of the generational narrative, there are many differences between the form of *Total Loss Farm* and the other, historically based, chronologically linear autobiographies written by members of this generation. In form and style, the only other autobiography that resembles it is *What the Trees Said: Life on a New Age Farm* (1971) by Stephen Diamond, Mungo's erstwhile co-worker in Liberation News Service and his present (1971) neighbor on a sister commune across Vermont's border with Massachusetts. Both of these books cover a period that begins with the breakup of LNS in August 1968 and ends in the spring of 1970, a few months after the suicide of LNS co-founder Marshall Bloom. And both books represent an apparently radical departure from the usual political orientation of generational autobiographies with their emphasis on collective life *in* history. *Total Loss Farm* and *What the Trees Said* focus on the communal experiment Mungo, Diamond, and their friends undertook in the woods of New England. Imitating Thoreau's *Walden,* both authors use the framework of one year in what they call "The Life" (their term for the postconversion New Age, as distinguished from pre-conversion History) as a metaphor for their new identity. It is an identity characterized by harmony with nature and a rejection of the individual ego in favor of a collective self. Since they relate similar stories, I will look at only one of the books here—Mungo's—because Mungo is more thoroughgoing than Diamond in his attempt to find an adequate literary form for the new self and because in his use of the autobiographical sequel he invites comparison with other two-book autobiographers among his contemporaries.

The major sections of Mungo's autobiography are called "Fall," "Winter," "Spring," and "Summer," an organizational choice that is intended not only to echo Thoreau's *Walden,* but also to reflect Mungo's postconversion belief that cyclical time, nature's time, is superior to the left's belief in history's progressive movement toward the revolution and a socialist utopia. As a reborn primitivist, the narrator has entered a mythic time in which the self is annually renewed in harmony with nature, and the "revolution," now internalized, occurs in an eternal present rather than in some imagined and inevitable future. But in spite of his insistence on cyclical time and structure, the circle of the seasons is actually a much less apt metaphor for Mungo's purposes than the journey, a linear metaphor that, in any case, dominates his perception of self in this book. The first chapter of *Total Loss Farm,* for example, although entitled "Fall," is not a studied meditation on that season on his Vermont farm. Instead, it describes a river journey (modeled on Thoreau's *A Week on the Concord and Merrimack Rivers*) through contemporary, industrial New England. It is the first stage of a journey toward a truer understanding of the generational self and its relationship with America. The lessons of this river trip, inserted into the narrative by the born-again narrator, are that America's imperialistic and capitalistic values are destroying the landscape and will eventually undo the society itself: "The American people, in taking revenge on the gooks, have all but destroyed the paradisial [*sic*] terrain and refined culture of Vietnam; now they will turn on themselves and do the same at home. What is ambiguously called 'the system' will crumble and fall, it is all too clear" (45). The "Fall" of this chapter refers, in other words, much less to an annual season than to the fall of the American empire.

Having learned those lessons, Mungo opens his second chapter, "Winter," with a description of another journey—this one by car across America to California, a place where "millions of Americans" are going every day, "racing across the planet headed for the Apocalypse, . . . they want to be in a safe place to go mad" (63). Following them, Mungo and his friends retrace the mythic journey he has already taken in *Famous Long Ago* because even though "we've been there before . . . we left something behind" (63). Like other Americans, they too are seeking a "safe place." California, where it is never "winter," represents here, just as it did in the earlier book, a possible alternative to that other generational haven, Vermont. Getting there, however, teaches Mungo more lessons than the place itself does, and California is afforded very little attention in the narrative. Whereas the first chapter describes the decline and "fall" of American society, the second charts what Mungo perceives to be a generational "winter," necessary in spite of his own efforts to escape it in the eternal summer of America's western dreamland. And his perception of that necessary "winter" is intensified by his growing awareness of the generation's need to wean itself "from all the awful things we've been deliberately and systematically taught to need—everything from additives in the food to a car for every really 'independent' person" (79). "Withdrawal" and death thus become the primary metaphors of this chapter. The journey across America aids this withdrawal by confirming Mungo's suspicion that the two primary elements of the American dream—California, where "it's always summer," and the belief that a "change of place would bring in its course a change of psychic season" (62)—hold no real promise. California teaches him something else as well: that linearity and progress—the fundamental metaphors of all leftist politics—are always an illusion: "Had I come through hell and cold, through darkest Pennsylvania, bebop Nashville, tepid Alabam, through treacherous Oklahoma and uncomfortable New Mexico, Arizona, California, to arrive at the same place I had left? Was not San Francisco just like Cambridge?" (104). So even though this section of the book is structured around a journey motif, its final direction, in Mungo's reading of it, is circular.

In the final section of "Winter," Mungo and his friends return to the farm and sacrifice their individualistic, addicted American egos. This section, entitled "ideath," is part mythopoeic fantasy, part literary allusion, and part fact. Employing a prose style consistent with his belief that mythic "truth" is truer than the "facts" that dominate more historically minded generational autobiographers, Mungo describes how the commune members cut off their hair, abolish couples, engage in group sex, scrap their television and telephone, stop eating processed foods, begin "phasing out cars and electricity," and cancel their newspaper subscriptions (119).[19] In the end,

> we are dead—strangled, burned, drowned, frozen. In hiding under the crusted Earth, though something more wonderful than our death was terrifying: and more impossible to describe [sic]. We are not authors of books, farmers or freaks anymore; we are life waiting to burst wildly and beyond control into nobody's vision, not even our own. We know nothing yet, compared to what we shall be. . . . We are the eye of the storm and we are coming your way. (120)

"Winter," then, is Mungo's generational death just prior to resurrection. Once through it, he and his friends will have transcended the historical and social outrage that "leads to action, and action leads to . . . where? Usually into a morass" (20).

The last two sections, or seasons, of *Total Loss Farm* describe and mythify "the Life" into which the reborn communalists awaken. Here, Mungo finally abandons the journey motif, informing his readers that "we've sailed the wild Conc and Merry, bumped across the great divide, even died in the process, now it's time to stay home for a spell" (128). Home, as he describes it, is actually a "state of mind," a fairy-tale locale (allusions to J. M. Barrie's *Peter Pan* are abundant) in which the narrator's friends are magically transformed into "children" who have built a "clubhouse" in the woods where they are free from "all the dead weight of the past—all the schools, factories, newspapers, jobs, religions, and movements—which would drag us under" (133). Their Emersonian dream of an escape from history is also unabashedly a dream of escape from responsibility and adulthood, and Mungo proselytizes for the advantages of remaining a child forever:

> I am never quite free of the forces attempting to make me grow up, sign contracts, get an agent, be a man. I have seen what happens to men. . . . I would rather know nothing of the cold cruel world I will someday just have to deal with, same as everybody else. Children take life by the short hairs. They are the real makers of life, they believe in it. And all of us know how it was, so each of us can remember. Innocence is our only possible hope. (136–37)

In more prosaic terms, the life Mungo describes is centered on a communal house where between five and twenty-five communards live. Their community is characterized by flexibility and mobility. It supports itself on garden farming, limited animal husbandry, and occasional "burn schemes" (including possibly *Total Loss Farm* itself). Their social life features freedom: freedom to be crazy, freedom to leave, freedom to be idle, as well as freedom from ideological hard lines, sexual inhibitions, and fixed gender roles. But it includes a prohibition on private property and sexual pairing. Clearly, the persona of *Walden* is given a different face when Mungo adopts it as a model for the collective self of his New Age generation.

Mungo's second conversion narrative, therefore, is organized around the four seasons partly to reflect the "new time," both nature-worshiping and cyclical, that he believes he and his friends (and potentially the entire generation) have entered. The new time also calls for a new calendar, so both Mungo and Diamond invent one that redates January 1, 1970, as Day One of the Year One. The change of calendar occurs during Mungo's trip to California. After stopping to celebrate the new year in Texas, he and his friends continue their trip, only to discover as they cross the border into New Mexico that a new time zone sets them "back in 1969 by 30 minutes!" Contemplating the arbitrariness of linear time, Mungo wishes "the world were round & wide enough for us to be born into Year One again and again, why stop at only *two* New Year's Eves in an hour's time, why not keep going, keep dying & being reincarnated *all* the time?" (89). The old time, historical time, is too full of trauma to be useful, and Mungo insists on the right "to call the past over & irrelevant to the present and future." Remembering actual events such as the Holocaust, he says, can lead to nothing but more of the same, but declaring them irrelevant allows for the possibility of renewal: "we've got to start again or none of us shall survive, we're making the Year One a convenient excuse for a new age of reconciliation on the planet" (90).

In spite of Mungo's efforts to leave history, his narrative is vitally engaged in a dialogue with it. That dialogue is obvious at once if one compares Mungo's book with Annie Dillard's contemporary *Pilgrim at Tinker Creek* (1974).[20] Dillard's book, which has none of the self-consciousness or evangelicalism that characterizes Mungo's withdrawal from history, accomplishes precisely what Mungo claims he has set out to do: it ignores politics, history, society, and it pays "attention to trees," an occupation that both Mungo and Diamond offer as the only kind of program that may yet "save the world" (*Famous Long Ago*, 189).[21] Dillard's prose is so focused on the natural rhythms of the valley in which she lives that she manages to place her readers completely outside of the world in which newspapers, calendars, and political events mark time. Indeed, if Dillard's book makes any comment on that "reality" at all, it is so indirect that most of her readers are apt to miss it. The ahistorical life Mungo describes on his New Age farm, on the other hand, is an engaged and explicit response to the "historical situation."

This apparent contradiction at the heart of Mungo's book is most evident in the two metaphors that determine its structure: the journey and the seasonal cycle. The former, linear metaphor implies change and evolution; in short, it implies history. The second suggests repetition and eternal renewal. Mungo longs for the latter but cannot disengage himself from the discourse with Western society that determines historical consciousness; he is always watching for the response of the society he claims to be rejecting and the peers whose minds he hopes to change. In the end, his proselytizing for the back-to-the-land movement represents not a flight from history, but an attempt to be at its very forefront. Reporting a conversation with a communard friend in California, Mungo self-congratulatingly reports that

> even fabulous Mendocino and glorious Vermont are not good enough for us anymore, no a new generation of city dropouts is coming along and it is for them that Mendocino remains; for us, who flatter ourselves with the notion that we are always a coupla years ahead of the real stampedes (*viz.*, antiwar movement, dope, rural relocation), for us there must be higher and further-out places: B.C., Ireland, Greenland, whatever. (107)

This is the essence of generational vanguardism underlying Mungo's mask of ahistorical pastoralism. The real collective self of *Total Loss Farm* is not one that renews itself annually in harmony with the seasons, but one that is on a perpetual journey; one which, in spite of its constant iteration that "we are the last life on the planet" (171), is ever mindful of the future: "Our great adventure after all is in searching for something not only better but new, nothing less than the next step in the evolution of the race" (133).

Psychological Renunciation: Jane Alpert's *Growing Up Underground*

Published in 1981, Jane Alpert's *Growing Up Underground* was the first of a new stripe of renunciation narratives written by onetime radicals in her age group.[22] Although they repudiated their past identities just as Mungo did, their aim, unlike his, was to reintegrate themselves into mainstream America. Alpert (b. 1947) attempts to restrict the repudiation to herself. Later writers, keeping faith with at least one collectivist element of their former generationalism, first reconstruct their sixties selves, highlighting now their typicality, and then reject their own onetime values (both countercultural and political) and the generation that held them.

During the late 1960s and early 1970s, Alpert, like Rader and Mungo, had seen herself as a member of a generational vanguard whose attitudes and actions represented the direction in which history was inexorably moving. She belonged at that time to a small group of radicals whose activities began with peaceful protests in mass demonstrations against America's involvement in Vietnam and ended with a series of bombings that was intended to "smash a hole in the wall of imperialism, through which the liberated armies of the world would march" (175–76). Although this group consisted of barely a dozen members, Alpert firmly believed that its actions would be applauded by "thousands" who "would support us, cheer us, imitate us" (176). In short, she felt that her group was representative of a large constituency of youth and that her participation in terrorist acts demonstrated that constituency's real, though often unexpressed, desires.

The initial bombings brought Alpert's group a good deal of anonymous notoriety. Alpert recalls thinking at the time "that the bombings had made us the toast of the movement and the talk of all New York. Our identities were the subject of speculation wherever radicals gathered" (222–23). Between August 20 and November 10 of 1969, the group set off bombs in New York City buildings owned by United Fruit, Marine Midland Bank, Chase Manhattan Bank, Standard Oil, General Motors, as well as the Whitehall Military Induction Center and the Federal Building. On November 12, Alpert and several of her friends were captured by the FBI and the New York State Police and brought to court. In an attempt to get a reduced sentence, she pled guilty to the federal charge of conspiracy to destroy government property, which carried a maximum penalty of five years' imprisonment, but later jumped her $20,000 bail (provided by her parents) in order to join the radical underground. Alpert spent the next five years as a fugitive, constantly moving, changing her name, and adopting disguises. In November of 1974, she resurfaced in order to "resume my own identity" (353) and pay her "debt to society" (368). After a new hearing, she was sentenced to twenty-seven months in prison (with an additional four months added later for refusing to testify in the trial of a co-conspirator). Of those thirty-one months, she eventually served twenty-four.

Much more thoroughgoing in its rejection of its author's former generationalist self-construction than either the Rader or the Mungo volumes, Alpert's book is consequently the most conventional of the works we have so far considered here. It also conforms more fully than the texts examined so far to the paradigmatic structure of the autobiography of renunciation, as Alpert herself makes clear in her prologue: "How I came to believe and act as I did—and later, in a spirit of renunciation, to surrender and go to prison—that is the core of this autobiography" (18). As we have already seen, both Rader and Mungo, in spite of their rejection of New Left models of identity, adopt new selves that retain many generationalist assumptions, including the importance of representativeness and the preoccupation with the self's alignment with history. Alpert's narrator, in contrast, renounces both of these aspects of generationalism in order to adopt a psychological model of human development that is much more in the mainstream tradition of twentieth-century autobiography. As a result, her book reconstructs the author's life from early childhood in the 1950s up to her release from prison in 1978 in a fairly strict chronological fashion (only the book's prologue, set in 1968, is anachronic). Consistent with its psychological model, it also devotes considerable space to childhood, marking a significant departure from earlier generationalist narratives that give childhood scant attention.

Like conventional autobiographies, Alpert's text consistently employs the past tense, for the identity with which she is primarily concerned is neither her present identity nor any *prospective* identity. In this, too, her book differs not only from those examined in Chapter 3, but also from Rader's and Mungo's, all of which retain a concern for the realignment of the generation's social and political agenda with a still reified, even if modified, notion of history. Like most renunciation narratives, Alpert's avoids focusing on her present self in order to give an insider's view of a repudiated former self and the ideology with which it was aligned. That insider's view is made available not only by her experience as a true believer in the repudiated ideology, but also by the psychoanalytic model she employs to examine it. Such a model is ideally suited for someone who perceives herself as having broken the social contract. Its purpose is to uncover the originary causes of the breach and to reveal patterns developed in early parental, sibling, and peer relations that have led to the transgression. The identification of these patterns acts therapeutically, allowing the writer to understand herself and to avoid future recurrences of antisocial behavior. It is also intended, of course, to elicit the readers' understanding of, if not sympathy for, the writer.

Although Alpert's narrative conforms to the renunciation form with its narrator's tell-tale hostility toward her former self, that former self is itself composed of a series of selves, all of which are united, according to Alpert, by a single psychological profile: that of a person who needs a totalizing theory of life and the approval and acceptance of a strong mentor figure. Extreme leftism and militant feminism had provided the totalizing theories of two of Alpert's former selves. Sam Melville and Robin Morgan had served as their "strong mentor figures." Her present attitude toward both of these former selves is uniformly belligerent, but the narrative reveals that each of the former selves had itself exhibited a similar belligerence toward its immediate predecessor. The adolescent Alpert renounced her familial identity in order to adopt one offered by Sam Melville and the militant left. Later, she repudiated her leftist identity to adopt one offered by Robin Morgan and militant feminism. Finally, she repudiates her militant feminism to adopt her present, moderate, feminism. Alpert informs us that this final self represents a real change; it is a triumph, she says, over her earlier need for a totalizing "ideology through which to interpret the universe" (370). One wonders whether this is really the case. Although Alpert does not proselytize for her present psychological perspective, her acknowledgment that psychiatrist Suzanne Schad-Somers provided "professional assistance with childhood material and in unraveling the major relations described in this book" (7) makes one suspicious that she has not fully overcome her need for "one strong personality who would keep assuring me that my chosen system worked and that I was brave and right to follow it" (347). Alpert's present marshaling of experience into pat psychological categories looks suspiciously similar to the cast of mind she claims to have cast away.

Finally, the identity that Alpert constructs is more individualized than those so far examined. Like Mungo and Rader, Alpert claims that she has abandoned her erstwhile penchant for generalizing from her own experience to that of her peers. But unlike Mungo and Rader, she appears to mean it. As Alpert herself confesses toward the end of the book, she had been "notoriously poor at figuring out what 'everyone' thought" (350). Her now chastised self even feels compelled to place "everyone" in inverted commas. In part, this gesture of individualization seems to be the result of her status as an ex-criminal and her conception of herself as a revolutionary comrade. Although by the time of the book's publication, the statute of limitations had run out on the crimes she and her friends were accused of committing, the criminal and revolutionary codes of honor both prevent her from incriminating others. That is, any claim that she might make to represent others would, in her case, look suspiciously like informing. Always sensitive to such accusations, Alpert tries to head them off in her prologue by announcing that she writes not "in the service of any particular ideology or with the intention of discrediting any persons or movements, but rather to set the record straight on my own role in a turbulent period of American history" (18).

The desire to avoid informing on one's immediate friends does not necessarily entail a refusal to make observations about one's peer group, but for Alpert, that desire and the fear of once again falling prey to generationalist assumptions prevent her from intentionally offering an analysis of anything beyond her own case. In spite of this, Alpert's book contains a fairly clear political subtext, and its self-construction was inevitably received and discussed by reviewers in terms of its representative status.[23] So in spite of its author's protestations to the contrary, the book is only fully understandable when it is read as a voice in the dialogue over generational identity. A contextual reading of Alpert's book, therefore, must begin by perceiving that it performs a task that its own author disavows.

In some respects, of course, this disavowal is disingenuous. For although Alpert insists that she intends to clarify only her own role in "a turbulent period," she frequently uses her self-analysis as the basis for observations about the feelings and behavior of her peers. Only an incredible naiveté could have prevented her from foreseeing that her story would confirm the conservatives' claim that the social and cultural disruptions of the sixties had more to do with bad parents and permissive child-rearing theories than with real political problems. By defining her earlier rad-

ical views as the result of psychopathological impulses rather than political injustices, she inevitably naturalizes the status quo and the structures
of reform already in place while casting doubt on the motives of all of her
leftist peers. But the narrative itself neither takes this explicit political
stance nor does it actively solicit its readers' allegiance to such a stance in
the manner of a conversion narrative.

The book's confirmation of conservative judgments of the sixties is,
however, readily apparent in its overall concerns, which echo in some respects those we have already seen in Rader's books. Like Rader, Alpert
structures her autobiography in part as a psychological case study. Part
1, entitled "Origins," details Alpert's early relationship with her parents
and her early sexual experiences in order to identify the sources of her
later susceptibility to the pathology of generational vanguardism. Part 2,
"Revolution," examines her slide into the fringe left in the late sixties and
makes ample use of the psychological patterns established in part 1 to explain her attraction to extremist ideas and the men who advocated them.
Part 3, "Underground," describes Alpert's life as a fugitive and her eventual repudiation of the left with the aid of insights provided by militant
feminism, another totalizing theory to which she is drawn for reasons
that are, in her view, more pathological than political. In a final epilogue,
Alpert briefly describes her present views and lifestyle, and includes a further renunciation of her earlier militant feminism. Whether or not she intended it, the overall effect of this structure and its focus on the psychological underpinnings of Alpert's politics is to redraw the generational
portrait offered by the writers examined in Chapter 3. Where they sketched
a self concerned with justice, freedom, and equality, Alpert draws one
that is self-obsessed, insecure, and full of repressed and irrational rage.

This approach differs in some ways from what we have seen in
Rader's *I Ain't Marchin' Anymore!,* which attributes the author's attraction to terrorism to an oppressive political culture and only obliquely
suggests the possibility that his actions spring from merely personal
sources. The rage Rader displays in the anti-Wallace demonstration at the
end of that book is shown as the direct result of his rejection by his young
girlfriend, but that rejection itself, he claims, is the result of an impotence
imposed on young men by a militaristic and repressive society. Even in
Blood Dues, which focuses more fully on the psychological deformations
brought about by involvement in the Movement, he avoids directly confronting the role that childhood and familial factors might have played in
his self-conception. In Alpert's narrative, however, the slide into terrorist
vanguardism is caused by childhood "themes." These she recounts in a
story that appears to follow the format of accounts elicited from patients
in therapy. Her themes include her desperate need as a child for her father's affection; the emotional damage inflicted by his early absence from
the home; a painful sense of herself as an outsider and a Jew; sexual in-

security; her family's financial difficulties; and an overweening desire to belong and to have the approval of her superiors that resulted in a ready willingness to compromise herself. Each of these themes, she claims, contributed to the pattern of repressed rage and destructive relationships that characterized her later behavior in the Movement. In addition to these more conventional psychological themes, Alpert points out one fateful intellectual influence from her early years: Ayn Rand's *The Fountainhead,* which first planted in her mind "the idea that bombing a building could be a morally legitimate form of protest." All of Rand's pro-capitalist books, Alpert adds (with little apparent sense of the irony involved), provided important role models in "brilliant, powerful, yet sexually passive heroines who submit to the men they love" (37).[24]

The connection between these childhood themes and her later involvement in generational politics is made clear in the very first description she provides of her political activity. While at Swarthmore College, she joins the Swarthmore Political Action Club (SPAC) and participates in a protest against the segregated and poverty-stricken conditions at a black public school in Chester, Maryland. In the midst of the demonstration, she writes, her emotions take on an intensity out of proportion to the occasion:

> I was prepared, or so I thought, for arrest, even for police brutality. But I was not prepared to find a wellspring of anger inside me, tapped by the chanting. As if hypnotized, I was frantically stamping my feet, cheering "Freedom! Now!" long after I was too hoarse to make a sound. I had stopped thinking about Franklin School, the citizens of Chester, the evils of racism and poverty. The utopian vision that had tugged at me yesterday was gone. In its place was something else, a fury that tore out of me with a life of its own, primitive as infancy. I was screaming against everyone and everything that had stood in my way—the boys who had rejected me, the man who had fired my father when I was nine, my absent father, my mother, my brother. (55–56)

The passage reads much like Rader's description of his attack on the busload of George Wallace supporters in *I Ain't Marchin'.* There is a difference, however; Rader's narrative retains its author's belief in the political and social etiology of generational rage. Alpert's narrative, like that of many later renunciatory authors, asserts that her radicalism was merely a mask behind which she acted out a personal neurosis. In many ways, of course, this characterization suggests a desire to avoid the generational dialogue altogether, as if to say that she, for one, was never anything but a confused adolescent and she's mighty sorry she ever bothered anyone with her problems. But even this early in her text, Alpert forgets her intention to present only her own case and claims that she was not alone in the displacement of childhood rage onto social causes: "I wasn't the only one in the crowd who temporarily lost control. When the police arrived, the entire mob sighed audibly, as at a long-awaited climax" (56). Whatever her announced intention, it is upon this displaced infantile rage that readers eager to attack the politics of the period pounce with glee. Narratives written by ex-generationalists, it would appear, are nearly impossible to read as solely self-referential. Stefan Kanfer, for example, uses his review of the book as an opportunity to denounce New Left politics as a whole. Merely making explicit the underlying message of Alpert's text, Kanfer writes that *Growing Up Underground* "shows on all of its banal pages, beneath the pounding, driving beat of the revolution, those who listened closely could always hear the hard bang of a spoon against a high chair."[25]

Interestingly, this new vision of herself as a person acting out her personal grievances on the political stage is not so far from the psychologized version of generationalism espoused by her now repudiated political self. Even before she came to see her political activity as based in non-related personal issues, Alpert believed that American terrorists were an avant-garde precisely because they were able to express their class grievances and had liberated themselves from bourgeois "hang-ups." She and most of her peers, in contrast, were filled with a repressed rage against the "system." When she was a graduate student at Columbia, the New Left demonstrators had appealed to her initially on this level; she looked to them as people who were "less repressed than I, who were acting out their beliefs by hanging flags from the buildings at Columbia, passing out flowers in the streets of Prague and San Francisco, or . . . risking jail by resisting the draft. They seemed to me joyous and free as well as principled" (122–23). Like Rader, she believed that they were a historical vanguard *because* they were able to act out what everyone else half consciously felt. Their uninhibited actions, she believed, would reveal to the generational mass its historical destiny and spur it to take up arms in imitation.

This theme of generational repression is present throughout much of the book, and it contributes to a portrait of the younger Alpert as a person addicted to the psychological perspective. Unfortunately, that perspective does not seem to have been of much use to her. Incredibly, for example, she suspects very early on that her lover, Sam Melville, the man for whom she initially takes up the terrorist cause, is emotionally unstable and that his terrorist commitments have little to do with the Vietnam War or any other of the various causes in whose name he has acted. As the group's ostensible leader, she says, he "clung to the movement not because he believed its ideas, but because he needed its rationale for his insanity" (180). After recounting his first clumsy bombing at the Marine Midland Bank, in which twenty persons were injured, Alpert acknowledges that she knew even at the time that his action had more to do with her dating another man than with politics:

> his behavior had nothing to do with the ideology we supposedly shared. He had given no thought to what Marine Midland meant to the left or to the general public, nor had he thought of how he might explain his action to our group, to the press, or if necessary to the courts. Because I had threatened to abandon him, even for one night, by sleeping with another man, he had taken revenge on a skyscraperful of people. (208)

In retrospect, she understands that she was no more stable than Melville, for while she believed at the time "that bombings could serve a useful political purpose," she is now aware that she "was attracted to bombings out of a deep irrational rage, not unlike Sam's own" (203). In her radical period, whenever her insights into her friend's behavior threatened to undermine her politics, she ignored them; after Melville demonstrates his instability, for example, she takes over the bombing in order to show him how to do it right. As an autobiographer she simply reverses this procedure, ignoring her peers' politics in order to focus on their social and psychological pathology.

The weakness of Alpert's psychologism, of course, is that its almost exclusive focus on the personal prevents her from examining the relationship between the extreme left and the Movement as a whole or even from exploring the implications of her early belief that thousands of Americans stood behind the underground movement. At one point, she criticizes two radicals "who had publicly endorsed violence against the state" and then refused to give her aid when she was a fugitive. "They claimed," Alpert writes, "to represent the revolutionary movement for the sake of which I had become a fugitive, and it could be argued that they bore some ethical responsibility for helping me to stay out of jail" (287). This is about as close as she comes to a discussion of the political atmosphere that allowed her to believe in and assume the role of revolutionary vanguardist. So when it is read in isolation, Alpert's book is not particularly revelatory except as a curious case study in aberrant psychology. Reading it in the context of other generational autobiographies, however, necessarily engenders a greater understanding of her former self than her narrator is willing to allow. For although Alpert claims she was acting out a "deeply irrational rage" over childhood disappointments, it is doubtful that she would have expressed that rage in the absence of the fantasies of revolution contained in those autobiographies and widespread in the culture.

One of the more poignant aspects of Alpert's autobiography is its depiction of the younger Alpert's dawning awareness of the gap between those fantasies and the realities of American cultural and political life. Unfortunately for her, that awareness did not begin until she had already committed herself irretrievably to her revolutionary identity. The begin-

ning of Alpert's doubts about her conception of herself as generational
vanguardist occurred when she realized that the left "had nothing that
could be called an army, no national unity or organization" (242). By the
time that had occurred, however, it was too late to shed the role she had
assigned herself:

> I came to see the unlikelihood of revolution at precisely the moment when I
> could no longer abandon my commitment to it. Already under arrest and fac-
> ing some seventy years in prison and in the spotlight of movement attention
> besides, I would have had to explain any change of heart to those whose eyes
> were fixed on me in the months before the trial. And any show of disillu-
> sionment might have hinted that I was getting ready to inform against Sam,
> Nate, Pat, and others—and that, of course, was anathema. (242)

Alpert's reemergence from a conception of herself as a member of a revolutionary vanguard was, in other words, retarded by the fact that she was
committed to it in a way that other generationalists were not, both by her
own choice and by the judiciary system's sentence, which guaranteed that
she would remain labeled as a "criminal revolutionist" for several years.
The deferral of that emergence was further prolonged by her decision to
go underground, where she had to assume a succession of false identities
to avoid detection by the authorities. Those disguises, however, presup-
posed the hidden existence of a "real" self, always in danger of public exposure. That self was, of course, "the revolutionary Jane Alpert," a self
that could be shed only within public discourse, where it was initially
taken on.[26] Living underground, Alpert found her ability to engage in
public discourse severely restricted by the requirement that she be someone other than herself. Given these factors, it is not surprising that she
emerged from her revolutionary identity as slowly as she did.

   Much of the confusion attending this identity drama, however, was
the direct outcome of the identity construction practices we have seen in
other generational autobiographers, particularly those who espoused
mythmaking as a better method than grassroots organizing for bringing
about political change. Writers such as Rubin and Hoffman, who were in
the business of "selling" the myth of generational revolution, employed
a strategy of media manipulation that was, at best, ambiguous. Part of
their strategy, as we have seen in Chapter 3, involved the use of Madison
Avenue advertising techniques to create media images of an America on
the verge of social and cultural collapse. Employing a time-proven advertising method, they sought to topple American institutions simply by
portraying them as having already toppled. According to their own explanations, the actual work of revolution—bombs, sabotage, civil war—
wasn't really necessary. The words alone, couched in mass media images
and in books like *Revolution for the Hell of It, Do It!* and *We Are Everywhere,* would suffice to bring about a new world.

As much as Rubin and Hoffman stressed a media-created social breakdown, however, they also indulged in revolutionary rhetoric that seemed quite serious. They supported, as Rubin said later in *Growing (Up) at 37,* "the Vietcong and selective violence here at home" (85). In the end, they seemed unable to distinguish between myth, parody, and reality, and their strategy of media manipulation, which had originally been undertaken to bring about a new world order, became an end in itself. Eventually, it didn't matter what image was broadcast so long as the Movement made the six o'clock news, which (as they predicted) responded only to the most sensational of "media events." So while Rubin and Hoffman originally constructed an image of youths as sexually promiscuous, drug-ingesting, bomb-throwing revolutionists as a self-conscious parody and with the intention of advertising more serious, though never clearly defined, social goals, that image eventually had the unintended side effect of trapping its creators in its own likeness. Rubin later wrote in *Growing (Up)*:

> for years I had successfully manipulated the media to serve the antiwar movement. Now I found myself a victim of the media: people saw me as crazy, dangerous, violent, insane. The image was driving me mad, until I realized that I believed it, too. As long as I believed I was a revolutionary hero, I would criticize myself for not fulfilling my own self-image. (5)

Read as parody or as a metaphor for revolution, Rubin's and Hoffman's books were, some might argue, amusing and provocative intellectual exercises. But read as political tracts, they were as manipulative and self-serving as the institutions they criticized. Much of Rubin's *Do It!* for example is devoted to imperatives that Rubin himself would never have followed and that had catastrophic consequences for many people who did: "When you're going through a toll booth on a freeway, pay the toll for a few cars behind you. Or better yet, dynamite the toll booths, because they charge people to get across free land. Blow up Howard Johnsons on the turnpike—the universal oppressor of everybody" (126). Rubin may have believed at times that such imperatives were merely tropes emphasizing America's need for complete cultural and social change, but many people, including Alpert and her friends, took them quite literally; that she ended up with a good deal of Movement prestige would seem to argue that others also took the revolutionary rhetoric seriously. Looking back at her group's first act of robbery, Alpert remarks:

> We, seven ordinary movement people, indistinguishable in our ideas, behavior, and ability from thousands of others across the country, were suddenly, by virtue of a harebrained robbery, a vanguard. Not one of us was capable of handling this new power; not one of us was brave enough to back away from it. (197)

Nor was her group alone. Between June 1969 and June 1970, Rader tells us, outrage over the continuing war in Vietnam led to over "4000 bombings in the United States" (*Blood Dues*, 22).[27] In the context of other generational works, Alpert's revolutionary violence was not merely a manifestation of aberrant psychology, but the consummation, however misguided, of the mythic and apocalyptic fantasies abundant in the collective autobiographies of Movement writers. No one over the age of forty can read Rubin's and Hoffman's books, or *I Ain't Marchin', The Wedding within the War,* or *Trial* today without being vividly reminded of how thoroughly the image of revolution had taken over the imaginations of the young during this period. All of these writers saw their work as attempts to "articulate a myth" of the generation; by 1969, a central feature of that myth was the vision of civil war between the generations.

It would be a mistake to conclude that those who acted out what others only wrote or talked about were typical of the entire Movement. Relatively few people were actually willing to act out the violent images of Movement rhetoric as thoroughly as Alpert and her group did. What Movement rhetoricians such as Rubin and Hoffman did represent, however, was the tendency of this generation to become so enamored of rhetoric, so caught up in the creation of images of themselves—as the oppressed, as victims, as persecuted purveyors of truth, and finally as guerrillas and revolutionaries intent on smashing injustice—that they forgot that images of the self beget selves in fact. Alpert acted as she did because she was convinced she was a member of a revolutionary vanguard, with the mass of her generation firmly behind her actions. Insofar as many of her contemporaries shared her revolutionary fantasies, she was correct. But neither Alpert nor the large mass of Movement-identified people who moved from protest to resistance was aware of what the dream of revolution entailed. When violence actually did break out sporadically all over the country, it was relatively short-lived, and it did more to kill the Movement than any of its enemies.

The God That Failed Revisited: John Bunzel's *Political Passages* and Peter Collier and David Horowitz's *Second Thoughts* and *Destructive Generation*

Alpert's book was published just one year after the election of Ronald Reagan to the American presidency in 1980. During the campaigning for that election, American conservatives had already begun a full-scale reconstruction and reevaluation of the sixties. It was a process to which Alpert's book contributed its own small mite. Even with its focus on the author's personal behavioral patterns, the book shared with the president's party a vision of the sixties as a malignant period in American history. The elections of 1984 and 1988 were also significant occasions for a vigorously partisan struggle over the control of America's national plot. According to the conservative rhetoric that dominated these elections, the sixties generation had offered a false plot, a version of America's past that focused unreasonably on racial oppression, slavery, Indian genocide, capitalistic greed, nuclear recklessness, and imperialism. Using this national plot as the larger narrative within which to construct their own generational plot, sixties radicals had cast themselves as a heroic resistance; freedom fighters struggling against a monolithic, all-powerful parent nation; allies of the downtrodden and oppressed. This plot, according to conservative rhetoric, was an outrageous libel. The real America, conservatives said, was the one that had existed in the minds of Americans in the immediate aftermath of the Second World War—the land of the free, the champion of democracy, the light of the world. They called nostalgically for a return to the pre-sixties Eden of the 1950s and a revival of American nationalism and pride.

That return should also be accompanied, they argued, by a focus on America's external enemies, particularly international communism, and a renewal of commitment to the arms race with the Soviet Union. They saw internal critics of American history and policy as the agents of an external power who should be treated as a fifth column. The "sixties" version of the American past was merely a propaganda tool, designed to weaken America's will and undermine its faith in its own world mission. In addition, they saw the radical critics themselves as seriously flawed characters, motivated by desire for personal gain, jealousy, envy, and bad faith. Such a vision (or political tactic) had worked well in the fifties, when politicians like Richard Nixon had founded their careers on the exposure of an internal communist threat. There were, however, significant differences between the conservative rhetoric of the two periods: in the fifties, the internal communist threat was depicted as coming from subversive political groups, most of them aligned with the Soviet Union; in the 1980s, although the threat was sometimes depicted in similar language, it was more often constructed in broad generational terms.

As in the fifties, a significant voice in this conservative reevaluation belonged to ex-members of the threatening group itself, and it once again expressed itself in autobiographies of renunciation. In the works that followed the relatively individualized revisionism of Alpert's narrative, the critique of the sixties became collective. In 1988, John Bunzel, a political science professor whose classes were targeted by student radicals during the 1969 strike at San Francisco State College, put together an anthology of renunciatory narratives written largely by members of the sixties generation and entitled *Political Passages: Journeys of Change through Two Decades, 1968–1988*.[28] As an anthology, it is one of the first collective efforts after *The Port Huron Statement* to engage in the struggle over generational identity. According to Bunzel, the book, in which "thoughtful

men and women" reflect on what the late sixties and early seventies . . .
meant to them and how and why they were changed by what they lived
through," was inspired partly by Richard Crossman's *The God That
Failed* (1950),[29] and, indeed, Bunzel's book and similar ones that followed in its wake are insistently reiterative of the themes, language, and
generational emplotment that characterized the work of all of the renunciatory autobiographers mentioned at the beginning of this chapter—
Chambers, Gitlow, Budenz, Massing, Bentley, and Dodd.

Like Crossman's book, Bunzel's provides narratives that begin with
the author's conversion to a secular ideology and end with his or her deconversion away from it. Bunzel's authors show how, through a single
crystallizing experience or series of experiences, they finally came to reject the political and philosophical assumptions underlying the New
Left's vision of generational identity and mission in the 1960s.[30] That organizing principle places the essays of Bunzel's book squarely within the
tradition of the older anticommunist memoirs to which they frequently
allude and also within the even older tradition of American evangelical
revival meetings, where born-again Christians stand to tell the story of
their conversion for two reasons: to bolster the faith of the already converted and to bring unregenerate audience members to an awareness of
the mortal danger in which they stand. Indeed, the Christian tradition
can cite Saint Augustine as an even older example of this use of "witnessing." It was by means of hearing the story of his friend Ponticianus
that Augustine was brought to a conviction of his own sinful nature. Directly addressing the divine author of that conviction, Augustine describes both the story's effect on him and the hoped-for effect of his own
confession on his readers:

> You, Lord, while he was speaking, were turning me around so that I could
> see myself; you took me from behind my own back, which was where I had
> put myself during the time when I did not want to be observed by myself, and
> you set me in front of my own face so that I could see how foul a sight I
> was—crooked, filthy, spotted, and ulcerous. I saw and was horrified, and I
> had nowhere to escape from myself. If I tried to look away from myself, Pon-
> ticianus still went on with his story, and again you were setting me in front
> of myself, forcing me to look into my own face, so that I might see my sin
> and hate it.[31]

Unlike Christian witnesses, however, Bunzel's collection of modern-day
Ponticiani are not particularly interested in persuading their readers to
convert to a particular faith; rather, they wish to *warn them about* a
heretical faith—the sixties ethos—that they feel is demonic and dangerous.

That sense of their present mission underlies most of these autobiographical narratives. Having once pitched their tents among the enemy,
they believe that they can now provide information about that enemy's

intentions and its typical means of infiltrating healthy American society. Most of the authors believe that these enemies, the purveyors of the sixties ethos, are now ensconced in the universities. Edward Shils claims in the book's opening essay that they are maintaining a purposefully low profile: "They are now less melodramatically expressed, but they still exist, and they are now entrenched in universities, as they are in American life" (25). In "A Virtucrat Remembers," Joseph Epstein echoes Shils, describing the sixties as "an enormous wave that rolled over the country, then slowly rolled back, but not without leaving a vast amount of debris on the beach. The university, I now at first hand came to see, was the beach" (54). Peter Collier, seizing the marine metaphor, warns his readers in "Looking Backward: Memories of the Sixties Left," that

> people from the sixties are still out there—the dark shapes under our political waters. After my years as a New Leftist, I could never join another movement or subscribe to another oxthdoxy [sic]. But I feel that I still have a small role to play—keeping an eye on these deep swimmers, and, when I see one of them come to the surface, pointing out who he is, what he is doing, and what the consequences are likely to be. It may not be much to show for a fifteen-year indenture to the New Left, but it is the only way I know to put that perverse experience to use. (186)

What emerges from the narratives is a reconstruction of "the sixties" as an entity analogous to the "communist threat" of 1950s cold war rhetoric, and it is depicted, in language borrowed directly from that rhetoric, as a "fifth column" within or a "cancerous growth" on the body politic. It is, according to this rhetoric, being led by a cadre of determined intellectuals, working in conjunction with an international socialist-communist movement, and its most powerful asset is its position within the education system, where it continues to sow the ideas and attitudes that predispose American youth to the weaknesses of socialism and relativism. Indeed, at times Bunzel's group's debt to the renunciatory works of the fifties almost undermines their own claims. Their assertion here, for example, that the universities have been infiltrated by cadres of socialistic relativists echoes Bella Dodd's 1954 renunciatory work *School of Darkness,* which depicts the university system as a "beachhead" controlled by communists (58) and ends with a warning to her readers about the insidious role of educational institutions in undermining true American progress:

> Now I saw in true perspective the contribution that the teachers and the schools of America have made to its progress, just as I was sadly aware of the darker picture some of the educators and the educated among us have presented. Justice Jackson has said that it is the paradox of our times that we in modern society need to fear only the educated man. (246)

According to the Bunzel anthologists, of course, this takeover did not occur for at least two more decades, when the sixties generation moved out of their hippie communes and Marxist cadres and into the previously uncontaminated universities.

The audience to whom all of these warnings are addressed is in part composed of those Americans unfamiliar with the nefarious techniques and beliefs of the enemy. In "Errand into the Wilderness," Michael Novak says that his audience is not the left itself, which is unlikely to be "persuaded through reason and an analysis of cases. . . . It is, rather, the younger ones, still open-minded and searching, the questioning and the self-affirming, who know in the depths of their minds that self-hatred, alienation, and resentment [all characteristics these authors assign the sixties generation] are signs of an illness of the spirit" (244). Most of the authors, however, are more actively engaged in an intragenerational dialogue, addressing their essays directly to their unreconstructed peers. David Horowitz, for example, uses a technique we have already seen in Cowley, Hoffman, Rossman, and Mungo, and couches his narrative in the form of a "Letter to a Political Friend," a red-diaper leftist who has not forsaken the faith, and James Finn's "Why Did You Sign That Ad?" is addressed to leftist ex-friends who had written an open letter in *Christianity and Crisis* demanding to know why he had signed an ad applauding President Reagan's policy in El Salvador (273).

Because of their status as "second generation" apostates from the leftist faith, these writers are highly conscious of their anticommunist predecessors and eager to mark their differences from them. Touchy that they might be accused of Manichaeanism, just as their elders were, they are uncomfortable with the notion that they are constructing conversion narratives, which smack, in their view, of religion or some other totalizing ideology: Christians and Marxists can write conversion narratives, but it is just such cosmic thinking imported into the realm of politics that they are repudiating. In fact, however, their narratives mostly conform to the conventional renunciatory-conversion pattern. As Novak says in his narrative, deconversions away from leftism may not be as deep as religious conversions, "but they are deep enough," affecting "all of one's judgment and actions as a citizen," and embodying "different senses of reality, different views of human nature, different senses of historical narrative, and quite different forms of self-knowledge" from those held previously (272 n. 3).

However, because they don't want their deconversions to be taken as irrational leaps of faith, very few of these authors admit that their change occurred as a conversion of the Pauline variety. Instead, they almost all portray their conversions as a gradual process of self-discovery and intellectual reexamination. Epstein notes that in his case it was a simple process of maturation, "nothing dramatic—no falling star, no shaft of sunlight on the forest floor, no weekend spent staring at the ocean—caused me to shed what I now think the political illusions of earlier years.

Instead, as illusions most often do, mine decayed and fell away, rather like baby teeth" (53). In "The New Left: Reflections and Reconsiderations," Jeffrey Herf echoes Epstein while at the same time distinguishing himself from his political forebears. His deconversion, he writes, involved "no clear 'before and after,' no 'Kronstadt' comparable to the Hitler-Stalin pact, the Russian invasion of Hungary in 1956, or Khrushchev's secret speech that led to a massive exit from the left. Nor can I report any sudden revelation or overnight conversion" (121–22).[32] In his own essay, "A Liberal in the Middle," Bunzel likewise claims that he experienced "no radical swing from left to right, no conversion to a new political church. Nevertheless, there was significant change" (155). James Finn avers that he had "no Damascus experience, no single incident, no sudden insight that triggered the changes. . . . It was rather the accumulation of a number of incidents" (280). And Novak writes: "If I had been knocked from a horse by a blinding light on a single memorable day, it would be easier to say. Instead, it was quite gradual, through examining my own left-wing presuppositions one by one. Underneath this questioning, perhaps, lay a pursuit of self-knowledge, a drive to be faithful to my family and my roots, to be myself" (248). The one author who admits to a single deconversion experience is Carol Iannone, who describes in "The Wide and Crooked Path" her falling out with her generation over the issue of feminism. An interview with two "radical lesbian man-hating feminists" during her application for a college teaching post served as her "Kronstadt experience" (316).

As in most conversion narratives, many of these authors exhibit an unusually high degree of animosity toward their former selves. But by couching their self-renunciation in narratives about collective identity, they manage to deflect their self-contempt not only onto the group to which they once belonged, but also onto anyone who still holds the values of that now repudiated group.[33] This project involves a number of the authors in a rather contradictory endeavor, for even as they condemn the sixties generation for the collectivist sin of imposing stereotypical identities on various groups, they engage in the same practice, first constructing a despicable version of their earlier selves and then putting this caricature forward as the embodiment of the worthless values of the entire generation. The range in treatment of the spurned former self is, however, rather wide. Like Alpert, several of the authors are appalled by their younger selves. In "Notes of a Journey," Julius Lester, for example, expresses "disbelief and shame" (74) over an essay he wrote in 1967 calling upon blacks to kill in the name of love and brotherhood. Others are somewhat kinder if no less rejecting. In "On Hanging Up the Old Red Flag," Ronald Radosh adopts an ironic tone, highlighting his younger self's exaggerated rhetoric, intimidating political tactics, and contradictory behavior with a fine sense of the ridiculous. Epstein, with less grace, attempts something similar, portraying his deluded younger self as "a down-the-line, pull-the-lever man of the left" (36).

The real animus of these essays, however, is reserved for those who once held and continue to hold the ideals of that rejected younger self, and this is the methodological axis on which almost all of these autobiographical essays turn. The former self of the author is reconstructed and repudiated, and then the author's self-disgust is turned outward, against those he or she perceives as complicit with this former self. This deflection from self to other is captured neatly, even if unconsciously, by Epstein's description of a walk he took in the late eighties through the Haight-Ashbury district of San Francisco. That area, he says, is still inhabited by "denizens" of the sixties, "sad and aging hippies, who seemed to be standing around awaiting a bus into the past." In spite of his own now reformed appearance as he strolls through their neighborhood, he reports that he sensed no hostility from them. But toward them, he says, he felt "a sense of revulsion, and loathing, and above all depression" (33). Such deflections are a typical aspect of the identity politics in which all of these renunciatory texts are engaged. Their authors are not merely renouncing their own earlier selves à la Alpert; they are also responding to the recent reconstruction of the sixties by those who retain their "nostalgia" for the period (and to whom we will turn in the next chapter). Reacting against such nostalgia, these twelve apostles of neoliberalism and neoconservatism employ renunciatory autobiography as the primary means to expose the "true" nature of that period and the generation that was its protagonist.

Bunzel's selection of writers itself reveals an attempt to engage the proponents of identity politics on their own grounds, for surely these particular authors, representing a veritable ethnic rainbow, were chosen at least in part for their collective affiliations. Since one of the oft-repeated themes of these essays is that the sixties generation erred by judging people according to such affiliations, one can hardly miss the reason for the choices here. Members of various ethnic, religious, and gender groups are called upon to speak out against such methods of discussing and assigning identity, especially if it is done to the exclusion of attention to individual identity. Thus, two of the authors are women, five are Jews, four are Roman Catholics, one is an African American, one is Irish American, one is Italian American, at least two are Anglo-Americans, one is Slavic American, and one is Hispano-American. In fact, the selection procedure was sufficiently wide-ranging to include several contributors who were not, strictly speaking, members of the sixties cohort at all, but who nonetheless felt themselves to be its representatives for having adopted, and then discarded, a portion of the decade's Zeitgeist.[34]

From the very outset, however, Bunzel's authors are at a rhetorical disadvantage in this autobiographical dialogue. One might imagine that the most effective way to counter the left's construction of generational identity would be to deny that the left was representative of the period. But as ex-leftists themselves, they cannot do that, and their language already concedes the left's representative generational status. "The sixties generation" and "the sixties," for example, are phrases these authors use interchangeably and tellingly with "the New Left," and "the Movement." Although both of these phrases have finally come to signify for them a whole cluster of leftist and countercultural values that they find abhorrent, they continue to grant them a generation-defining status. In other words, in spite of the reversal of their attitudes toward those values, the authors remain entrapped within the framework of a leftist vocabulary and worldview. In fact, many of them believe that their own voices are the only ones offering a competent version of the generational past precisely because it is ex-leftist, as though the generational experience of the 1960s is fully comprehensible only within the confines of a dialogue between leftists and ex-leftists.

Peter Collier (b. 1941) sums up what he takes to be the characterization of that generational experience by "the nostalgia artists who write pop history." Their portrait, he says, is of a generation that is "passionate and caring, a collection of dewy-eyed idealists driven to extreme remedies by a world of cruel power. These radicals were right more often than they were wrong, we are told, but whether they were right or wrong is almost irrelevant because they were above all *authentic*" (163). The task Bunzel's writers have taken on is the reconstruction of the generation's plot together with the wholesale revision and reevaluation of its character. Their point is not that the generation is not defined by Movement values, but rather that those values are themselves improperly understood. As Collier goes on to say, the truth about the sixties is that they "were anything but an innocent time," and its leftist leaders were, "at least by the middle of the journey, confirmed cynics. They never really believed *in* anything. Certainly by the end of the decade their commitment was negative: they were *against* patriotic commitment; they hated the *idea* of America" (163).

Aligning themselves with what they claim is the mass of "American people" (a collectivist construction these essays oppose to the "sixties generation"), Bunzel's writers seek to reevaluate the generation from the point of view of American "traditionality, nationality, normality, civility" (31). Horowitz, for example, claims that the left's scorning of his characterization of the sixties only demonstrates "contempt for the majority of Americans" (196). Shils dismisses out of hand the moral high ground the left has always assumed in discussions of generational identity; the truth, according to Shils, is that the sixties were worse than the thirties. Both generations gave in to what he refers to as cultural-political "temptations." The earlier generation fell to the temptation of "totalitarianism"; the latter, to "antinomianism," which calls for a "life of complete self-determination, free of the burden of tradition and conventions, free of the constraints imposed by institutional rules and laws and of the stipulations of authority" (15).

Several of the writers construct narratives demonstrating that their sixties selves were guilty primarily of the sin of "adolescence," a term they prefer to the Movement writers' "youth." Epstein's construction of an adolescent collective whose members projected their personal problems onto society strikes a note already sounded in Rader's and Alpert's narratives. In Bunzel's book, Alpert's focus on the psychological is generalized to include the political culture of the whole epoch. Epstein quotes Joseph Conrad's comment in *The Secret Agent* that "the way of even the most justifiable revolutions is prepared by personal impulses disguised into creeds" to explain his and his peers' behavior. His construction of his sixties self includes the notion that his political identity was, in large part, the result of an "impulse . . . toward nonconformity" (41). Julius Lester, like Alpert, perceived generational motivation as aberrant even at the time he was a part of it. As Stokely Carmichael's traveling companion in 1966, he noted the militant leader's destructive narcissism and wrote that Carmichael's "anger is not one person's aberration, but the ethos of a generation. That is frightening" (70). Collier claims in his essay that "What we called politics in the sixties was . . . an Oedipal revolt on a grand scale; a no-fault acting out. We liked to think of ourselves as characters out of Malraux. As I think back on it now, it seems to me that we were always political Katzenjammer kids whose mischief turned homicidal somewhere along the road" (163).

Martha Bayles' essay, "How I Spent My Summer Vacation," also continues Alpert's reconstruction of the generation as one defined more by adolescent "acting out" than by genuine political considerations. One of two women represented in the anthology (the other is Carol Iannone), Bayles narrates her experience working for an organization that sent white college students from the North into the Deep South to help underprivileged black children; that summer of 1969 becomes a metaphor for everything that was wrong with the sixties and the person she was at that time. Like Alpert, she dismisses the politics of her earlier self as a mask behind which she acted out her emotional problems. Although she includes, as Alpert does, the disclaimer that "such psychological motivations were not typical" (92), the narrative's inclusion in Bunzel's anthology and its language—particularly her recurrent use of the "we"—both suggest that she believes they were *quite* representative.[35] But it was not only her psychological problems that served as the basis for her onetime identification with, and present condemnation of, the Movement. That identification was also encouraged, as she sees it, by the permissiveness of her parents and the institutions that affected her life (92–93). Reacting to the failure of the adults around her to be "authorities," she turned to liberals. Two such surrogate authorities were the Caplans, a couple who oversaw the Georgia operations of the southern program she worked for. Bayles claims that her younger self (and by extension, her generation) needed good disciplining to keep in line. The Caplans, instead of providing it, only encouraged her immaturity: "There was I, a young woman in emotional and cultural free fall. And there were the Caplans, elderly do-gooders mistaking my plummeting for exhilarating flight" (95). Without strong parental figures, she was simply an adolescent girl rebelling against bourgeois rules and living out her sexual fantasies. The futility of her efforts to change the world for the better was amply demonstrated, at summer's end, when she allowed a young black boy in her charge to drown in a local pond.

Perhaps the most striking overlap between Bayles' narrative and Alpert's, however, is her focus on her younger self's translation of political values into a sexual mythology. In Alpert's case, the translation ended with the author's idealization of and sexual submission to her unbalanced terrorist lover. In Bayles', it leads to a political version of "jungle fever." She becomes sexually infatuated with an uneducated, married black worker named Quennel. In retrospect, she sees this infatuation as doubly emblematic of late-sixties Movement politics: it embodied a generational tendency to overlook individual persons in favor of collective identities derived from simple oppressor/oppressed models, and, insofar as Quennel lived within a subculture that stressed family values, it signified an unconscious desire for the very "normality" that the sixties pretended to challenge (105).

This tendency to see others as embodiments of collective identities is undoubtedly the sixties characteristic that the writers in this anthology are most intent upon first reconstructing and then attacking. Julius Lester, for example, excoriates his former black militant self for "mouthing platitudes in clichéd prose" and for having allowed his individual self to be "swallowed by the savage appetite of the collective" (75). One of the more experimental pieces, Lester's essay uses Rossman's windows-into-time form, juxtaposing diary entries from the sixties with his present (1987) ruminations on them. But where Rossman wanted to demonstrate continuity and growth, Lester is intent on showing the convert's sense of discontinuity between his sixties self and his present perspective. Nonetheless, even the early diary entries evince a serious conflict between the collective self the Movement was pressuring Lester to adopt and his own sense of individual difference. In the end, the struggle for the survival of his "authentic" individual self leads to his repudiation of the Movement's collective identity, and he opts for "the agony and the joy of democracy. It attempts to confer collective identity even as it gives one the space, encouragement, and support to oppose the collective" (87).

More typical of the book are Collier's and Horowitz's essays, which censure the sixties penchant for collective idealizations even while engaging in their own collective denigrations. Both Collier and Horowitz (b. 1939) pepper their narratives with emblematic events—"crystalline moments" as Collier calls them—that serve as deprecatory metaphors for the collective self of the generation. Occasionally, these simply provide a literary veneer for political mudslinging as, for example, in a sketch provided by Collier echoing Epstein's description of his walk through the Haight-Ashbury district. Like Epstein, Collier returns to the San Francisco Bay area, where the sixties were continuing to "happen," and notices that "a sewer had broken and spewed human excrement onto [Berkeley's] Telegraph Avenue. People were stoically walking through the mess, pretending not to see or smell it. The scene was right out of Kundera and offered itself as a metaphor for Berkeley civic life" (164).

However, even more typical than stories that serve as metaphors for the sixties collective self are stories intended, like Bayles', as metaphors for the sixties collectivist errors. For Collier and Horowitz, the most blatant of these was the left's idealization of African Americans, particularly militant black nationalists. Both Collier's and Horowitz's autobiographies contain episodes describing how African Americans "hustled" the Movement by exploiting the Movement's belief that blacks enjoyed a special moral status because of their oppression. Collier, for example, tells a poignant story of a summer he spent in the South teaching at a poor black college; it is, as he now sees it, a "summary moment" in his civil rights experience, though he "didn't fully understand the lesson until later on" (167). After enthusing wildly over the compositions of one of his young students and devoting himself to taking her "away from all this," he discovers he has been had; all of her papers had been plagiarized from an anthology of Harlem Renaissance writings. Back in California several years later, something similar happens in his relationship with the Black Panther Party, which manipulates him easily because of his projection of a fantasy "about 'avant gardes' onto them" (179). A crucial turning point for Horowitz and Collier occurred after they convinced the Panthers to hire a white friend of theirs, Betty Van Patter, as their bookkeeper. When she discovered that the Panthers were doctoring their books and confronted them about it, they murdered her and dumped her body into the bay. A similar fate awaited two other women acquaintances of theirs, Fay Stender, the lawyer who defended "Soledad Brother" George Jackson and was later murdered by one of his followers for having "betrayed" him, and Ellen R., a social worker in New Jersey who was killed by one of her black clients. For both writers, these murders served as a wake-up call not only about the true nature of the blacks they idealized, but also about themselves. They had imposed an idealized collective identity on black thugs and gangs, and those people had killed their friends. In

Horowitz's reconstruction, Ellen's murder serves as a metaphor for generational history: "Our progressive mission had been destructive to others and, finally, destructive to us. It had imbued us with the greatest racism of all—a racism that was universal, never allowing us to see people as they really were, but only as our prejudices required" (204).

Herein lies perhaps the most glaring inconsistency of the text as a whole: it repeatedly excoriates constructions of collective identity even though its own primary aim is to bash the collective identity of the people who came of age during the sixties. This contradiction should, at this point, come as no great surprise, for if anything can be said to characterize the books I have examined in this chapter, it is that as they move increasingly toward the right politically, asserting as they do so the preeminent value of individualism, they also engage more and more vehemently in collective identity construction, culminating in the revealingly collectivist title of Collier and Horowitz's neoconservative *Destructive Generation*.

The same year in which Bunzel was putting together his anthology, Collier and Horowitz demonstrated the accuracy of Michael Novak's observation that deconversions affect a person's "sense of historical narrative" by founding the "Second Thoughts Project," a group explicitly devoted to the construction of narratives that would counter the autobiographies examined in Chapter 3 as well as some of those we will look at in the next chapter. *Second Thoughts: Former Radicals Look Back at the Sixties* (1989) contains the proceedings of the project's first conference, held in October of 1987.[36] In its introduction, Collier explains that the meeting intentionally coincided with the publication of James Miller's *"Democracy Is in the Streets"* (1987), Maurice Isserman's *If I Had a Hammer* (1987), and Todd Gitlin's *The Sixties* (1987). All of these books, Collier claims, are "affirmative, indeed euphoric, views of the New Left experience." The conference was organized to present what he calls an

> equal and opposite reaction to these celebrations of SDS and the Movement, a voice of experience challenging the voice of innocence these authors adopted in talking about an era they insist was motivated primarily by an earnest radicalism and moral passion they seem to believe is sadly lacking in the present day. (xii)

In order to marshal this "equal and opposite reaction," the editors borrowed heavily from Bunzel's contributors. Several essays are in fact reprinted in revised form and with new titles from the earlier work. Jeffrey Herf, Ronald Radosh, Carole Iannone, Julius Lester, and Michael Novak (all contributors to the earlier work) provide new pieces for this one. Ex-leftists of the older generation, represented by Martin Peretz, Hilton Kramer, William Phillips, Irving Kristol, Norman Podhoretz, and Nathan Glazer, get their own section here, entitled "Second Thoughts: A

Generational Perspective," in which they draw historical parallels between the delusions of the sixties and those of the thirties. Most of the proceedings, however, consist of brief renunciatory autobiographies offered by ex-members of the New Left, the civil rights movement, the feminist movement, the counterculture, and the pro-Hanoi and pro-Sandinista factions of the American left. Like their generational counterparts in the thirties (to whom they make frequent reference), these writers all claim that they allowed themselves to be seduced by false gods, and their stories, like those in Bunzel's book, recount how they came to see the light. Their convocation here in some ways echoes, albeit with an added tone of beleaguerment, the original *Port Huron Statement*. They've held a conference to produce autobiographies that together constitute a collective confession-cum-manifesto; they too are announcing a new identity to which they wish to attract others. As Michael Medved writes, using phrasing that echoes New Left formulas for the representation of their collective identity, "Many others have made—and are making—similar journeys. The great value of the 'Second Thoughts' project comes in assembling these stories, and demonstrating that we are not isolated aberrations, but part of a considered, and inevitable response to the trauma of recent history" (24).[37]

While they may make broad annunciatory gestures, most of the autobiographical sketches in this work, like those in Bunzel's, focus their energies on revising the generational narrative and conform to the conversion and renunciatory modes we have seen in other books. In spite of that, almost all of the writers again worry lest their stories be taken as irrational "conversion experiences." Their present attitudes, they claim, are the result of careful deliberation. Setting the pace, Collier points out in the foreword that the writers generally had "no single conversion experience; no epiphany on the road to Damascus. Rather there was a slow glacial action of doubt whose cumulative effect was to alter the personal political landscape, subtly at first and then decisively" (xiii). But revealingly, he then goes on to list the various "triggers" that brought about these decisive changes, and these "triggers" sound suspiciously like Damascus road experiences. "For many," he writes, "the trigger . . . had been what happened in Southeast Asia in the aftermath of the U.S. defeat in Vietnam" (xiii); for others, it was the Soviet Union's imperialistic aggression in Afghanistan. In any case, "almost all of those who participated in the Conference had experienced a crystalline moment which embodied the new and disturbing insight they had had into the nature of the left, an insight which would ultimately cause them to turn their back on its smelly little orthodoxies" (xiv).

These "triggers" not only resemble the turning points of conventional conversion narratives; they also signal a recapitulation of the generational plot constructed by their predecessors, the ex-communists of the thirties generation. Much of this is clearly intentional, reflecting the authors' belief that the New Left blindly repeated the errors of the old left, and their own generational conversions are, as a consequence, simply more of the same old story. Thus, these "triggers" are not merely moments of conversion and revelation, but repetitions of earlier such moments in leftist autobiography: Kronstadt, the Moscow Trials, the Hitler-Stalin Pact, the Khrushchev revelations, and the invasion of Hungary for the earlier writers. To these, defectors from the sixties generation may now add the killing fields of the Khmer Rouge, the Vietnamese invasion of Cambodia, and the Russian invasion of Afghanistan. All of these are experiences that reveal, in neoconservative narratives, the "true" nature of the leftist tendency to genocide and brutality.

The book's primary difference from Bunzel's lies in the fact that more of its autobiographical essays are directed at specific political issues. Many of them, in fact, are identified by Collier as "position papers." This is evident even in the book's organization. After its opening section, with its narratives of defection from the left, the book offers a section on Vietnam, one on Nicaragua, and one on political culture in general. The last two sections are reserved for "second thoughts" on the sixties from the point of view of members of the older generation, and a kind of envoi, such as we have seen in many other generational autobiographies, in which several of the sixties defectors suggest a "political agenda" for the future. Unlike the calls for action that were so conspicuous in the texts examined in Chapter 3, however, these are mostly cautionary sermons warning readers against all forms of belief in a better world, with special emphasis on the dangers of utopianism, socialism, and communism. In short, like most renunciatory works, their focus is retrospective, full of warnings about the dangers of the faith they have abandoned, rather than good tidings of the faith they have found.

As their final contribution to the "god that failed" theme, Horowitz and Collier published a collection of their own essays entitled *Destructive Generation: Second Thoughts about the Sixties* (1989).[38] The ideological gist of the book is most clearly articulated in the book's second section, entitled (once again) "Second Thoughts." There, the authors outline their arguments against sixties leftism and its consequences in specific political arenas. After treating the inherently treasonable nature of American leftism in "The Fifth Column Left: Divided Loyalties," the totalitarian tendency of the leftist use of the term "McCarthyism," and the disastrous effects of municipal leftism in "A Tale of Socialism in One City: Slouching toward Berkeley," they turn to a direct engagement in the generation's autobiography wars. For these writers, autobiography is indeed perceived as a battleground in which the nation's political soul may be won or lost. In an essay entitled "Radical Innocence, Radical Guilt," they target the

celebratory generational narrative being reconstructed in recently published Movement autobiographies, singling out as particularly heinous
examples Todd Gitlin's *The Sixties: Years of Hope, Days of Rage* (1987)
and Tom Hayden's *Reunion* (1988). Both of these writers, they claim,
took up autobiography during a mid-eighties "resurgence" of leftism in
order "to recapture lost innocence by asserting that whatever excesses they
had committed had resulted from America's madness, a social insanity
that had temporarily diminished their capacity. 'Explaining' the past was
thus a means both of self-revisionism and of self-rehabilitation" (240).

According to Horowitz and Collier, Gitlin attempts to achieve the
appearance of self-scrutiny while at the same time maintaining the innocence of the left by admitting to small sins and ignoring larger ones. And
even for the smaller sins, they say, Gitlin (like his entire coterie) manages
to find excuses. Thus, in his autobiographical reconstruction of the period, Gitlin focuses briefly on the Movement's accidental killing of a
graduate student when it bombed the physics building at the University of
Wisconsin. The killing of this "first" innocent person, says Gitlin, was a
turning point for the Movement. Collier and Horowitz point out that
there were many more such innocent victims and that most of them were
far from accidental. The Black Panthers, for example, were heroes to the
New Left and well known to be involved in murder before the Wisconsin
incident. Gitlin, moreover, was aware that the Movement-idolized North
Vietnamese had carried out massacres during the 1950s. But even when
he acknowledges Movement "excesses," they say, Gitlin finds an excuse
for them in the Vietnam War and the assassination of America's liberal
leaders (243). They are even harder on Hayden's memoir since they believe he omits more than mere sympathy for terrorism. Hayden, they
write, "omits . . . his own efforts to incite paramilitary insurrections in
Berkeley and other American cities" (244). And unlike Gitlin, who tries
to rehabilitate the entire left in his memoir-history, Hayden is, in their
view, a mere opportunist, "a one-man cult of personality" who "has
made his rehabilitation effort for himself alone" (245).

As their first maneuver in the autobiography wars, then, the authors
alter the rationale for placing events within the generational plot. In most
of the autobiographies I have discussed so far, the writer includes characters or events in the narrative because they are *representative* or *typical*
of the collective identity that is intended to be celebrated. But in these
neoconservative books, the authors insist that characters and events
should be included because the collective identity being reconstructed is
responsible for them. The impetus for this insistence clearly derives from
conservative backlash, as evidenced by the invariably unsavory excesses
for which these writers find "the sixties" responsible. According to
Horowitz and Collier, these excesses most clearly reveal the generation's
reprehensible character. Recognizing the possibility for such conclusions,

Jane Alpert offered a halfhearted disclaimer of representativeness in her book that allowed her peers to deny that her narrative implicated them. Horowitz, Collier, and their political allies, however, focus precisely on extremist groups such as Alpert's, the Black Panthers, the Soledad prisoners, and the Weathermen because they see the Movement as directly responsible for their actions. Indeed, as their attack on Gitlin reveals, they are eager to go even further: even the crimes of totalitarian regimes and terrorist guerrilla groups such as the North Vietnamese Marxists and the Cambodian Khmer Rouge can be blamed on the sixties generation, since it sympathized with and/or excused their actions. This conflation of the extreme left with the Movement as a whole culminates in Collier's glib observation that not only the Black Panthers but the "Left as a whole" were a kind of "gang" (271).

It is this shift in the rationale for selecting representative characters and events that underlies the book's first section, "The Dancers and the Dance." In it, Collier and Horowitz recount the stories of leftists whose histories were, for them, the direct outcome of Movement logic and thus apt metaphors for generational identity. Here, however, the metaphors are intended as object lessons in the sins of the sixties rather than as self-vaunting models of generational destiny. The first two are very readable investigative histories: one about Fay Stender, the well-known Bay Area activist lawyer—she defended "Soledad Brother" George Jackson and Black Panther Huey Newton—who was eventually riddled with bullets by one of Jackson's followers; and one about the Weathermen, the SDS offshoot that turned to terrorism in the late sixties. Stender they depict as a radical so blind to reality that she eventually got herself gunned down by the very people she had idealized. Her sixties politics consisted, as the authors have it, of the fantasy that black pimps, hoods, drug pushers, rapists, and murderers were really intellectuals, poets, and political philosophers oppressed by the dominant white culture. It comes as no surprise to them, then, that these gangsters should have eventually revealed their true natures or that Stender should have suffered for her blindness. Just as Hayden becomes, as these authors construct him, the "Everyman of the Movement" (219), Stender becomes "a radical Everyperson" (65) whose life and death raised "issues that were too lacerating" (65) for most of her peers to confront. Like Stender, the sixties generation never fully understood the implications of their beliefs or were willing to accept responsibility for them. In the end, these beliefs proved both self-destructive and destructive of American institutions.

Lest one miss the present-day relevance of the Stender biography, the book's second essay on the Weathermen repeats it: the sixties were bad enough when we were living through them, but they continue to do harm because the generational leaders of the period have never fully acknowledged their errors. The second essay therefore follows two of the Weathermen's leaders, Billy Ayers and Bernadine Dohrn, from the early days of their involvement with SDS, through the most orgiastic and terroristic underground period, to the present. And what this investigation reveals is that even in 1987, after so many of their harebrained schemes have literally exploded in their faces, these two survivors are incapable of facing the truth about themselves and the past. For Collier and Horowitz, Dohrn especially embodies the narcissism and self-delusion of nostalgic New Leftists. To make their point about Dohrn—and coincidentally about the Movement as a whole—they quote repentant ex-SDS leader Mark Rudd:

> "her ego was still totally involved with all that dead history. How little she had looked at herself all those years. She should have had to confront what she did to people—manipulated, maneuvered, and isolated them, fucked them up; she should have had to admit how wrong her ideas were, how *meshuga* her self-conception was. A great revolutionary leader! She had no great revolutionary ideas. None of us did. She was just the daughter of a credit manager of a Milwaukee furniture store." (117–18)[39]

This, then, is the primary political aim of these biographies: not simply the moral and political condemnation of the sixties generation, but the insistence that its onetime leaders acknowledge their crimes and errors, and thus help to purge the liberal cancer from American society.

Finally, however, these exercises in politically tendentious biography give place to a more subjective account of the period. They begin their work following Emerson's famous dictum "There is no history, only biography," but later abandon it, agreeing with Thoreau that "there is really not even biography, . . . just autobiography" (320). The last section of the book, consequently, is devoted entirely to their own stories, two of which are reprinted here from the earlier Bunzel and *Second Thoughts* texts.[40] Given what they have said about others, one would expect these stories to be exercises in careful self-scrutiny. And certainly Collier's autobiographical essay maintains a consistently ironic tone toward his former self. Horowitz's essay, however, is less given to self-criticism and more to apologia; he claims that even in his most fully committed leftist phase, a part of his self was always withheld and alone: "I was alone because I never stopped thinking about the ambiguous legacy we all had inherited" (291).

But even with their mea culpas (particularly concerning their relations with the Black Panthers), Collier and Horowitz make the transition from repentant radicals to self-righteous radical bashers with astounding ease. Foremost among the motes they see lodged in the eyes of their ex-comrades is autobiographical whitewashing; but they are curiously blind to the log of self-exculpation that dominates their own texts. According to their version of the past, they may have been sixties radicals, participants in the collective self their autobiographies seek to expose, but they were not really responsible for the epoch's worst excesses. "In the Sixties," their joint autobiography claims,

> we were radicals, but radicals who stopped short of the most radical behavior. . . . Most of us who had come of age in the Fifties could never quite accept the admonition that so appealed to the second wave of activists, who appeared a few years later amidst assassination, war, and racial strife: "Do it!" We were more comfortable thinking or talking about it. We might store weapons for groups like the Black Panthers or hide their armed fugitives but "Pick up the gun" never became more for us than a slogan. In an anti-intellectual movement we were closet intellectuals who always held a piece of ourselves apart from what was going on. Some "bourgeois values," such as responsibility for one's acts and respect for the truth—not revolutionary truth but truth beyond considerations of ideology—were hard to get rid of. We never succeeded. (319)

This self-description, simultaneously admitting error and claiming moral superiority (they tried to be bad, but were impeded by the ineradicable effects of good breeding and natural virtue), is almost identical to one made by Tom Hayden in *Reunion,* the autobiography they condemn so roundly for its evasions. Hayden's final self-assessment is that "the lure of violence and martyrdom were powerful subterranean forces in my makeup. But deeper still was the lure of life, family, a future." If anything, Hayden's is the less self-congratulatory, for he attributes his avoidance of the worst sixties excesses not to superior values but to a rather less heroic "survivor's instinct."[41]

In their efforts to recast the generational narrative, Horowitz and Collier depict scenes of intragenerational conflict and borrow heavily from their autobiographical antecedents, so that the voices that inform their text include not only their own and those of their peers, but also those of the ex-communists of the thirties generation. Of course, these latter voices are also present in Bunzel's text and in the *Second Thoughts* anthology as a whole, in the form of essays by members of the thirties generation. But in Horowitz and Collier's joint essay "The Middle of the Journey" (the book's only new autobiographical piece), the older voices are more thoroughly integrated into the sixties narrative by means of allusion and the imitation of their generational plot.

The essay's title is itself borrowed from Lionel Trilling's 1947 novel of ideas, *The Middle of the Journey.* Dealing with the movement toward the left among intellectuals in the thirties, Trilling's novel presents its main character, John Laskell, as a man suffering from a life-threatening illness that gives him a new perspective on the major ideas—history, progress, communism—confronting his peers. Friends representing these ideas attempt to win him to their beliefs, but in the end he resists the temptations of leftism because it fails to recognize life's limitations, complexity, and intractability. The novel's title refers, as Collier and Horowitz see it, to the conservative belief that history offers no utopian future—no glorious ending—toward which we must work; the present—or middle—is all there is. That is the nature of the human condition. John Laskell's great illumination comes when he realizes that that is precisely where he is and always will be—in the "middle of the journey." In this novel and Whittaker Chambers' anticommunist confession *Witness* (1952),[42] Collier and Horowitz find the great touchstones of experience for their own generation. They call upon the plots of these narratives to supplant the "socialist romance" (320) of an inevitable forward march toward progressive ideals that has been tediously offered up by other sixties autobiographers.

The precise nature of this counterplot is most adequately captured in Chambers' unfortunately neglected anticommunist classic. An occasionally unwieldy mixture of confession, apologia, political tract, and courtroom transcription, *Witness* presents Chambers' life story as the background for his participation in the two perjury trials of Alger Hiss in 1949 and 1950. As an ex-Communist Party courier and a voluntary witness before the House Un-American Activities Committee, Chambers accused Hiss of supplying the Soviet Union with government documents while working in the Roosevelt administration's State Department.[43] Chambers, however, transforms his confrontation with Hiss into a major episode in what he sees as a cosmic struggle between democracy (backed by the Christian God) and communism (backed by Satan). In this struggle, secondary forces such as socialism, liberalism, reformism, and the Democratic Party itself ultimately serve, often unwittingly, the powers of darkness. As the Armageddon that will determine mankind's future approaches, all outward appearances indicate that the forces of evil will triumph, and those who oppose them must, like Chambers, be prepared to suffer for having done that which they know is right.

Seeing contemporary history as a struggle of such cosmic dimensions was, in Chambers' view, absolutely necessary if the battle against evil was to have even the slightest chance of success. Unfortunately, the public's vision of the struggle is impaired by the communists' habit of disguising their true intentions behind liberal ideals. It is this nefarious practice that justifies Chambers' belief that only communists and ex-communists can fully understand contemporary history. By speaking out, he believes he can force his erstwhile comrades to

> stand up in face of the nation and confess what we had been that it might take alarm, throw off its apathy and skepticism, see that the enemy really was embedded in its midst, and be given time to act and save itself. That was the least that we could do in atonement. That we must do. That my testimony would force the others to do, but that was all that it would force them to do. Moreover, I believed that most of them would do it. . . . (534)

When his efforts met with skepticism, he blamed it on America's "failure of the will to live, a failure of the power of this dying world to survive, a failure of more than intelligence, a failure of the force of life itself." Seeing that failure, God would decide "to plough [America] in as a man might plough in a smutted crop." Chambers saw himself at such moments as an American Jonah, a "rejected instrument" of "God's purpose to save this nation" (769–70).

It is the imposition of this cosmic spiritual design upon the Hiss trials that is most characteristic of Chambers' narrative. Those who disagreed with him failed, in his view, to see the history-shattering ramifications of the "great socialist revolution" that had taken place during the Roosevelt administrations, and they now constituted the weakest link in the armor of American democracy. Most of them were liberals who had foolishly associated themselves with communism, and Hiss's exposure threatened their own self-conception. In accusing Hiss of communism, Chambers wrote,

> I had attacked an intellectual and a "liberal." A whole generation felt itself to be on trial—with pretty good reason, too, for its fears probably did not far outrun its guilt. From their roosts in the great cities, and certain collegiate eyries, the left-wing intellectuals of almost every feather (and that was most of the vocal intellectuals in the country) swooped and hovered in flocks like fluttered sea fowl—puffins, skimmers, skuas and boobies—and gave vent to hoarse cries and defilements. (789)

It is clear, he wrote, "that what most of the world supposed [the Hiss trial] to be—a struggle between two men—was precisely what it was not. It was a struggle between the force of two irreconcilable faiths—communism and Christianity—embodied in two men, who by a common experience in the past, knew as few others could know what the struggle was about" (699).

It is precisely this vision (complete with its marine metaphors) that Horowitz and Collier impose on the generational plot of their own times. Like Chambers, they see their generation as one that has put the future of democracy in grave danger. Like Chambers, they see liberalism as inherently tainted by its close association with communism. Like Chambers, too, Collier and Horowitz perceive themselves as members of a generational elite—now curiously split into two warring factions—that alone fully understands the wider political and spiritual implications of the present struggle. Their own role in this struggle, like Chambers' role in his time, is to expose the hidden generational conspiracy—the one being carried out, in Collier's words, by the "deep swimmers," the slimy sixties people moving surreptitiously in our midst.

In *Witness,* Chambers depicts the Hiss trial as the arena within which his generation's identity was being contested. Whether or not the country ultimately confronted and understood the true nature of that trial would determine, as he saw it, history's treatment of his generation and the future viability of American democracy. In Collier and Horowitz's essay, Nicaragua's Sandinista regime serves the same rhetorical purpose. According to the authors, where one stands on Nicaragua reveals where one stands on the momentous issue of how the generational plot is to be constructed. Collier and Horowitz structure their own narrative around a journey whose undertaking they accept, as a duty to their country and the Reagan administration, in order to encourage and advise opponents of the Nicaraguan government. Once in Nicaragua, they conduct a series of interviews designed to demonstrate that the Sandinista regime is a repressive and corrupt totalitarian dictatorship. The directors of the opposition paper *La Prensa* and Violeta Chamorro tell them that the Sandinistas, not Somoza, were responsible for Joaquin Chamorro's assassination and are now guilty of carrying out tortures worse than any that occurred under Somoza.[44] Miskito Indian land reformers criticize the leftist regime's intolerant political measures. An independent human rights commission claims that the Sandinista jails are packed with political prisoners. All of these revelations are to be expected from writers traveling on behalf of the Reagan State Department, but they by no means form the essay's central focus, which is not, after all, particularly concerned with Latin American problems.

What really interests Collier and Horowitz is the demonstration that Nicaragua has become the most recent example of the sixties penchant for representing third world totalitarian regimes as embodiments of an idealized leftist "future." It is their intention to dismantle this myth and to expose the American fans of Sandinismo as schemers intent on obscuring Nicaraguan realities and as political renegades responsible for the perpetuation of totalitarianism. So even though this journey takes place in Nicaragua, its real subjects are the sixties and its leftist survivors, and it is to these that each of their interviews with Nicaraguans finally turn. The Miskito land reformers may be angry with Daniel Ortega's government, but they are even more angry with American sympathizers, the "Sandalistas" who are "more Sandinista than the Sandinistas" (311). In meetings with opposition youth groups, the writers suggest protests not against the Nicaraguan government, but against the American "internacionalistas" who have come to support Daniel Ortega's administration. Such a demonstration, they argue, would reveal to the world just how little support the American sympathizers have among the Nicaraguans and how far-fetched their picture of the Sandinista utopia really is.

When the writers finally deal directly with their American rivals, they employ ad hominem tactics every bit as exaggerated as those used by Rubin and Hoffman. Interviewing an American nun who runs the Sandinista Human Rights Office, they pay more attention to her physical idiosyncrasies than they do to her words: "Her Adam's apple," they write, was "bobbing convulsively and her words [were] punctuated occasionally by a smacking sound like a glottal click" (312). They later describe encounters with several other American sixties figures—Thomas Harkin, Tom Bates, Loni Hancock—and report the petty exchange of name-calling and mutual accusations that these meetings produced.

Finally, and as if to remind their readers of the typological continuity between their generational narrative and that of Chambers, they relate the story of how, upon their return to the United States to give lectures on their Nicaraguan experiences, they were picketed by "an ancient man in a baggy suit" who turned out to be none other than the "gaunt and dour" Sender Garlin, "the man who Whittaker Chambers says recruited him into the Communist Party in 1925" (317). When he asks them why they "really" went to Nicaragua, they reply, in the coded language of ex-communist renunciation narratives, that they went "because it was the middle of the journey" (318).

The most significant variation that Horowitz and Collier introduce into the Chambers plot lies in the composition of the two "armies" that face each other in the final struggle. In their revision, this struggle is not between communists and ex-communists but between members of the same generation—"between those who have had second thoughts about their experiences in the Sixties, and those who have not" (334). Consequently, the most salient aspect of their construction of a counter-generational narrative is their insistence that the collective has split into two groups, each vying to implement its own set of political values. This insistence manifests itself in vignettes that embody such confrontations (Collier and Horowitz engaged in political bickering with Bates and Hancock, or unidentified leftists in a Managua hotel, or an unreconstructed—or at least unresponsive—Susan Sontag), direct written attacks on their left-leaning peers (Ayers, Dohrn, Gitlin, Hayden, Rudd, etc.), and an entire section responding to the critics of the Second Thoughts conference. Their efforts to read the sixties as a repetition of the generational plot of the thirties lie at the heart of their response to Alexander Cockburn, who wrote a column critical of the conference in the *Nation*. They attack Cockburn, their contemporary, by employing three pages to attack the integrity of his father, Claud, "who was the other side of his generation's coin to Whittaker Chambers." This attack is, as they see it, a legitimate way to criticize the son, since the son's "only inheritance was his father" and the son had "modeled his style on that of his father" (331). Thus, the failings of unreconstructed thirties leftists are ample evidence of the bankruptcy of unreconstructed sixties people.

Like Chambers vis-à-vis his ex-comrades, Collier and Horowitz hope that their text will encourage other sixties defectors to "confess" in order that the American public may be made aware of its mortal danger.

And finally, they see themselves, as Chambers saw himself, as likely to suffer martyrdom in a losing cause: democracy is on the wane, individual liberties are falling before collective ideologies, political conservatism is doomed to lose, and they have chosen to go down with it. In the closing pages of their memoir, they quote Chambers' remark to his wife after he has decided to abandon communism: "'You know, we are leaving the winning world for the losing world.' Later, he explained, 'I meant that, in the revolutionary conflict of the 20th century, I knowingly chose the side of probable defeat'" (335). This, too, is Collier and Horowitz's sense of their own situation in America.

Whether or not the politically active survivors of the Movement (or the generational remnant for which it still speaks) actually enjoy as much power as these two writers claim is precisely one of those issues over which the autobiography wars are being waged. It is an odd contest, for in it Horowitz, Collier, and their neoconservative friends all claim the position of underdog, a rhetorical strategy that implicitly acknowledges that moral superiority is possible only for those whose voices have been repressed. It is ironic evidence of the pervasive legacy of late-sixties identity politics (especially its manifestation in what has recently been called the "culture of victimization") that even conservatives now represent themselves as marginalized outsiders. Reading Horowitz and Collier's assurances of their own doom, one is reminded of the contemporaneous (though more extreme) upside-down politics of David Duke, the former KKK grand wizard from Louisiana whose NAAWP (National Association for the Advancement of White People) claimed that white males were systematically disempowered and discriminated against in America. Horowitz and Collier's claims were being made, it should be remembered, at the beginning of the third consecutive Republican administration (all three of which had won elections on the basis of campaigns that included considerable sixties bashing), and they were enjoying much more media attention than Hayden, Gitlin, Bates, Hancock, or any of the other sixties subversives they represent as tramping gloatingly toward culture war victory. The left may have dominated the struggle over how the sixties were going to be characterized, but by the mid-eighties the evaluation of that "character" was largely in the hands of writers like Collier and Horowitz and their allies among conservative politicians.

5
Generational Autobiography as Elegiac Narrative

Lawrence Kasdan (b. 1949), the screenwriter of such popular Hollywood films as *The Empire Strikes Back* and *Raiders of the Lost Ark*, was a student at the University of Michigan in the late 1960s, shortly after that school had established itself as one of the premier academic havens of New Left leadership. Tom Hayden was an alumnus, as were several other SDS luminaries including Todd Gitlin, Carl Oglesby, Dick and Mickey Flacks, and Alan Haber. Twenty years after his graduation, Kasdan wrote and directed *The Big Chill* (1983), a film that reflects the conventional wisdom about the effects of the passage of time on the sixties generation. It tells the story of seven ex-radicals and Michigan alumni who spend a weekend together in the early 1980s after one of their group, Alex, commits suicide. The reasons for his suicide are never entirely clear, but it appears to have been the result of his inability to live in a society that does not conform to his sixties ideals. At the funeral, one of the group eulogizes Alex, saying that "he was too good for this world." In the background, we hear his favorite song; it's the Rolling Stones' "You Can't Always Get What You Want."

The scene sums up Kasdan's take on his peers: naively idealistic in their youth, they have had to make a difficult adjustment to the compromises of adulthood. The film suggests that the Movement's politics were unsuited to the "real" world, and that in order to "move on" the sixties generation has had to give up the illusion that life consists of passionate relationships lived in the midst of a melodramatic battle between the forces of good (themselves) and the forces of evil (other middle-class Americans and their comfortable bourgeois allies). During the course of their reunion, each of these erstwhile revolutionaries reveals how he or she has made the adjustment that Alex failed to make. None of them has been entirely successful; all are nostalgic about the sixties and confused about the disparity between their earlier generational identity and the selves they have become. As one of them says at a postfuneral chat, "I was at my best when I was with you people." Another responds, "I lost my idea of what I should be when I lost touch with this group."

Still, all but one have made an uneasy peace with society. Michael (Jeff Goldblum) is now a confirmed cynic who writes sleazy articles for *People* magazine. Sam (Tom Berenger) is an unhappy actor who plays a beefcakish Tom Selleck-style detective in a puerile Hollywood television series. Karen (JoBeth Williams) has had to abandon her dreams of becoming a writer to take care of her businessman husband and their two children. Meg (Mary Kay Place) is a public defender who has come to the very un-sixties realization that her clients are "scum." Harold (Kevin Kline) and Sarah (Glenn Close) have married each other; he has inadvertently gotten rich in small business, while she has become a successful pediatrician. It is at this couple's beautiful country home that the group holds its memorial reunion. Other than Alex, the one character who has failed to adjust is Nick (William Hurt), a wounded and impotent Vietnam War veteran who makes sneering comments about the group's nostalgia even as he remains neurotically and anachronistically true to sixties attitudes. He still thinks, for instance, that the police are the enemy, and he is helplessly addicted to drugs. In one of the film's more revealing scenes, Nick has been picked up by the town sheriff for speeding, and Harold has to mollify the officer in order to keep him out of jail. Afterward, when Nick upbraids him for having befriended a cop, Harold responds with an anger that puts the sixties "politics" with which Nick is identified in a distinctly eighties perspective: "You're a fucking idiot," he says, and then explains that the lawman is a "hell of a guy" who has prevented the country house from being "ripped off" twice. "I live here," he yells at Nick; "I'm dug in." The implication is clear. The sixties were valuable not for their politics and lifestyle, both of which are unattractively and simplistically embodied in Nick's recidivistic maladjustments, but for the feelings of camaraderie and idealism that they engendered. Having come of age in the sixties was like belonging to a fraternity or sorority; it was a good place for making lifelong friends and for having fun. Sixties attitudes are more appropriate fodder for nostalgic reunions than for successful living. Once "real" life begins, one must "dig in."

Autobiographical narratives written during the third phase of the generational dialogue reveal a somewhat more complex array of plots as well as a wider array of notions about what constituted the "real" 1960s. Some of them, in fact, are conscious deconstructions of the "big chill" plot underlying Kasdan's story. But all of the narratives I will look at in this chapter have at least two things in common with Kasdan's film: they return to the sixties in an elegiac mood, and they employ various death tropes to figure the demise of their former sixties selves. In Kasdan's film, this demise is figured in the suicide of Alex, who expires after indiscreetly slitting his wrists in his friends' bathroom ten years after the sixties have ended. His is a suicide of social maladjustment. Some written versions of the sixties legacy feature similar endings: David Harris' *Dreams Die Hard*, for example, includes a central representative character whose story ends in violence in the early 1980s, and like Alex's suicide, his violence is attributed to an unsuccessful resolution of sixties issues. Other elegiac autobiographers, however, suggest that the demise of the era (and its attendant representative figures) occurs at the end of the sixties themselves, rather than in a delayed, out-of-joint-with-the-times fashion. Instead of figuring that demise in characters suffering from personal disorientation, writers such as Tom Hayden and Todd Gitlin figure it as a public event. In these plots, the sixties end in a binge of self-destructive violence, and their exemplary figures are portrayed either semiromantically in the style of George Roy Hill's Butch Cassidy and the Sundance Kid (the sixties ended in a blaze of romantic violence) or disparagingly in the style of Charles Dickens' Madame Defarge (the sixties ended when the revolutionaries became precisely what they claimed to hate). Still others will figure the demise of the sixties as a "murder" and will point to specific sites, times, and perpetrators of the "crime." Michael Rossman, for example, sees the killings at Kent State as an apt figure for (and probable actual cause of) the era's end. Yet others, such as Joyce Maynard, see the death as a natural one, the inevitable result of the aging process and the displacement of one generation by another.

In some ways, this focus on the death of the sixties resembles aspects of the renunciation narratives examined at the end of Chapter 4, for both kinds of narrative seek to construct a former generational self that has "died." There are, however, significant differences. The authors of renunciation narratives see their generational death as very salutary. It is a kind of ritual self-sacrifice carried out in order that a new self might be constructed. More important, they believe that in spite of the death of their individual sixties selves, the sixties generation and its spirit have survived (often by moving underground or disguising itself) and continue to threaten the larger social body as a malignant growth. Renunciatory authors once believed this collective was a vanguard of good; now they see it as a cabal of evil. As we have seen, they write both to renounce their former collective self and to warn the public of its continuing existence within the body politic.

The authors of elegiac narratives believe that those who survived the death of the sixties have suffered a diminution of collective focus and identity. Like the characters in Kasdan's film, they have lost their sense of their historical task. Nostalgia is often a primary sentiment in such narratives, as is a wistfulness about and an idealization of the earlier self. The tone of such works is one that Northrop Frye identifies as common to the elegiac mode: "a diffused, resigned, melancholy sense of the passing of time, of the old order changing and yielding to a new one."[1] The writers of elegiac autobiographies look back on the generational experience from a vantage point that assumes a good deal of distance, either emotionally (as in Joyce Maynard's *Looking Back*) or temporally (as in David Harris' *Dreams Die Hard*). Writers who work in this mode often ponder what they conceive to be the "end" of the generational moment as they attempt to establish continuity with their earlier experience and identity. There may be criticism in their accounts of this earlier identity, but it is a criticism couched in an overall effort to recover and recuperate.

Unlike autobiographies of conversion and renunciation, elegiac narratives provide their authors not so much with a "life plot" as with an attitude toward the former self. It is usually a sympathetic one, as these authors set about to reconstruct the former self, to assess its life and actions, and to record and mourn its death. As the authors move away from the coming-of-age experience, the autobiographies they produce become more intimate and reflective, more taken up with the individuating emotions of the private self, and less concerned with the active manipulation of history. Because of this, they tend to make use of more traditional autobiographical conventions: they are more concerned with individual identity, they generally cover longer periods in the author's life, they are less overtly political in their perception of identity, and they are less overtly prospective than generational works in either the annunciatory or the reactive mode. Nonetheless, it is useful to look at them in the context of earlier generational autobiographies because, unlike conventional retrospective autobiographies, they remain focused on generational identity; elegiac generational writers are anxious to understand that earlier period in time, to find out why they were the way they were *then,* to defend their earlier selves against their detractors, and, in some cases, to understand the lasting impact of that generational experience on their present and future identities.

In the elegiac texts of writers who emerged from the Movement, we may also find elements of apologia. David Harris, Tom Hayden, and Todd Gitlin, for example, all wrote generational autobiographies during the 1980s that reflect the other side of the argument made in renunciatory works written in that same decade by deconverted Movement autobiographers. All three of these writers employ exculpatory narrative strategies to deflect the kinds of criticism leveled against the "sixties generation" by contemporaries like David Horowitz and Peter Collier. I will look at some of these strategies later in this chapter.

Other potential readers, however, include people from later generations who were either too young to appreciate the momentous events of the sixties or not yet born when they were occurring. Faced with this audience and its potential for boredom over the "sixties fuss," writers often adopt a somewhat different strategy from the ones they use when talking to other members of their own or older cohorts. One such strategy is figured in Kasdan's film in the way the sixties characters deal with Alex's lover. Chloe (played by Meg Tilly) is some twenty years younger than her companions in the movie, and she completely lacks the social conscience that they believe defined their coming-of-age years. By contrast, her life as she enters her twenties revolves around a search for simple and immediate gratifications. Symbolically, she stands in for the eighties generation and their relationship with the sixties generation. Often, the sixties characters simply talk to each other in her presence, and if the film suggests an intergenerational dialogue, it is one in which the younger generation simply eavesdrops on the nostalgia of its elders. At other times, the sixties characters' stance toward her seems more defensive, as if to say: "You had to be there in order to understand what it was like; the sixties experience is really noncommunicable." Writers in the wistful, elegiac mode often make such disclaimers, providing at least partial protection against the charge that the period is overrated or that its chief protagonists were foolishly deluded about their historical uniqueness. Michael Rossman, for example, writes of his attempts to reconstruct the experiences of the 1964 Free Speech Movement:

> I always felt awkward and frightened when I tried to speak of it to others, and soon stopped trying. I felt like a crazy man alone with an unverifiable reality. . . . I never found words to describe what is still my most vivid feeling from the FSM, beyond even the intense surprises of fraternity, community, and power over my citizen life—the sense that the surface of reality had somehow fallen away altogether.[2]

David Harris likewise interrupts his narrative *Dreams Die Hard* to lament the impossibility of his autobiographical task:

> It is hard for me to describe us and what we were about that summer without lapsing into what now sounds trite. The intervening decade and a half has reduced much of the language we then used to describe ourselves into a rubble of jargon that, however I try to arrange it, now reads like parody. . . . We weren't a parody, whatever has since become of our words. We were the "real thing." As far as we were concerned, no one had ever done what we were doing.[3]

And Todd Gitlin, employing the nineteenth-century convention of direct address, does the same in *The Sixties*:

> How can I convey the texture of this gone time so that you and I, reader, will be able to grasp, remember, believe that astonishing things actually happened, and made sense to the many who made them happen and were overtaken by them? Statistics are "background," we do not feel them tearing into our flesh. The years 1967, 1968, 1969, 1970 were a cyclone in a wind tunnel.[4]

Not surprisingly, however, the claim that the sixties are not susceptible to representation is always made in the midst of just such a representation, for whatever they may say about the impossibility of reconstructing the period, all of these authors are dedicated to that project. They really have no alternative. One of the primary lessons of the identity politics of the sixties, after all, was that those who do not represent themselves are inevitably represented by someone whose interests are unlikely to coincide with their own.

The real show, however, is not the individual author representing his unique identity, but rather the intergenerational dialogue that self-consciously focuses on the construction of generational experience and identity. In that dialogue, no one person can own generational memory, for it is by nature collective, and it is up for grabs. Its definition and characteristics can only be negotiated and argued; they cannot be possessed. All of the people who came of age during the sixties had experiences. Many of these experiences were shared, but many others were not. There are as many "sixties" as there are members of the sixties generation. If one wants to make something collective out of what happened then, it is obviously a "something" that will have to be constructed through communal negotiation and dialogue.[5]

Generational Geriatrics: Joyce Maynard's *Looking Back*

Joyce Maynard's *Looking Back: A Chronicle of Growing Up Old in the Sixties* (1973) declares itself to be above the kind of political rhetoric that marks the annunciatory and reactive autobiographies of Chapters 3 and 4, and certainly her book seems less overtly concerned with the kind of generational politics that is so central to those autobiographical modes. Maynard's intention, like that of all of the elegiac narratives I will look at in this chapter, is primarily retrospective and analytical. Although at nineteen she is the youngest of any of the authors I am considering, she wants to provide the full story of the generation from its childhood in the early 1950s to its "old age" in 1973. To carry out this task, she assumes an ironic superannuated persona reminiscent of several twenties-generation memoirists. F. Scott Fitzgerald, for example, says that readers of his generational essays, written when the author was in his late twenties, may suspect him of "premature arteriosclerosis," and John Glassco, writing in 1932 at the age of twenty-one, calls his memoir the "chronicle of my dead youth." "I would like," he writes, "to continue my record of those years—the years in which I really lived—before the onset of death or the inevitable dullness of a mature outlook: this is to be the book of my youth, of my golden age."[6] Maynard (or her editor) exhibits a similarly wry humor not only through her persona's air of premature venerability, but also on the book's cover jacket, which features what appears to be a pubescent photo of the author gazing precociously at the camera. However, while striking the geriatric pose of writers like Fitzgerald and Glassco, Maynard eschews their nostalgia. Her elegy is written from the perspective of disillusioned objectivity. Her tone is, in fact, flatly valetudinarian, her text a sixties generation's *Goodbye to All That*. Bidding a veteran's weary farewell to political activism (Maynard achieved her political experience campaigning for McGovern's presidential campaign in 1972), she settles in now to figure out what all the fuss was about. In some respects, therefore, her book resembles Raymond Mungo's *Famous Long Ago*, with its dismissal of radicalism and its ironically assumed distance from the very recent past. But unlike Mungo, whose valetudinarianism is employed in the service of a countercultural avant-gardism, Maynard devotes herself almost entirely to the elegiac mood. Mungo is out to sacrifice his earlier radical self. As far as Maynard is concerned, that self passed away of natural causes. She can afford, therefore, to be more understanding. Ignoring politics, Maynard claims that her generational portrait is constructed "reluctantly" and out of concern for the present and future: "[T]he fact is that there's no understanding the future without the present, and no understanding where we are now without a glance, at least, to where we have been."[7]

To construct that understanding, Maynard presents a picture based on her own experience of what life was typically like for members of her age group as they grew up. Characteristically, her chapters are organized around an account of a major psychosocial issue or theme such as peer pressure or sexual maturation. At the same time, Maynard's perspective is not restrictively local; she always looks at these issues and themes as they are affected by larger national and international events. Her generation had a unique identity, she says, because it came of age in the context of the Cuban missile crisis, the Kennedy and King assassinations, the Vietnam War, and the peace movement. Consequently, Maynard's narrative follows both a chronological, year-by-year pattern (some chapter headings are "1963," "1965," "1966," etc.) and a thematic pattern (other chapters, not always headed, deal with coming-of-age issues such as menstruation and awakening sexual awareness). Maynard does not, however, maintain a clear-cut distinction between public and private histories. The chronological chapters are not exclusively concerned with national events. The year 1963, for example, is characterized as "the year of rationality, the calm before the storm. Boys still had cooties and dolls still tempted us. That was the year when I got my first Barbie" (28). And the unheaded chapters occasionally deal with public events. According to Maynard, such mixing is an essential characteristic of her generation's identity. "National and personal memory blur," she claims, "so that, for me, November 22, 1963, was a birthday party that had to be called off and Armstrong's moon walk was my first full can of beer. But memory—shared or unique—is, I think, a clue to why we are where we are now" (15).

In spite of Maynard's claims of political neutrality, her pose of superannuation and her elegiac reconstruction of growing up "old" in the sixties ultimately underwrite a kind of "do-nothing" political agenda. By pretending to superannuation, Maynard can take advantage of a cultural narrative that allows "retirement," "leisure," "self-indulgence" to the aged. They have passed beyond the productive stages of life and can justifiably begin to pamper themselves. Maynard's claim that she wants to "understand" the present by examining the past is also conventional, but her further claim that she wants to understand the "future" by reviewing her own generational history is telling. Behind its apolitical facade, Maynard's narrative performs the same function as those of her more activist contemporaries: it constructs a past that justifies Maynard's political plans for the future. The difference, in the end, is that she no longer shares any of the political passions that concern these other writers; her generationalism is not infected by Marxism, leftism, or historicism. She constructs her final acceptance of the political status quo as the pure product of generational experience.

Such a stance is much more likely in the elegiac than in either the annunciatory or the reactive mode of autobiography. The latter modes are both typically activist; their authors are intent upon changing the world. Annunciatory authors are just starting out, and their texts inform the world of their intentions for the future. Reactive authors generally have been out long enough to discover the errors of their ways, but it is not too late for them to reconstruct themselves and undertake, once again, the reform of the world. The elegiac writer, by contrast, is typically a person who has been out long enough to be somewhat humbled by experience. Writers like Maynard, who assume an attitude of *weltschmerz*, may have suggestions for the future, but they are generally very chastened suggestions, and their real focus is on the past.

This is not to say that Maynard's narrative includes no plans for the future. It does, but these plans are the passive consequence of another "future," the one that dominated her childhood. Like that of the framers of *The Port Huron Statement*, Maynard's childhood was overshadowed by the imminent danger of nuclear holocaust and the apparently inevitable destruction of the environment by overpopulation and industrial pollution. This horrific future-to-end-futures was a given condition of her generation's coming of age. It shaped, she says, their consciousness of human possibilities: "We were a generation unused to thinking ahead, incapable of visualizing even our twenties, and faced suddenly with the prospects of the year 2000 and forced, in youth, to contemplate the bleakness of our middle age" (121). It is the presence of this terminal "future" in her past that allows Maynard to "understand" the future for which she is planning. It explains, in part, her weariness with political activism and provides the justification of her desire for retreat into the middle-class values and comforts she has inherited from her academic New England parents:

> I want to be happy. And I want comfort—nice clothes, a nice house, good
> music and good food, and the feeling that I'm doing some little thing that
> matters. I'll vote and I'll give to charity, but I won't give myself. I feel a sud-
> den desire to buy land . . . a small plot of earth so that whatever they do to
> the country I'll have a place where I can go—a kind of fallout shelter. (155)

For Maynard, the past constitutes an argument that justifies the collective persona she has constructed for her generation: the world-weary, disillusioned mask that prevents her and her peers (whom she defines as
"we, the young, affluent, and educated" [125]) from maintaining any belief in the efficacy of political solutions.

   This construction of her peers as a group to whom things have happened (rather than as a group who will make things happen) is further un-
derscored by another feature of Maynard's generational plot. Her group,
she says, arrived on the historical stage too late, well after their older and
more politically active brothers and sisters had made their mark. This late
arrival is so significant in her narrative that she thinks of her immediate
peers (those born around 1953) as a distinct age group and restricts the
use of the term "generation" to her high school class, the seniors who
graduated from American schools in 1970. "We inherited," Maynard explains metaphorically,

> a previous generation's hand-me-downs and took in the seams, turned up the
> hems, to make our new fashions. We took drugs from the college kids and
> made them a high school commonplace. . . . And we inherited the Vietnam
> War just after the crest of the wave—too late to burn draft cards and too
> early not to be drafted. The boys of 1953—my year—will be the last to go.
> (14–15)

Having passed their childhood, rather than their late adolescence, during
the sixties, they entered the political arena just as Movement writers like
Mungo, Diamond, and Rader were concluding that political activity was
pointless. In a sense, then, the elegiac mode is the only one possible for
Maynard's peers. Everything of importance for her generation is already
over and finished. Her plot, therefore, is the story of a generation of
Johnny-come-latelies: history was made before they had a chance to participate in it. They are willy-nilly cast in a passive, spectatorial role; they
cannot hope to emulate their older and more accomplished brothers and
sisters. They can only look back. They can only memorialize.

   Unlike their older siblings, her "generation" is consequently less concerned with effecting social change than with simply getting by. They are,
as her subtitle implies, prematurely aged victims of history. Maynard's
narrative begins with a summary of the past that attempts to explain how
the "traumas of our childhood" (15) caused this apathy:

> The Kennedys were our fairy-tale heroes, integration and outer space and
> The Bomb the dramas of our first school years. It was not a time when we

could separate our own lives from the outside world. . . . We were dragged through the mud of Relevance and Grim Reality, and now we have a certain tough, I've-been-there attitude. (13)

And the narrative ends with the conclusion that only personal satisfactions and answers are possible: "As some people prepare for their old age, so I prepare for my twenties. A little house, a comfortable chair, peace and quiet—retirement sounds tempting" (155).

Besides the emphasis on her generation's passive molding by history, Maynard typifies the elegiac mode in her attitude toward her generational constituency and in her perception of what constitutes the significant past. As we have already seen in Chapter 3, annunciatory writers such as Hoffman, Rubin, and Rossman generally present themselves as *representative* of the generational "we." But being representative is not the same thing for them as being *like* their contemporaries. Annunciatory writers see themselves as members of a vanguard that is separate from the generational mass. That vanguard constructs itself as a group that stands, by dint of its youthfulness, its geographical position, and its historical insight, on the "edge of the future"; they are responsible for shaping it and ushering it in. The annunciatory autobiographer claims representative status because he (it is almost always a "he") and the vanguard to which he belongs mediate between that future and the larger generational mass. They arrive at the "edge" slightly before their peers, who will inevitably follow in the vanguard's footsteps. The generational "we" in these books is, therefore, partly a rhetorical tactic and partly political cajolery. Annunciatory autobiographers construct a "we" that they believe *will be true* of the collective they represent. This is not to say that such autobiographers never construct themselves as typical; those usually brief portions of their texts that treat childhood almost always construct that part of the self's experience as "typical" (i.e., white, middle class, male). It is only when the self enters history (during the period Kenneth Kenniston refers to as "youth") that its status changes from typical to representative, i.e., one that exists on the forefront of historical change.

As a member of the generation that she constructs as having arrived "too late," Maynard cannot cast herself in the vanguard. Too late to assume the political activism of their older siblings, her contemporaries are cast instead as passive victims of shared history. In this plot, Maynard is forced to put herself forward as *typical*, rather than representative, of the generation. Generational identity, she says, is the result of a passively shared past, not a consciously chosen future, so her claim to typicality is necessarily based on the belief that her past has been, after all, very much like that of everyone else who was born around 1953. In spite of her insistence on typicality and passivity, however, Maynard manages to suggest both her own uniqueness and agency. Generational identity, she tells us repeatedly, is the product of social forces, yet among the strongest of those forces are the media, which by naming the generation, call it into existence. "Generalizing is dangerous," she says. "Call us the apathetic generation and we will become that" (15). Yet that is precisely what she is doing. By constructing the generation—an act that she suggests is always somewhat arbitrary—she asserts her own agency as one who shapes generational identity and behavior. "Say times are changing, nobody cares about prom queens and getting into the college of his choice anymore . . . and you make a movement and a unit out of a generation unified only in its common fragmentation" (15).

What I have just said about Maynard's straddling of the agency/ passivity opposition may also be said of her treatment of the representativeness/typicality opposition. For one of the paradoxes of Maynard's narrative is that even in the process of claiming to be typical of her contemporaries, she constructs an image of herself as most emphatically not like anyone else. Maynard's difference, she says, stems from her alienation from her own typicality; she is a detached observer of her own subjugation to the Zeitgeist. It is her difference, finally, that allows her to transcend the identity historical and social circumstances have imposed upon her generation. It is what allows her to be the generation's elegist. Maynard introduces this image in her first chapter:

> In truth, what I have always been is an outsider. Midnight on New Year's Eve I would be reading record jackets or discussing the pros and cons of pass-fail grading with an earnest, glasses-polishing scholar who spoke of "us" and "we" as if I were just like him. . . . Sometimes I pretend [to be like others], but I can always hear, off in the distance, the clicking of a typewriter. I see myself in the third person, a character in a book, an actor in a movie. (17)

That there might be something odd about claiming difference while constantly employing the first-person-plural pronoun does not escape Maynard's self-analytical gaze, but she explains the apparent contradiction by asserting that her generation is, like herself, composed entirely of self-perceived outsiders, people convinced that they are alone while everyone else lives in the "Thornton Wilder dream [of belonging and community] that never really existed" (17). "We all," Maynard claims, "have something of the observer in us, the detached outsider" (43). By constructing a "we" in which everyone suffers from a sense of alienation, Maynard manages to portray even her own feelings of difference as typical.

Maynard's explanation of the contradiction between her simultaneous claims to uniqueness and typicality is only partially persuasive. For perhaps the most important aspect of her relationship to her peers is that she seems not to be writing *for* them but *about* them, and she does so as one whose real identification is with the parental world to whom she is making her report. While her American classmates abandon their virginity, succumb to peer pressures, overindulge in drugs, and celebrate destructive sports, she remains aloof and mature. "It must seem, to people who don't know me," Maynard admits, "and even more, perhaps, to the ones who do, as if I'm a cold-blooded traitor, informing on a world that trusted me enough to let me in" (17). Although such tattling is understandable in a young person who writes so well, in the final analysis the youthful "we" Maynard constructs, and to which she claims to belong, is really her ticket to the adult world she longs to be permitted to enter.

Since Maynard constructs herself as typical rather than representative, her notion of the significant past differs from that of most annunciatory and reactive writers. For the two latter groups, as we have seen, reality consists primarily of life in what Rossman calls the "growing bud of the historical tree." The significant past, therefore, is the one that has taken place within the public realm. Since the private pleasures and pains of childhood lack that reality, their significance can usually be summed up in a page or two. Indeed, the primary elements of the collective childhood constructed in *The Port Huron Statement* are repeated fairly consistently by those annunciatory and reactive autobiographers who give childhood any attention at all (Jane Alpert is the exception). In short, insofar as these writers deal with childhood, they do so only to discuss those aspects of it that were collective, and therefore historical in their own right. For Maynard, however, it is precisely this collectively shared childhood that is typical and significant. Most of her generation, after all, did not live in Berkeley or take part in the trial of the Chicago Seven or even attend Woodstock. But they almost all attended American high schools, experienced sixties-style peer pressure, had feelings about the senior prom, and so on. Her book, therefore, focuses on that phase of life rather than on the generation's active entrance into history. Consequently, she mostly ignores the great generation-defining events that so concerned the writers in Chapters 3 and 4. Insofar as she does comment on the generation's entrance into the historical arena, Maynard presents it as just one more incident in their childhood—rather like going to the prom—and she treats it with the same jaded eye for petty motives that characterizes her treatment of high school cliquishness. "I am suspicious-natured," Maynard admits, "I look for the lowest motives, aware of what they are as only one who feels them herself can be aware. So when I saw the Haiphong demonstrators, reruns of 1969, it seemed to me . . . that what they were involved in was nostalgia" (149).

Maynard's method of constructing her typicality is amply demonstrated in her memory of a photograph on the cover of *Life* magazine. The photograph, she says, played a crucial role in the formation of her sensibility by the mass media:

> They were the first shots ever taken of an unborn fetus, curled up tightly in a sack of veins and membranes, with blue fingernails and almost transparent skin that made the pictures look like double exposures. More than the moon photographs a few years later, that grotesque figure fascinated me as the map of a new territory. . . . If I were asked to pinpoint major moments in my growing up, experiences that changed me, the sight of that photograph would be one. (51–52)

While the exposure of a young mind to a strong impression may be a part of the individualist autobiographical tradition, in generational autobiographies the signal characteristic of such experiences is its shared quality. The shaping event is one that has affected her entire age group.

> Ask us whose face is on the five-dollar bill and we may not know the answer. But nearly everyone my age remembers a cover of *Life* magazine that came out in the fall of 1965, part of a series of photographs that enter my dreams and my nightmares still. (51)

Characteristic of Maynard's elegiac vision, however, is her sense that this shared experience has irremediably damaged her and her contemporaries, robbing them of the rich imaginative experiences of childhood: "Having had so many pictures to grow up with, we share a common visual idiom and have far less room for personal vision. The movie versions of books decide for us what our heroes and villains will look like, and we are powerless to change the camera's decree" (52). The elegiac tone of Maynard's text derives, therefore, not only from her sense of having passed out of an important phase of generational experience, but also from her sense of generational losses. Specifically, she laments the loss of the possibility of individual identity and uniqueness.

In this, she distinguishes herself markedly from most annunciatory and many reactive autobiographers. Their generational "we" frequently represents the positive values associated with community, belonging, and shared political purpose. Like Cowley before them, these writers depict the lost romantic individualism that Maynard pines for as the agent responsible for the evils of bourgeois capitalism. True happiness, for them, is to be found in community. Raymond Mungo's *Total Loss Farm* and Stephen Diamond's *What the Trees Said*, for example, are replete with photographs of unidentified communards working or playing together, but neither autobiography includes photographs of the individual authors. This visual strategy merely features photographically what such writers proclaim doctrinally in their texts: individual identity is to be subsumed in togetherness and community. But where writers like Mungo and Diamond celebrate collective identity, Maynard views the loss of uniqueness entailed in collective identity as regrettable. "I'm saddened," she writes, ". . . knowing what [the photograph of that fetus] did to me" (52).

Instead of attributing collective identity to a consciously adopted political agenda, she attributes its formation to peer pressure and the ubiquity of contemporary mass culture. That, finally, is the general stance of Maynard's book. She seeks to establish the collective identity of her age group, but even as she does so, she laments all of the losses that that identity entails: loss of individuality, loss of responsibility, loss of belief, loss of optimism, and loss of innocence.

Maynard's gender—she was the first female generational autobiographer of the sixties—may help explain her book's emphasis on quotidian typicality. Certainly her choice of subject matter is frequently dictated by her sex, as can be seen in her sections on Barbie dolls (28), menstruation (29–32), and fashion (71–82). Like her male counterparts, however, Maynard often seems unconscious of the ways in which the generation might look different to its male and female members. Her "we" usually does not exclude men in spite of its frequently female slant, and her perspective is occasionally conspicuously masculine. At one point, for example, she explains that "we" did not feel outraged by Nixon's mining of Haiphong harbor because "the draft no longer threatened so much" (148). What Maynard attempts, without specifically articulating it, is an ungendered, universal generational construct.

One could argue that the *passivity* of Maynard's generational concept is at least partly the product of a gendered vision. Often excluded from positions of leadership in the Movement, female generationalists were more likely than their male counterparts to construct a generational self that is acted upon rather than acting upon. Even Jane Alpert, who played a fairly active role in a self-proclaimed generational vanguard, constructs a plot in her *Growing Up Underground* that emphasizes her unconscious passivity and manipulation by authority figures. Although a onetime militant leftist, she accounts for what she now sees as her activist delusions by reconstructing her behavior as the result of dysfunctional childhood relationships and cultural forces. In Alpert's case, however, this emphasis on passivity is probably the result not so much of gender as of Alpert's adoption of a psychological model of selfhood.

Maynard similarly portrays herself and her peers as wholly the products of their times, and she logically focuses her narrative on the most impressionable, powerless, and vulnerable phase of life, but as in Alpert's case, gender roles only partly explain the passivity of her generational construct, for the real cause, as she herself insists, is her peers' late arrival in a collective narrative whose main action is already winding down. In adopting this plot, Maynard consciously rejects alternative narratives of identity offered by the newly emerging feminism. Although these narratives sponsored an identity actively taken on rather than passively absorbed from environing circumstances, Maynard claims that feminism fails to provide a viable model of selfhood. The "sisterhood" it proclaims, she says, is based only on "negative feeling, . . . bitterness, and sometimes hate," (151) and, besides, it denies the undeniable differences between men and women. "The truth," she confides, "is that the methods of the feminist movement turn me off" (150). Her dismissal of feminism, like her dismissal of the left in general, does not absolutely dictate the construction of a passive plot, but it certainly predisposes her toward a narrative in which the self submissively aligns itself with the twin forces of history and nature. However, as already noted, in constructing a plot that in some ways underscores conventional notions of female passivity, Maynard also transcends it by identifying herself with the very forces she claims determine her generation's consciousness. By constructing her own generational narrative—by naming the generation—Maynard becomes one of those reality-shaping forces that she credits with the formation of generational attitudes. Maynard thus manages simultaneously to assign her peers the role of victims of history and herself the role of generation maker.

A Postrevolution Divorce Story: Michael Rossman's *New Age Blues*

Michael Rossman waited until 1979 to publish a second autobiographical work, but like his earlier *The Wedding within the War, New Age Blues: On the Politics of Consciousness* is a collection of essays that show the evolution of his thinking on generational issues over the course of a decade. The second book, however, shies away from the earlier work's claims of prophetic power and generational representativeness, and it is, as Rossman himself says, more "modest in ambition and narrow in scope" (xi) than its subtitle implies. In addition, Rossman goes on to explain, while "its stance is personal, it deals, on the whole, very little with my own experience" (xi). The evaporation of Rossman's earlier vision of a generation united in its determination to create a revolutionary "wedding" of personal and social "therapies" is at least in part responsible for this retreat. Indeed, the primary subject of this collection is the "divorce" of these two forms of political strategy in the 1970s.

Rossman's greater caution in this second book highlights the degree to which he felt isolated by the historical forces of the 1970s. The synthesis that Rossman foresaw and celebrated in *The Wedding within the War* did not materialize: political activism, as Rossman says, "went into eclipse in the public mind" (xi), and the New Age consciousness fostered by the counterculture "seemed to evolve more in response to the conclusion that the social movement had failed" (xii). Like many of his peers, Rossman seems to have lost his sense of generational community. Indeed, one underlying theme of *New Age Blues* is loneliness. The "we" of *The Wedding within the War* becomes a very personal "I" in *New Age Blues*: "more than it usually is," Rossman laments, "writing these essays has been lonely—for this decade has left me, like many others, more alone than I would like to be to shape my understandings from its conflicting evidences" (xiii).

The sources of this loneliness also reveal themselves in the kinds of metaphors Rossman employs to describe what it means to be a part of history. As long as Rossman felt that he and the movement to which he belonged were aligned with the direction of collective history, he wrote generational autobiography using a collective voice. However, when that alignment of identity and history was disrupted after the Kent State killings, he was forced to use a different voice: *New Age Blues* is still concerned with generational issues, but it takes them up as the subjects of culture criticism. In both books, Rossman claims that his intention as a writer is to be a "conscious swimmer in history,"[8] but in the earlier book he is clearly swimming with the current, and this sense of belonging affects the nature of the identity he constructs: the self is not an "I" but an ecstatic, victorious "we." In the later book, Rossman has found himself in a side eddy from which he skeptically watches the main current. He is still subject, willy-nilly, to its force, but the self of the second collection is more observant than active, more static than ecstatic. It is not that Rossman sees no possibility of community in the new direction the generation has taken, but it is a different kind of community from the one he experienced earlier. To make this difference clear, he uses one image to describe the democratic collective behavior of the sixties (a school of "fish swimming with the natural current" [49]) and another to characterize the authoritarian tendencies of generational behavior in the seventies (a sheep herd blindly following "the tinkling bells of leaders . . . toward the glorious pastures" [45]).

This brief glimpse at Rossman's invidious comparisons of the seventies and sixties should provide some hint of the book's elegiac elements. The essays in this collection are mostly concerned with the present direction of generational thought and behavior, but those that are concerned with the past (particularly the essays "A Father for Our Time" and "Looking Back at the FSM") are elegiac and nostalgic rather than annunciatory or reactive. The narrator constructs himself and the generation as identities in transition. He is working his way out of the sixties, but he seeks continuity with whatever generational identity the Movement created in the earlier period.

In this transition period, Rossman tries to position himself as someone who can help the generation avoid imbalance by continuing his argument with other generationalists over what he perceives as an unnecessary and harmful split between political and New Age generationalism. Some of this argument is conducted by means of representative biographical pieces, accounts of the direction in which various generational spokespersons have moved since 1969. Thus, the first three essays in the section entitled "Notes from the Public Carnival" are devoted, respectively, to Rennie Davis (one of the Chicago Seven), Arthur Janov (originator of primal scream therapy), and Richard Alpert aka Ram Dass (who with Timothy Leary did much to make psychedelic experience an integral part of counterculture identity in the late sixties).

In "But How We Talk Now Together!" Rossman continues the generationalists' convention of incorporating dialogues with peers into their narratives. Here, he uses not the hypothetical or epistolary dialogue we have seen in other works, but an actual dialogue between himself and two acquaintances. He renames these representative interlocutors "St. Aquinas" and "Genghis Khan." The former was a founding father of humanistic psychology; the latter a New Left leader in the mid-1960s who—like Rubin and Hoffman—"went on to national organizing, government indictment, and media stardom." Genghis' books, he tells us, "made a mint" (38). The dialogue itself is meant to tell us how the generation has dealt with the two great issues of its times: personal growth and social reform. Genghis is representative of the generation's efforts to move beyond the merely political: "Since Kent State, Genghis has pursued the picaresque odyssey of our generation, and has gotten heavily involved in old and new therapies of mind and body, and with perspectives on inner revolution" (39). Recently, however, he has visited the People's Republic of China, and the present conversation focuses on that trip. Rossman is appalled by the uncritical quality of Genghis' account of China, which merely echoes the official propaganda purveyed by that country's leaders. The account is, he says, like Genghis' first book, full of the "rudimentary consciousness of sloganizing" (40), and it reveals that he has not changed significantly from his earlier days in the Movement:

> he's again found another Answer, flat and absolute, to the human problems of the day, and he's urging it on us with all his old enthusiasm. First the antiwar effort, then the youth revolt, then the inner quest, now it's China: the problems, the meaning of what we're doing, everything is to be evaluated in light of the Chinese experiment, not as if it were something more to richen the mix, but as if it were all that mattered. (40)

Aquinas, from whom Rossman expects a critical response, instead responds positively to Genghis' story. Rossman is "stunned" by this, especially since Aquinas has been very critical of the methods of EST (Erhard Seminar Training programs), which taught people "to pursue their private interests exclusively, and to reject responsibility toward others as illusory" [41]). According to Rossman, the China "answer" simply reverses this by recognizing only public interests and altogether ignoring the individual. Aquinas' lack of a critical response is so disappointing to Rossman that he ends up wondering what the evening has to say about "us, how we see, how we say, what we do" (42). The answer, he muses, is that "the qualities of mind, of temper, of imagination which [Genghis] now attaches to China—the uncritical enthusiasm, absolute, programmatic, superpositive, one-dimensional, un-self-reflective, ephemeral, unrooted—rule the day now, attached by the hungry to every item on the New Age table" (42). Looking back on his own role in the New Left during the sixties, Rossman realizes that his career was built "upon those energies of unquestioning hungry fad which Genghis was so deft at arousing and feeding with slogans" (43).

Such self-criticism and the despairing thoughts that follow his conversation with Genghis do not, however, prompt Rossman to write a deconversion narrative, for he remains a largely unreconstructed child of the Movement. He remains committed to the synthesis of private growth and public justice that he believes characterized the Movement at its best. So while it is true that most of the essays in this collection criticize what he sees as a New Age tendency to authoritarianism, Rossman's own enthusiasm for New Age consciousness at times seems to blind him to the very thing he is criticizing. He never abandons his faith, never questions the fundamental principle that world reformation along radically democratic lines is possible. And what is his evidence that it is possible?—a fleeting experience during the early days of the Free Speech Movement, "the early Fillmore, the Haight, People's Park, my wedding" and "a dozen other gatherings of encounter and conflict" (65). Pushing himself for further evidence that a perpetual renewal of such experience is possible on a larger scale, Rossman looks to the very place he has criticized Genghis for idealizing, the People's Republic of China:

> Only in the past decade has a metarevolutionary vision begun to form. Now we speak of revolution in the revolution, of Mao's attempt to renew the "permanent revolution"; we grasp at the concept of education as a continuous unmetered process of growing beyond old frames and integrating new ones, and try to imagine an institutional vessel for this universal solvent. (65)

It is this unreconstructed vision of a permanent revolution that underlies the nostalgia of the two essays devoted to a retrospective examination of the Free Speech Movement (FSM) of 1964, the event that marked, for Rossman, the real character of the sixties.

In "A Father for Our Time" and "Looking Back at the FSM," Rossman returns to the generational experience that was so central to his earlier *The Wedding within the War*. In "Father," he harkens back to a theme I have already noted in early annunciatory narratives, the loss of adequate fathers and models of authority in American culture, and blames this loss for his generation's vulnerability in the seventies to religious gurus and political authoritarians. The failure of the generation's fathers is finally embodied, for Rossman, in the downfall of President Nixon after the Watergate fiasco, an event that was "as much as the Kent State killings, . . . [a] part of the mythic climax to the Movement of the 1960s" (48). The loss of adequate fathers, he says, has created a hole in the generation's soul:

> I too have a hole inside. . . . But my center survives it, and I am not moved to flock with a herd. For everyone I see has a hole somewhat like mine, and I don't expect to find anyone to magically fill it. I think the hole is there because my culture is falling apart, and as a creature of my culture I too am dissolving inside. (50)

In spite of this sense of present loss, Rossman recalls the FSM, that moment during the sixties when democratic leadership was a reality. The FSM's significance, he claims, is in danger of being lost because of media distortions, which transformed the FSM participants into a mere "campus mob organized by a disciplined cadre of radicals and inflamed by a brilliant young charismatic leader," Mario Savio (45). The real FSM, he counters, was born of a "new vision of community and of culture" (45). It was composed of "thousands of people, self-organized into a hundred spontaneous groups" that coordinated themselves into "an intense web of learning and action" (45). But the degeneration of the Movement did not come about solely through the action of the media. It was also, he says, the result of a failure of will on the part of the participants, who allowed themselves to become the media caricature they ostensibly despised.

Like "Looking Back at the FSM," "Father" is motivated by the central intention of elegiac narratives. It honors the "true" narrative of a past self threatened by the competing narratives of its detractors and distorters. The construction of this narrative is meant to reveal the "real" nature of that threatened self. Almost ten years after it occurred, Rossman believes he has come to understand the central meaning of the FSM. "Years later," he writes in "Looking Back," "I see that in some partial way—yet a way broader and perhaps deeper, humanly speaking—we succeeded together for more than a moment in what Castaneda's don Juan calls 'stopping the world'; and that the strange second consciousness which haunted me was at least akin to what he calls 'seeing'" (63). Although clearer to him now, his understanding of the new consciousness created by the FSM is still incomplete, and he wonders in retrospect whether it was simply his "imagination," a "solitary experience" (64), or something shared by everyone who participated. If it was a shared, collective event, then some "awesome questions open" (64). These questions have to do with the potential power of collective action to transform worldviews, integrate psychic "realities" (such as those being revealed by New Age consciousness), and create a "permanent revolution" (such as might be occurring in China [65]). All of the academic fields are already contributing to the breakdown of customary modes of perceiving reality and have shown that it is always a collective "process of interpretation"

(65) whose manipulation might lead to new worlds, new powers, and new social arrangements. In short, Rossman seems to believe that if we truly understood the significance of the sixties as it was manifested during the FSM, we might be able to break through to another plane of consciousness (66).

Generational Nightmares: David Harris' *Dreams Die Hard*

Born in 1946, David Harris was among the youngest members of the sixties generation of student radicals. He was also one of the first of this group to win the student presidency of an elite university. One of four founding members of the important antidraft organization the Resistance, he culminated his radical career by marrying Joan Baez and going to prison for refusing to serve in the American armed forces. For all of these reasons, Harris received a good deal of public attention in the sixties. When it ended, he found himself at a loss about how to "move on" (297). In this, he was not so different from many of his leftist peers who took up new identities after the disintegration of the Movement. In his elegiac *Dreams Die Hard: Three Men's Journey through the Sixties* (1982), Harris writes that in 1973, "I was an ex-convict, ex-husband, ex-civil rights worker, ex-student body president, and ex-organizer against an ex-war. I was proud of what I had done, but I somewhat desperately wanted a future to go with my past" (297). If Harris had written an autobiography at that point, it might not have differed much from those written by Rader, Mungo, or that other ex-convict, Jane Alpert, all of whose books reflect the "desperate" need to create new identities and all of whom use narrative structures that pit a new self against an old one. Harris, however, differs from them in two respects: he is "proud of what [he] had done," and he waited almost ten years after emerging from his Movement experiences to write about them. For both reasons, the text he produced is remarkably free of the animus against a former self that characterizes reactive conversion narratives. Harris reconstructs a past self and a past era that he has lost, but it is not one that he violently rejects. As he says in the book's final sentence, the sixties were years that he will miss.

Harris undertakes his autobiography, therefore, not to repudiate his former self, but simply to recollect and understand it. In his first chapter, he aptly characterizes the nature of his backward glance with a buried biblical metaphor: "When I suddenly wanted to remember [the sixties]," Harris writes, "I had to look back across a long plain and against a fierce glare" (2). Recalling the fates of Sodom (that "city of the plain") and Lot's wife, Harris' comment suggests the cultural taboo against looking back at a condemned past. In the biblical story, Lot's wife is transformed by Yahweh into a pillar of salt because she has violated the Hebrew God's injunction against looking back at the flaming city he has instructed her and her family to flee (see Genesis 19). By employing this figure, Harris seems to concede the story's commonsense point: a culture cannot move forward if it fixes itself nostalgically on the past. But given the social context in which he was writing, the figure more probably suggests the difficulty of Harris' task: reflecting positively on the sixties in 1982 was clearly going against the cultural grain. Early in the Reagan administration, when conservatism was experiencing a strong resurgence and the sixties were widely regarded as years of cultural chaos, moral degeneration, and national backsliding, Harris was aware that what he was doing was comparable to looking back favorably on Sodom. The story he reluctantly constructs is one that he is not sure anyone wants to hear. In his first paragraph, he notes that were it not for a particular incident, he would "have left this story [of the sixties] alone." It is a period that "had long since receded into the past"; it was "long gone" and "finished off." Nevertheless, he adds, the usual treatments of that era "tend to be glib and miss all the actual vastness that coming of age in such times implied." So however much we may wish to ignore that decade, it is "still much too important to ignore" (2).

The "long plain" of Harris' metaphor also suggests the difference he perceives between the historical landscape of the sixties, so full of momentous life-changing events, and that of the seventies, when no identity-jarring occurrences interrupted the psychic and social terrain. In deconversion narratives such as those we looked at in the last chapter, a single event conventionally catalyzes a radical change of identity. But in an elegiac narrative like Harris', the self experiences change in less dramatic ways. Change is brought about by the simple accumulation of events; more than anything else it is the result of the passage of time. One looks back at one's past and realizes one is no longer who one once was. This is how Harris constructs his situation as he begins the task of reassessing the self he was in the sixties from the vantage point of the self he is in the eighties. "Times change and I am no longer the same person," Harris writes, "but my past and I are still directly related" (148). Still, there exists a large gap between the two selves. The older narrating self marvels "at how young I was and how much happened to me." The younger self, he says, "was comfortable making definitive statements about important subjects to large groups of people who were prepared to believe me." His present self, on the other hand, is a sadder and wiser one: "at the age of 36, my precociousness is gone, . . . the rest too complicated, and I am now old enough to know better. I only want to backtrack and string it all together piece by piece" (5).

The "it" that Harris wishes to "string together" is not only his own past. Like other generationalists, he wishes to reconstruct the times during which he came of age and the issues that helped define his generation. To do this, Harris interweaves his own story with the stories of two other men with whom he had close ties in the sixties. One of them, Allard Lowenstein, was his political mentor at Stanford University and a major behind-the-scenes figure in liberal Democratic causes of the 1960s. The other, Dennis Sweeney, was a fellow student at Stanford and another Lowenstein protégé whose political career in the Movement was similar to Harris' own. Harris and Sweeney had both been recruited at Stanford by Lowenstein to work in the Mississippi civil rights movement, both had returned to Stanford radicalized by their experiences in the South and anxious to establish independent political identities, and both had become involved in the antiwar cause that led them eventually to the founding of the Resistance. Not long afterward, however, their positions on how to oppose the war and the draft led to disagreements. Sweeney believed in complete noncooperation and felt that draft resisters should not submit to the system of justice that enforced the draft laws; Harris was convinced that going to prison represented a moral act that would have a substantial impact on American public opinion. At the end of the sixties, Sweeney drifted out of political work, and Harris went to federal prison for refusing to cooperate with the Selective Service System. After his release in 1971, he lost touch with both of his former political friends. At the end of the decade that followed, the one Harris describes as a "long plain," Sweeney suddenly reappeared in the national news when he assassinated Lowenstein in the latter's New York law offices.

In weaving the stories of these others with his own, Harris is only exploiting more fully a convention of the subgenre already noted in other generational autobiographies: a shift of focus from the self of the author to a friend or acquaintance whose story is representative of some aspect of generational identity. By constructing a narrative that interweaves three life stories, Harris constructs what he considers to be a more fully representative portrait of his times than would be possible in a generational autobiography based solely on his own experiences. The three men, Harris claims, "typified three strands of behavior that, when wrapped about one another, made the decade what it was" (3). Allard Lowenstein was

> the older liberal, wedded to the Democratic party, convinced that the citadels of power could be stormed from the inside out, his world view framed by a belief that articulate reason, recourse to the constitution, benign leadership, and enlightened self-interest were the ultimate hole cards. Dennis [Sweeney] was the young man, idealistic, moved by the sufferings of others, and disillusioned with the compromise inherent in the liberal approach. He divorced himself from the status quo and eventually became consumed with the need to create a communal identity in which he could submerge himself in the radical task of immense change on all fronts. I was the even younger man, romantic too, disturbed by the hypocrisy of what was and unwilling to accept the degradation of working my separate peace with it. I was drawn to the ex-

emplary existential act as a means of transforming both myself and the world around me. (3–4)

Lowenstein, who is not actually a member of the generation, is a central figure in Harris' narrative partly because he represents a political option that would have allowed the generation's leftist wing to remain a part of American mainstream politics. The rejection of this option was one of the more important choices that the New Left made in its definition of the generational self.

The other two characters, Harris and Sweeney, are members of the generation, and their lives and choices are meant to serve as a direct reflection of its identity and narrative. Harris represents the political conscience of the generation, while Sweeney represents its emotional life, and especially its deeply felt dreams and disappointments. Harris' primary contribution was made in the form of his strategy for opposing the war in Vietnam. He wrote to his draft board (the local arm cf the nationwide Selective Service System) that he would no longer carry his draft card or accept the student deferment it signified, that to do so would mean that he tacitly assented to American policy in Vietnam, and that he would not be party to the destruction of Indochina by allowing himself to be inducted. He did this with the full expectation that it would lead to his incarceration, but he believed that such an "existential act," if carried out by enough young men, would bring the war to an end (147–48). Harris looks back on his own earlier self with a degree of bemusement and respect; bemusement because the past is always, in his estimation, outside the reach of complete understanding, and respect because his earlier self acted with heroism in pursuit of his political and moral ideals. As he looks back on his defiance of the draft system, for example, Harris' tone of respect, unqualified by irony, is typical of this treatment:

> I feel as though I have explained that act of defiance a million times in the intervening years without ever quite capturing it. The repetition eventually burdened my explanation with a shell of distance and matter-of-factness that distorts what I did. It was an act of wonderment and impulse, taken in the calmest and most practical frame of mind. I was prepared to abandon what seemed a promising future and pit myself against the war one on one, believing that I would redeem my country and realize myself in the process. It seemed that to do anything else would have dishonored both. There was nothing matter-of-fact or distant about it that August. I took my life in my hands and it was the bravest I have ever been. It was also, I think, the most right. That I have never doubted. (148)[9]

One might argue that by focusing on his youthful virtues, Harris leaves out the psychological complexity and moral ambiguity we have seen in Alpert's and Rader's self-portraits, but one cannot accuse Harris of outright self-glorification, since he portrays his younger self as subject to the sexual and identity confusions typical of that age, and his moral heroism is constructed, at least in part, as accidental. It was thrust upon him, much as the presidency of the Stanford student body was thrust upon him, because Harris misunderstood the implications of what he was doing. Initially, his stands on various political issues were taken half in jest, as a kind of youthful fillip to the establishment, but once his public stance was endorsed by his "followers," he was trapped in the role of moral leader, and it was then that he began to take it with full seriousness. According to Harris, he never sought his own briefly held celebrity, and once he had attained it, he never felt comfortable with it. Moreover, in spite of the fact that Harris' self-portrait at times seems self-serving, his intention is at least partly to retrieve the generational self from attacks on its moral idealism, a feature of its collective identity that the autobiographies of Rader and Alpert, with their intense concentration upon psychological complexity, directly undermine.

Harris can also neglect his "inner" history because he does not have to rely solely upon it to construct the generation's emotional plot. That, after all, is one of the functions that Sweeney is most clearly meant to fill in the narrative. Sweeney's plot is tragic and extreme; it is, as Harris puts it, "one of the saddest stories I know" (337). The specific import of Sweeney's plot, however, is discernible only in the context of his relationship to Harris, for it is through the braiding of their stories that Harris conveys the two strands of the generational narrative. Where Harris' own plot represents the generation's moral and existential idealism, Sweeney's stands for its passionate, though often hidden, emotional life. Like other self-constructed outsiders of his generation—one thinks of Alpert, Rader, and Maynard—Sweeney is "consumed" by a "need to create a communal identity" (4), and it is this consuming need that typifies the generation's emotional life. Sweeney's dream of community gives his life and eventual madness their generational significance: it is the betrayal and loss of this dream that lie at the emotional center of Harris' elegiac narrative. Sweeney's isolation at the end of the sixties symbolizes for Harris the fate of a generation whose dreams seemed, for a brief time, possible.

In writing about a peer whose fall represents the entropic tendencies of the generational ethos and serves as a metaphor for its death, Harris is merely employing a convention used by other generational autobiographers who write *after* what they perceive to be the end of their era. Raymond Mungo's *Total Loss Farm* and Stephen Diamond's *What the Trees Said*, for example, both include accounts of the suicide of Marshall Bloom; Dotson Rader's *Blood Dues* recounts the descent of a friend, Jann Eller, and a hero, Jim Morrison, into drugs, madness, and death. The convention is also conspicuously present in Malcolm Cowley's prototypical generational narrative, *Exile's Return*, which, as we have seen, includes an entire chapter on the suicide of Harry Crosby. Sweeney's narrative most clearly represents the fate of the sixties generation's dreams of community and justice. His initial dedication to civil rights work, his disillusionment with conventional political solutions, his brief flirtation with political arson, and his final loss of purpose and sanity in the seventies all symbolize the fate of the New Left and its hopes. Like Bloom, Eller, Morrison, and Crosby, Sweeney is driven to extreme behavior by his times; his mind, like theirs, becomes a prism that refracts the issues and tendencies that give the generational decade its character and definition.

In addition, such "others" often serve as alter egos for the writers' own selves. The similarity between Harris' career and Sweeney's (like the similarity between Cowley's and Crosby's lives) made Sweeney a natural choice as alter ego. In conversion narratives, these alter egos become the sacrificial goats whose deaths allow the autobiographers to experience, at least symbolically, a form of rebirth. When the era in which the historical self comes of age dies, the author must, in some sense, also die and be reborn if he or she is to continue with life. For Cowley, Crosby's death symbolizes the death of the individualistic, decadent capitalism that characterized his and Crosby's coming-of-age in the 1920s. Only through some such ritualistic death could Cowley be reborn into the New Age of the Marxist proletariat. Though neither Diamond nor Mungo self-consciously uses Marshall Bloom's suicide as a symbol for the death of the political consciousness of the 1960s, they do depict Bloom, one of the co-founders of Liberation News Service, as a person whose efforts to maintain a foothold both in the old era of leftist politics and in the New Age are partly responsible for his death.[10] For them, rebirth in the New Age is possible only when politics and the "real world" are left behind.

The differences between Harris' treatment of Sweeney's act of assassination and Cowley's treatment of Crosby's suicide are instructive at this point. In Cowley's collective autobiography, Crosby's death serves as a symbolic climax to the twenties at the end of the book. Sweeney's assassination of Lowenstein, by contrast, is featured in the first chapter of Harris' autobiography, as well as on the book jacket where a photograph of Sweeney after his arrest is prominently displayed beneath photographs of Lowenstein and what appears to be a sixties peace march. In effect, this placement of a murder that represents the end of the sixties at the beginning of Harris' book sets up the problem of the autobiography. By going back and "stringing it all together," Harris intends to offer an explanation of generational experience by locating the cause of the murder in the decade when two representative men came of age dreaming of a better world.

Besides giving the deaths different structural locations in their texts, Cowley and Harris also choose deaths that occur at different times in relation to the generational coming-of-age experience. Crosby's suicide takes place in 1929, the same year that Cowley designates as that in which the generational ethos of the twenties came to an end. Crosby died, as Cowley says, "at the right time." Sweeney's act, on the other hand, occurred in 1980, ten years after the date that Harris, like most other sixties generationalists, would fix as the end of the generational heyday.[11] Unlike Crosby's well-timed act, Sweeney's gesture belatedly "finished off a decade long gone" (2). During the ten-year lapse, which Sweeney referred to as "ten years without change" (328), he was drifting rudderless around America, convinced that the ideals of the sixties had been betrayed (especially by liberals like Lowenstein), and tormented by the delusion that voices were being sent to him through a transmitter planted in his dental work by aliens. Among the voices he hears are those of Lowenstein and other acquaintances from the sixties.

That Harris constructs this tale as one that is rich in significance for the generational narrative is quite clear. He figures the murder itself, for example, as an autobiographical act, thereby drawing attention not only to its textuality, but also to the textuality of generational identity: "I would have left this story alone," he writes, "if it weren't for the ending Dennis wrote to it all so much later in our lives" (2). So when Harris asks the question "How did it all end up like this?" (5), he is asking himself what symbolic import can be attributed to Sweeney's bizarre version of the generational autobiography. The answer he provides, simply put, is that Sweeney's story (like the book's title) suggests that the dreams of the sixties—unfulfilled, betrayed, and finally killed off by the indifference and cynicism of the seventies—are likely to resurface as delusional, conspiratorial nightmares in the eighties.

Some readers may find Sweeney's plot too extreme to support its own symbolic weight, and one of the real problems of the book arises from what at times appear to be Harris' own doubts about its significance. Is Sweeney's tale one of individual aberration, signifying nothing more than the effects of "either an over- or underabundance of certain amphetaminelike chemicals in the brain" (294), or does it really contribute something to the generational narrative? Like almost all of the works written in the reactive and elegiac phases of the generational dialogue, this one is ambivalent about its own project. Harris occasionally claims that he is simply a journalist who wants to get the facts straight. He refers to the book in the last chapter, where he discusses its genesis and development, as "an extensive reporting effort" (329). He also characterizes himself, as we have seen, as someone who is "now old enough to know better" (5), by which he means that he no longer makes big pronouncements, that he has given up such avocations as generational "plotting." But big pronouncements about generational identity are precisely what this book would appear to be all about, for Sweeney's story would hardly be worth telling at all if the voices of the sixties that torment him do not also in some figurative sense haunt the lives of his peers. Unfortunately, Harris doesn't want to claim too much for his story, and his caution in handling the "ending Dennis wrote" (2) weakens the work as collective autobiography; it never quite lives up to the promise of its disturbingly suggestive triple story line.

Exile's Return Revisited: Tom Hayden's *Reunion*

In Chapter 3, I examined Tom Hayden's generational reading of the Chicago Seven conspiracy trial. Like many contemporary texts, *Trial* (1970) employed an apocalyptic tone and traced a generational trajectory from idealism and protest to outright generational secession and civil war. Within a few short years, however, Hayden (b. 1939) had changed his mind about the condition of American society. His acquittal on the conspiracy charges, the successful appeal of his sentence for contempt of court, and the ouster of Nixon and his top aides after the Watergate scandal all began to convince him that the "system had worked."[12] When Senator George McGovern ran for office in 1972, Hayden decided to commit himself to "working within the political system" (465). It was not until the mid-1980s, however, after enough time had passed for "those turbulent experiences to settle," that he felt able to reconstruct the generational plot once again in a narrative "outpouring" that is "partly personal, partly historical" (xvi–xvii).

This new narrative, *Reunion* (1988), retains a good portion of Hayden's earlier accounts of the generational plot, but it also makes some major modifications, many of them dictated by the changed circumstances of Hayden's political career and all of them colored by the elegiac tone of a writer meditating on the demise of an earlier generational self. Although by 1987 Hayden had become active in California state electoral politics, he was still suffering from the burden of having to woo voters who looked at him "through their own subconscious image of the sixties" (482). One of the primary aims of his narrative, therefore, is to persuade readers that he has returned to a "mainstream" that itself longs for a simpler, more harmonious, America. Hayden finally realized in the 1970s, he says, that the system

> had gone to the brink of breakdown, to the preliminary stages of civil strife, but now there were signs that working within the fabric of society was producing change. Now it was time, I thought, to make an adjustment to reality. . . . I was a "born-again" Middle American, emotionally charged by my reacceptance in the political mainstream. (465)

Designed to convince readers that his generation has made a successful return to American life after a period of catastrophic intergenerational misunderstanding, Hayden's narrative is also intended as a contribution to the "ongoing struggle . . . to define the sixties" (xvii). This 1988 text, however, reconstitutes not only the generational narrative, but also Hayden's audience and its attitudes. No longer made up of clearly opposed generations, it consists now of a less vilified older generation and of that part of his own generation who have shed their identities as "youth" in the process of becoming parents themselves. Acknowledging that his memories and his past are part of a collective text, Hayden invites this newly constituted readership to "participate through his or her own memory, searching with me for the meaning" (xvii).[13]

Hayden's book is structurally conventional, following his biography both chronologically and topically. The primary narrative moves from his childhood in the fifties (chapter 1) through the beginnings of his career in electoral politics in the 1970s and 1980s (chapters 18–19). The topics covered include the beginnings of the Movement and SDS in relation to civil rights protests (chapters 2–5), the SDS projects among the poor in northern cities (chapters 6–7), the Vietnam War (chapters 8–11), the Chicago protest and conspiracy trial (chapters 12–16), and a final section called "Reunion" that covers his gradual reintegration into society (chapters 17–20). Dispersed throughout the narrative are FBI memos Hayden obtained under the Freedom of Information Act; they detail the surveillance, harassment, and entrapment techniques the bureau employed in its efforts to discredit Hayden and the Movement throughout the period from 1960 to the mid-1970s.

Although they constitute the text's most curious generic "innovation," the FBI memos were oddly ignored by most of the book's reviewers. Perhaps they felt authorized to do so by Hayden himself, who offers the memos with virtually no comment of his own. In his introduction, Hayden says he includes them "to instill a sense of being personally hunted throughout the sixties by the very authority figures I was raised to respect" (xviii). As a rhetorical ploy, the juxtaposition of Hayden's construction of his activities with these government memos effectively skewers conservative arguments that Movement paranoia was an overreaction to acceptable government concerns about national security. They demonstrate graphically the state's vision of Hayden and his peers as dangerous subversives against whom any method of persecution could be exercised, no matter how flagrantly it violated the principles of democracy.

One reason Hayden does not focus a lot of rhetorical energy on the memos is his desire to avoid sparking old fights with his onetime political foes. His book is, as its title clearly suggests, about reconciliation and return. Although *Reunion* never mentions Cowley's 1951 version of *Exile's Return*, this theme is one that the two books have in common. Sharing the generational plot of Cowley's text, Hayden's elegiac narrative traces a journey that begins with youthful idealism, passes through a period of intergenerational misunderstanding and alienation, and ends with "reunion" (485), "reconciliation" (500), and a "coming home" (449). As

Cowley wrote in 1951 in his own book, "the story [these chapters] tell seems to follow the old pattern of alienation and reintegration, or departure and return."[14] Toward the end of his book, Hayden describes one of his 1970s political projects in terms that echo both the ending of Cowley's plot and its title. The project, Hayden writes, was "mostly composed of sixties veterans . . . who yearned to work again in the mainstream. In fact, the personal dimension of the project was akin to a rebirth for many, a return of exiles" (449).

Like Cowley, Hayden also combines his "exiles' return" plot with a nostalgia both for the early period of the generation's coming of age (he refers to this as the "Port Huron period" [430]) and for a bucolic Middle American past that preceded that period. This dual nostalgia reflects Hayden's belief that the values upon which his generation's rebellion was based were originally located in an older America, founded on radical democratic ideals of justice and fair play. These ideals were absorbed from the patriotic rhetoric promulgated in the public school system, in the old-fashioned nuclear family, and in the small community of the 1950s. Hayden's nostalgia for this small-town America runs throughout the text, but it is most evident in the opening chapters, where he depicts his own childhood, and in the final chapters, when he makes his "return." Visiting his mother's hometown after her death, Hayden writes,

> As I wandered across that Wisconsin hillside where my mother lay buried, I felt a form of personal relief. I saw the fields where I played as a boy, the railroad tracks I walked along, the blue lakes and tiny dams where I caught bass, the green yards where I threw the ball. It was all still there, beckoning me. The harmonies of my early life, disrupted by the civil wars of the sixties, were healing and reappearing, like blades of grass after a fire, in my middle years. (485)

This nostalgia for his fifties childhood also reflects Hayden's rejection of aspects of the counterculture he touted in *Trial* as essential to his generation's identity. The counterculture, after all, largely rejected the institution of the nuclear family, replacing it with various kinds of collective groupings, and Hayden himself belonged for a time to a Berkeley commune called the Red Family, in which parenting was shared by all members of the household. But this particular reimagining of social relations is discarded in *Reunion*, which holds the family up as the model on which full happiness and social responsibility depend. To underscore that message (and to exploit its potential electoral benefits), Hayden repeatedly emphasizes that his reconstructed self is a responsible family man, devoted to his celebrity wife, Jane Fonda, and his son Troy. In a way, this element of Hayden's rehabilitation project appears to be at odds with one of the book's underlying themes: that the generational excesses of the sixties were the result of dysfunctional family relationships. In retrospect, however, the dysfunction of the nuclear family appears preferable to him than that of the communal family. And one of the traditional plotlines of the dysfunctional nuclear family—"the return of the prodigal son"— clearly provides a model for his book that would appeal to those readers who would like to see him assume the role of repentant sinner. However, it is a model that never dominates the text because Hayden never casts himself in the role of errant child without at the same time casting social authorities in the role of overly rigid and authoritarian fathers.

Cowley handles the nostalgia of his text somewhat differently. A member of the twenties generation, he wrote, could return from exile to "his own country" and "live and die there like his ancestors," but the return is never complete: "the door was double-locked against him; the house would not take him back" (213). This passage and others like it constitute a leitmotif of Cowley's book that is first sounded in the opening chapter:

> Perhaps our boyhood is a stream in northern Michigan. . . . The water is swift and chill in July; a trout lurks in a hollow log, ready to take the grasshopper floating toward him at the end of your line. Perhaps we remember a fat farm in Wisconsin, or a Nebraska prairie, or a plantation house among the canebrakes. Wherever it lies, the country [of our boyhood] is our own; its people speak our language, recognize our values. . . . This is your home . . . but does it exist outside your memory? (14)

Cowley, in short, retains a skepticism about the possibility of full reintegration; he accepts nostalgia without succumbing to the illusion that one can reenter the pristine and innocent past.

The reasons behind these different treatments of nostalgia are not difficult to imagine. Hayden's book attempts to appeal to a popular audience that is itself nostalgic for "fifties values" and a family-based culture. Reintegration into the culture of these readers (and potential voters) requires that Hayden show his appreciation for those ideals. I am not saying that his nostalgia is predicated on a cynical pandering to his political constituency; it is possible that Hayden sincerely believes that he has returned to his roots and discovered true happiness in marriage and family values. Real life, however, has a way of undoing our efforts to construct personal narratives with the sort of pat "conclusion" Hayden offers here: *Reunion*'s plot "explains" Hayden's entire adult life as a more or less successfully completed journey back to family, yet he and Fonda were divorced within two years of the book's publication. The overall plot of Cowley's book, on the other hand, suggests that America underwent an irreversible change as it made the transition (sometime around 1914) from a predominantly rural to a predominantly urban culture. For Cowley and the literary audience to whom he writes, this is a demographic fact. The values represented by the former social landscape belong to an irretrievable rural past. One can feel nostalgia for this past, but one cannot pretend that it is possible to return to it.

As these modifications suggest, Hayden's new narrative has enabled him to expand significantly on his earlier generational texts. Like *The Port Huron Statement* and *Trial*, *Reunion* is finally not so much about class or ideological conflict as about old-fashioned Americanism and familial dynamics, as Hayden repeatedly reminds us by intertwining generational history, in which he played a major role, with his own family's story. Explaining his position during the Chicago trial, Hayden writes that his "decade of struggle" was carried out

> to end the apathy of the fifties, to make the Constitution and the Bill of Rights mean something, to put ideals into practice, to reach my parents. As I looked into the unexpressive faces across the courtroom, I realized that the jury was a microcosm of the same America that taught me to think and speak out and then broke my heart. (398)

The Chicago jury in this passage may serve as a microcosm for the parental generation across all of America, but in the text as a whole, it is his own parents who fill that role. Hayden's father at first rejected his involvement in reform and later broke with him altogether, refusing to speak to him for thirteen years. His mother, though slightly more understanding, never approved of his politics.

To underscore his narrative's familial focus, Hayden opens his introduction with two scenes set in the present, "twenty years since I battled on the streets of Chicago" (xv). In the first scene, he is playing baseball as a member of the Hollywood Stars team; in the second, he is coaching his fourteen-year-old son. He imagines yelling to the boy, as his father once yelled to him, "'That's okay, son. That's the way. You can do it, son. You can do it. That's the way'" (xv). Both scenes employ that icon of Americanism, baseball, as a conveniently apolitical activity that unites male Americans of all ideologies, faiths, and ages. The first scene portrays Hayden as a reborn American man actively involved in the favorite national pastime. The second scene employs a romantic image of generational continuity: fathers passing the lore of the game on to their sons, supporting them in their first fumbling efforts to master its techniques. But it also heightens the poignancy of the narrative's tragic plot, which depicts the failure of fathers to fulfill this role as the primary cause of the excesses and failures of the sixties. In a narrative replete with rhetorical "if only's," the most conspicuous is Hayden's suggestion that if only fathers had spoken the proper "you can do it, son" during his generation's coming of age, everything would have been different and better.

Reunion is, therefore, a domestic drama in which all of the characters are cast as members of a dysfunctional family in desperate need of counseling. "My simple hope," he says, "is that this book will stir a therapeutic chord in all those who lived through, or are still affected by, the unique trauma of the sixties" (xvii). In this therapeutic setting, Hayden casts various historical figures—Chicago mayor Richard Daley and Presidents Johnson and Nixon—as fathers whose "rigid" response to youthful idealism eventually forces the young to outright rebellion. Other fathers—John and Robert Kennedy, the socialist Michael Harrington, Senator Eugene McCarthy, Martin Luther King—might have been better, but they were either assassinated or too compromised by their pasts to be able to give the kind of support and encouragement the young needed. One other father figure plays a dominant role in this reconstruction of the national family circle: J. Edgar Hoover, the FBI director whose paranoid vision of the young as foreign subversives represents for Hayden the unconscious repressive "impulses" of the parental generation (xviii). The younger generation, of course, is cast as the family's "children" in this drama, but this group is further divided into "sibling rivals" (other male radicals [259]), siblings who have chosen another path altogether (soldiers [356, 418]), and those black sheep who represent the "id" of the young (the Weathermen [360]). In this reconstruction, the real tragedy of the late 1960s occurred because the conflicting forces that finally came to dominate the familial drama were those parental figures representing a hyperrepressive superego and those filial figures representing a hyper-Dionysian id.

As we have seen in previous chapters, constructing identity as the outcome of a family drama is a common characteristic of generational autobiographies. It was occasionally employed in the annunciatory and reactive narratives of Chapters 3 and 4, where writers like Jerry Rubin, Abbie Hoffman, and Raymond Mungo depict their politics as, in part, reactions to parental behaviors. We've seen generational politics psychologized before as well, particularly in the reactive narratives of Jane Alpert, Joseph Epstein, and Martha Bayles, all of whom conclude that their youthful politics were merely a facade for underlying psychopathologies unleashed by middle-class boredom and permissiveness. Like Dotson Rader, Hayden writes of his flirtation with violence and his romanticization of the Molotov cocktail as a way of "asserting a systematically denied manhood" (165), and like Rader, he sees the rebellion of the sixties generation as the result of a rigid patriarchal repression of sons.

Hayden, however, goes well beyond other generational autobiographers in his recasting of the sixties as a family drama, reading virtually every episode of generational history through the familial metaphor. Hayden's drama begins with an account of his typical fifties childhood in an America that is too good to be true. Outwardly idyllic, it was actually a suburban dead end where there "was nothing much to dream about or look forward to" (14), a place designed to "promote mediocrity" (21). The apparent "comfort and tranquillity" of this family-centered world did not last long. As a foreshadowing of dysfunction on a national level, Hayden first introduces the breakdown of his own family. His father, he says, became alienated from the boredom of family life by the "excitement and camaraderie of the war years" (7). Shortly after the Second World War, his parents separated and divorced, leaving him with a sense that "life was very much out of control" (8). America, for a while longer, continued to be a superficially placid and "one-dimensional" world, apparently "lacking in any real social conflict" (14), but its stifling conformism and the parental hypocrisy that it engendered eventually led to his generation's "resentment of the future that had been prepared for us" and laid the groundwork for a rebellion whose models were found in novels like J. D. Salinger's *Catcher in the Rye* and Jack Kerouac's *On the Road*, or in films like Nicholas Ray's *Rebel without a Cause*. Later on, when the middle-class young moved away from their homes and into the universities, these models of adolescent rebellion against ineffectual and hypocritical parents were replaced by models of political rebellion against ineffectual and hypocritical parent institutions. In the universities, Hayden and his friends encountered writers like Albert Camus and C. Wright Mills, whose books developed their political consciousness and social idealism. His own "conversion" to the New Left occurred at the University of Michigan at Ann Arbor, but young people all over America experienced a similar awakening: "Ann Arbor is one of the classic college towns where the sixties generation first commingled, where it was inspired and then alienated, and where it formed its distinct identity" (25). The generation's initial attempts to put their ideals into practice in the civil rights movement led to what Hayden refers to as the generation's "age of innocence" (32). Very quickly, however, they encountered a resistance by authorities that resulted in a "rip in the moral umbilical cord linking us with American society. We had not lost our vision or moral fervor, but we began to suspect that our parent society had" (72). Having been rejected by their actual parents, the young generation turned to sympathetic adults, but even these people turned out to have ideological commitments that led to intergenerational fighting: "We who had enough trouble gaining acceptance from our real parents were now rejected by our political father figures" (91). Other more distant and idealized father figures such as the Kennedy brothers were assassinated by vague forces that appeared to oppose everything the young were hoping to do. The Kennedy deaths, together with those of Malcolm X and Martin Luther King, led to "the tragic consciousness of the sixties generation" (114). The culmination of this rise and fall of generational aspirations occurred for Hayden, as it did for other generational writers, in the catastrophic Chicago demonstrations in 1968. At this moment of generational polarization, the repressive parental forces, represented by J. Edgar Hoover and Richard Daley, poised themselves against the Dionysian filial forces, represented by the anarchic Yippies and, shortly after Chicago, by the Weathermen.

What Hayden failed to see at the time of this polarization, and what his autobiography highlights as one of the tragic elements in the generational plot, is the difficulty of reuniting a "family" damaged by such feuding. Writing of his own family, Hayden says, "When one is young, or at least when I was young, there always seems to be a vast expanse of future time in which to reconnect with uncomprehending parents. I didn't see that, from their perspective, time was rapidly passing by" (49). Looking back, of course, Hayden can see many things, but perhaps the most important is that his parents' generation had been as determined by its historical moment (the Depression and the Second World War) as his own generation had been determined by the era of anticolonialism.

> In retrospect, there is even something idealistic in my parents' generation's willingness to support a war against such unbelievable odds. Experience had taken them prisoner, and they failed to see Vietnam as a popular and nationalist struggle, with elements of a civil war, against the new foreigners, who happened to be Americans. In my generation's world view, the most apparent and unwanted invaders were our own armed forces—"white boots marchin' in a yellow land," as Phil Ochs sang—the very opposite of the dynamics of World War II. (179)

And so it is not surprising that Hayden devotes the final section of his generational plot to his successful efforts to create a family of his own, to reconcile with his parents before their deaths, and to reaffirm both the fifties spirit of small-town patriotism and the early sixties spirit of idealism and reform. Such a reconciliation, he optimistically suggests, is precisely what lies in store for the nation as a whole. After a high school reunion and a return to the site of the Port Huron conference, he sentimentally ponders the future:

> The buildings at Port Huron had disappeared, but the yearnings of youth recorded there still remained alive, like spirits in Irish legends. I could feel them in the trees, in the paths, waiting for renewal. They were in the imaginations of my high school classmates who spoke the language of understanding, acceptance, reconciliation. The change was slow but secure, gradual but real. I felt at home again and waited expectantly for a new generation. (500)

This familial plot dominates Hayden's reconstruction of the history of the sixties generation, but his text also suggests another plot that replicates Harris' arc of hope followed by frustration, disappointment, and unrealized dreams. Hayden's discursive style, however, raises this plot to a tragic/epic level that Harris' sparse journalistic version never attains. In *Reunion*, the tragic/epic plot is based on Hayden's likening of the period to a "Greek drama": it begins "with legendary events, then raised hopes,

only to end by immersing innocence in tragedy" (254). More introspective than the familial plot, this aspect of Hayden's reconstruction finds in
the young generation tragic flaws that lead to their dowrfall. They fail to
see that the very things they criticize in society are present in themselves.
Like the institutions against which they are struggling, they are capable
of violence, cynicism, egotism, nihilism, arrogance, and they fall prey to
these weaknesses with an alacrity that is difficult to explain. On the one
hand, Hayden defends the turn to violence as a strategic reaction to "society's rejection and hypocrisy" (164), but he admits that as a strategy, the
use of violence is self-defeating. On the other hand, he suggests that intragenerational differences explain the transition to violence. The real
culprits in this tragedy are the youngest members of the young generation—those who appeared on the historical stage after 1966. Unim-
pressed by the "beloved community" that had comprised the leadership
of the Movement in the early sixties, the younger group of leaders, knowing "only the bitterness of the mid-sixties" (201), turned to "long-term
revolutionary doctrines" (205) and violently confrontational political
strategies.

Like Harris' plot, this one suggests that the identity of the sixties
generation in the postsixties period depends entirely on the way in which
the group copes with its failure to make good on its historical tasks. "For
those who went through it all," Hayden argues, the sixties experience is
"felt to this day in failed dreams, enduring hurts, unmet yearnings" (254):
"After 1968, living on as a ruptured and dislocated generation became
our fate, having lost our best possibilities at an early age, wanting to hope
but fearing the pain that seemed its consequence" (326). Like his familial
plot, however, Hayden's tragic/epic plot has a redemptive ending. Tragedy,
he says, "has another dimension, a noble one":

> Edith Hamilton described the "suffering of a soul that can suffer greatly"
> and the experience of loss for an entire generation that began with its soul
> fired with great hope. The two great periods of tragedy in Western culture,
> she pointed out, were Periclean Athens and Elizabethan England. Both were
> times, like the sixties, "when life was seen as exalted, a time of thrilling and
> unfathomable possibilities." Tragedy takes place only amid such possibilities
> of greatness. (326)

The failure, in other words, may yet be redeemed by the wisdom of a
chastened generational soul. So while Hayden's domestic familial plot
ends in reunion, his epic/tragic plot ends in greater spiritual depth and understanding. And the central character in this historical tragedy is, of
course, Tom Hayden himself. His story is the story of a man who dreams
big dreams, who puts forth a noble effort to attain them, who initially
succeeds, who eventually fails, and who then has to rehabilitate himself.
It is a classic statement of the rise and fall and rise of a generation.

186 Generational Autobiography as Elegiac Narrative

Hayden's book represents a further development of the elegiac plot developed in Harris' *Dreams Die Hard*. Harris ends his book in a nostalgic mood, summing up the sixties as a period of tragedy and of great historical significance. Dennis Sweeney and Allard Lowenstein, he says, "were both extraordinary people who lived through an extraordinary time, and the extraordinary thing that happened between the two of them finally convinced me that the extraordinary time had come to an end. I will miss it, too" (338). Hayden ends his book on precisely the same note: "Times filled with tragedy are also times of greatness and wonder, times that really matter, and times truly worth living through. Whatever the future holds, and as satisfying as my life is today, I miss the sixties and always will" (507). But as we have already seen, Harris' sympathetic look back at the sixties contains little hope that the generation has moved toward reconciliation and reintegration. Instead, he implies that the frustration of generational dreams and the cultural fear of reexamining the past bode ill for the American future. Harris' generational plot ends with murder and madness; Hayden's with reunion and a chastened optimism for the future.

A Tale of Two Sixties: Todd Gitlin's *The Sixties*

Although Todd Gitlin's elegiac narrative *The Sixties: Years of Hope, Days of Rage* (1987) covers roughly the same period as Hayden's *Reunion*, the two books differ significantly. For example, even though Hayden reconstructs an earlier self that is often both generational and collective, his book adheres more closely to the conventions of the traditional memoir, with its focus on the individual self as it intersects with the author's times. Gitlin (b. 1943) is more ambitious. Intent on presenting a full generational history, he weaves together several generic forms: political history, personal memoir, culture criticism, and pop culture analysis. Like other writers I have examined, he uses his own story as the baseline of the generational narrative, but he includes entire chapters that treat aspects of sixties culture—such as "the beats, the southern civil rights movement, the hippie scene" (4)—with which he had little personal connection. To produce his text, he says, he has had to work

> at the edge of history and autobiography, from inside and outside the Sixties, writing at different focal lengths, in first and third persons. . . . So this is part historical reconstruction, part analysis, part memoir, part criticism, part celebration, part meditation. Pride, chagrin, embarrassment have their places, but beyond them, I hope to have evoked the spirit of the time from the interior. . . . (4)

And it is also, like other generational works, "organized around pivotal moments" (4) that constitute both a narrative of the times and a foundation for the historical identity of the sixties generation.

Gitlin's *The Sixties* is a fitting book with which to end this chapter, for its publication spawned precisely the sort of argument among its readers and critics that makes generational autobiography an overtly collective—and always politically charged—project. If we are to credit its reviewers' contradictory responses, the generational portrait that emerges from Gitlin's book is rather open to divergent interpretations.[15] In the culture wars rhetoric of Peter Collier and David Horowitz, for example, Gitlin is a "sentimental revisionist" of the sixties.[16] In their view, he not only whitewashes the period and its youthful protagonists, but the "utter absence of irony" (246) with which he renders his earlier anti-Americanism clearly demonstrates his "unreconstructed" status. Gitlin, they charge, acts as a "mortician for the Movement" who "has taken it upon himself to compose the features of its corpse" (329). Other peers have reacted differently. James Miller declares that *The Sixties* is completely free of "false sentimentality" (13), and several others identify Gitlin's condemnation of New Left strategies and attitudes in the latter half of the decade as a central feature of his narrative. Indeed, Winifred Breines turns Horowitz and Collier's reading upside down when she demurs from the "undisguised disgust" with which Gitlin "condemns the movement for its own demise in an orgy of countercultural self-indulgence, lack of discipline, and mindless militance . . ." (539).

The gaping disparity between these readings of the book underscores the degree to which the construction of generational identity is inevitably freighted with political jockeying. For all of these reviewers, as for Gitlin himself, the "sixties generation" is a concept that embodies a set of political attitudes, a lifestyle, an approach to culture and authority. For each reviewer, that concept will vary depending upon his or her own political values. One's judgment of Gitlin's account of generational identity, therefore, constitutes a judgment both on the past and on the desirability of a future based on those political attitudes, that lifestyle, that approach to culture and authority.

Still, the inherently political nature of his subject only partly explains the discrepant readings of Gitlin's book. Some of the differences are also attributable to the polyvocality of the book itself. As Gitlin puts it, *The Sixties* is a "record of a conversation with myself, and with friends and comrades, teachers and students, colleagues and (sometimes) opponents" (4). He says he has "tried to convey the grain of other voices than my own, tried to be fair to those I have disagreed with (and to an earlier self, and those I agreed with but no longer do)" (7). To the degree that Gitlin succeeds in restraining himself from imposing his present judgments on these others' voices, one would expect ambiguity in the text. Likewise, the effort to depict a former self from "within" requires the suppression of at least some of the irony that would signal to readers like Horowitz and Collier an appropriately denunciatory attitude.[17] When they read Gitlin, they hear only those earlier voices, and they can find no significant distance between them and the present day Gitlin. Breines, on the other hand, hears primarily the voice of an "older and wiser" Gitlin who has abandoned his earlier radicalism to embrace a moderate social democratic stance. She feels toward this antisixties Gitlin almost as much animosity as Collier and Horowitz feel toward their prosixties Gitlin. Both Gitlins are in the text.

But there is yet another quality in Gitlin's book that encourages conflicting readings: he is ambivalent toward his subject. That ambivalence is suggested in the book's subtitle, *Years of Hope, Days of Rage*, whose juxtaposed phrases intentionally echo Charles Dickens' characterization of the French revolutionary epoch in *A Tale of Two Cities*. The Dickensian echoes continue, in fact, throughout *The Sixties*. For example, chapter 15, "The Spring of Hope, the Winter of Despair," begins with a paragraph written in direct imitation of the opening paragraph of Dickens' famous book:

> Everything was at stake, anything seemed possible, there was the promise of universal liberation, there was the profaning of everything holy, the end of time was approaching, nothing was changing, there was a leap toward equality, there was a degradation of standards. . . . (341)

If it weren't clear enough from other evidence, the borrowings from Dickens amply demonstrate the ambivalence that prevents Gitlin from creating anything resembling an unqualified panegyric to the period. For the literary technique that Gitlin borrows from Dickens is just that pairing of contradictory phrases that allows him to characterize the sixties both as the "best of times" and as the "worst of times."

Using Dickens as a textual model suggests that Gitlin also sees his narrative of the period as a repetition—perhaps an inevitable one—of another historical narrative. The history of the sixties recapitulates, by implication, at least some aspects of the French Revolution as depicted by the English novelist, whose own narrative is marked by a kind of fatalistic ambivalence. In the final chapter of *A Tale of Two Cities*, Dickens' narrator comments on the inevitability of the Reign of Terror:

> There is not in France, with its rich variety of soil and climate, a blade, a leaf, a root, a sprig, a peppercorn, which will grow to maturity under conditions more certain than those that have produced this horror. . . . Sow the same seed of rapacious license and oppression over again, and it will surely yield the same fruit according to its kind.[18]

Of course, the "seed" that is sown in Gitlin's narrative and the "fruit" that it produces are of a distinctly American sort. This seed may not have produced "la Guillotine," but Gitlin does entitle one chapter "The Decapitation of Heroes," in which he treats not only what is by now a conventional topic of the period's generational autobiographies—the assassinations of the Kennedy brothers, Martin Luther King, and Malcolm X—but also the rising culture of violence on both sides of the generational war. Gitlin's narrative here verifies Rader's depiction of his penchant for violence as typical of the mentality of Movement people in the late sixties, but his description of the new mood has a distinctly Dickensian flavor, as the originally hopeful revolutionaries come increasingly to mirror the violence that is directed against them and against those with whom they identify. They discover in themselves a "fasc nation with precisely what was feared": "why not seize upon violence, why not will what had first been experienced as a terrible destiny?" (317). Even Dickens' botanical metaphor is echoed in Gitlin's preliminary analysis of the fifties, which he refers to as the "seedbed" of the sixties (12), suggesting that he views the evolution of the latter period with a sense of Dickensian fatality. Picking up on this thread in the work, Maurice Isserman asserts that it is precisely its sense of predestination that sets Gitlin's narrative apart from other generational narratives of the late eighties.[19] But in fact the fatalism of Gitlin's work is of a piece with the historicism that marks almost every text I have looked at in this book. In earlier generational autobiographies, this historicism manifested itself in prophetic announcements of an inevitable generational revolution. In later texts of both the right and the left, generational writers look back with the same sort of fatalism that marked their earlier looking forward. For Collier and Horowitz, the violent end of the sixties was inevitable, given the leftist underpinnings of the revolution. For Hayden and Gitlin, the end was inevitable because the "Zeitgeist" of the fifties made it so. The irony, of course, is that the 20/20 fatalism of the retrospective view often demonstrates the fallibility of the fatalism of the prospective view.

Gitlin's ambivalence toward his subject is likewise apparent in a contradiction between the narrative body of the text and its discursive frame. In the latter, Gitlin is every bit the partisan eulogist that Collier and Horowitz claim he is. That is to say, Gitlin openly avows in his preface, introduction, and concluding chapter that he is an advocate of what he takes to be sixties values. These sections contain a strong element of both eulogy and apologia. The eulogistic strain praises a past self that has disappeared, enumerates its sacrifices, and lauds its virtues; the apologetic strain defends aspects of the former self that still exist, justifying as much as possible (or at least rendering understandable) those of its attitudes and acts that seem vulnerable to attack. If one takes away this discursive frame, however, neither the period nor the generational leaders who were its chief protagonists emerge as particularly admirable. For the book's central narrative—which focuses on the generation's "wrong turns" (xi) as it descends into something Gitlin variously calls "the maelstrom" (4), "the realm of the demonic" (403), or "the demonic side" (435)—lends itself easily to Breines' reading. What we end up with is a kind of textual collision between a narrative historian intent on critical insight and an autobiographical partisan intent on vindicating himself and his party.

Apologetic or exculpatory strategies are commonplace in elegiac narratives written by ex-Movement leaders after 1980. By that time, generational autobiography, conceived as a national project taking place within diverse media, had begun to incorporate conservative and non-Movement voices that had earlier been either silent or defensive; the Reagan administration and its spokespersons changed that by carrying out an effective campaign to reconstruct the sixties according to the needs of their own political agenda, which required the demonization of the period. (I examined several examples of this campaign, as it expressed itself in generational autobiographies, in the previous chapter.) The apologetic mode—taken up in response to these conservative voices—is certainly present in Hayden's *Reunion,* whose primary exculpatory strategy is the construction of a generational plot that might be characterized as a family-feud-with-a-happy-ending. For Hayden, the familial metaphor is intended to depict the generational agonists—him and his father—in ways that will make the two generations appear more human and understandable to one another. In his figurative one-child family, after many years of misunderstanding and alienation, father and son finally reconcile. The father forgives the son for his excesses; the son forgives the father for his authoritarian rigidity. The father passes peacefully to his grave, and the son takes his rightful place in the halls of power.

Gitlin also uses the familial figure for exculpatory purposes, but he gives it a distinct twist. Figuring the sixties generation as a family with *many* children, Gitlin casts himself as Oldest Brother, the one who tells the story of his siblings' coming of age. Most often, the parents in his metaphoric family are made up of the old left or older liberals (most of whom came of age in the 1930s), but occasionally they are the older generation as a whole. Describing the early New Left's argument with its elder sponsors in chapter 5, for example, Gitlin refers to his peers as a "'band of brothers and sisters'" engaged in a struggle with the

> moribund social-democratic segment of the Old Left. . . . From the "child's" point of view, nothing was more important than its claim to be taken seriously; from the "parents'" point of view, nothing was more important than the question of what to say and do about Communism and Communists. . . . The "child" flexed its muscles; the "parent" clamped down, losing its chance of control. (110)

In the course of this telling, Gitlin feels compelled to respond to a common perception that the children have badly misbehaved. Readers who come from large families will immediately recognize his defensive tactic: he blames the worst mischief on his kid brother. Which is to say that when Gitlin sets out to defend the generation, he does so in part by blaming its most serious problems on the younger element within it.

When one extracts the central plot from Gitlin's impressively dense account of the period, the way in which he implements this strategy becomes apparent. He simply breaks the sixties in two, creating a "good" sixties and a "bad" sixties, assigning different protagonists—indeed different generations—to each period. And here, too, we see how Gitlin subtly uses the Dickensian juxtaposing of phrases in his title so that it suggests not only his ambivalence about the sixties, but also something about his way of organizing the decade into two temporal components. The good sixties were the "years of hope" from 1960 to 1964, and its protagonists were, in Gitlin's terms, "the old New Left, the pre-Vietnam New Left" (26), or the "Old Guard" (186). Gitlin characterizes this group as one that

> aspired to become the voice, conscience, and goad of its generation. It was never quite typical: it was morally more serious, intellectually and culturally more ambitious than the rest of the generation. It shared its generation's obsessions, and then some, but focused them in an original way. (26)

The bad sixties were the "days of rage" (a phrase coined by the Weathermen to name their rampage through the streets of Chicago in October of 1969); for Gitlin, they began in 1965, triggered, among other things, by the failure of liberals to meet the demands of the civil rights movement (especially the Mississippi Freedom Democratic Party's bid for representation at the 1964 Atlantic City convention) and by the liberals' backing of the use of American military power in Vietnam. The bad sixties lasted until 1970, and their protagonists were the "late New Left," "prairie-power SDS," and Weatherman. He refers to this separate and later group as a "new generation," defending his use of the term because "campus populations undergo major shifts every two or three years" (186).[20] This group was

> younger than the Old Guard, they tended to come from the Midwest and Southwest, they were not Jewish, they were more likely to come from working-class families, and they were less intellectual, less articulate. . . . Many hailed from frontier country, had long, shaggy, swooping mustaches, wore blue work shirts and cowboy boots, and smoked marijuana. . . . they were instinctive anarchists, principled and practiced anti-authoritarians. (186)

According to Gitlin, these new members flocked to the Movement partly because President Lyndon Johnson escalated the war in Vietnam, arousing hordes of middle-class white youth who had paid scant attention to the civil rights and antipoverty struggles. The influx began shortly after the Washington antiwar march of April 17, 1965, when, Gitlin says, huge numbers of new people decided to join SDS. Their numbers were strengthened by the sudden appearance on the historical scene of the demographically significant "baby boomers," who were a few years younger than most members of the sixties generation.[21] By their sheer numbers, they allowed Movement thinkers to imagine a purer form of generationalism, free of the Marxist notion that only a revolution of the proletariat could bring about true social change. With youth as its "revolutionary" base, the vanguardist New Left could abandon its efforts to forge alliances with groups such as labor or the Democratic Party. When this happened, according to Gitlin, the New Left cut itself off from the social realities of American life and committed itself to "go it alone" (179). Since they no longer needed to appease adults, nothing restrained them from indulging in the fantasy of revolution. They were now free to indulge in social behaviors and political theories that were wildly divorced from mainstream American life, imagining as they did so that they constituted a new mainstream. In fact, however, the side eddy in which they had begun to twirl was quickly becoming a black "maelstrom" that would eventually engulf them and their movement entirely. Among members of the Movement, he writes,

> the largely unconscious intuition of 1965 was this: Suppose the New Left were only *apparently* small. Suppose it were actually the thoughtful, active "vanguard" of a swelling social force, one that embodied the future forming in the cocoon of the present the way Marx's proletariat was supposed to do. Suppose that SDS stood for students-as-a-whole, and students-as-a-whole stood for *the young*. . . . Then the unthinkable might be actual, the unprecedented possible. You could safely kick out the jams, dissolve the old hesitations, break with adults, be done with compromises, *get on with it*. (192)

"Kicking out the jams" and "getting on with it" were precisely the kinds of slogans that groups like the Weathermen called for in their infamous Days of Rage, when they ran amok in the streets of Chicago, convinced that masses of youth all over the country would rise up, imitate their example, and bring about revolution in America.

By placing himself and his coterie in the good sixties group, the one that "tried to keep the movement from running off its rails" (177), Gitlin avoids having to take full responsibility for the worst excesses and outrages of the bad sixties. Still, it would be misleading to characterize Gitlin's text as completely dominated by the familial metaphor and the exculpatory strategy it supports, since he uses it far less frequently than Hayden does. Indeed, generational apologists have good reason to avoid it altogether because it potentially trivializes the moral issues underlying the civil rights and antiwar movements (one could imagine leftists making such a critique of Hayden's book). As Gitlin himself says after considering the family backgrounds of members of the pre-Vietnam New Left, "if vulgar psychoanalytic interpretations were sufficient, the early SDS circle might have been a religious cult or a utopian commune," not the complicated "outward-facing community it was" (107). The traumas of the sixties were not reducible to either a family squabble or personal psychological problems, such an argument asserts, because they were the result of real clashes between the powerless (African Americans, Vietnamese, the poor) and the powerful (the America government and established American institutions).

Nor does Gitlin blame the excesses of the decade's final years entirely on the generation's younger members. If he did, he wouldn't be nearly as ambivalent as he is. In his efforts to be fair, Gitlin is also at pains to demonstrate that the bad sixties were partly the inevitable result of the "achievements as well as the paradoxes and tensions" (26) of the good sixties. One line of his plot, therefore, follows the evolution of late sixties problems out of these tensions in the old New Left. The first of the tensions Gitlin describes was endemic to all vanguardist groups: they had an elitist tendency to think of the mass of people "as ingrates" and of themselves "as spurned prophets" (70). Another was a pervasive sexism (108). A third was its early rejection of liberalism as the real enemy of social progress (127). A fourth was the lack of a clear political program behind the equally vague ideal of "participatory democracy," with its suspicion of all forms of authority and leadership (149, 166). A fifth was a commitment to an "expressive politics" that placed as much emphasis on the self-actualization of the reformer as it did on the reformer's cause. And a sixth was the old New Left's "soft" stance on communism (a position taken in part because its members could not imagine themselves vulnerable to doctrinaire ideologies) and romantic idealization of third world revolutions (121–22).

Gitlin implies that most of these tensions were initially invisible within SDS because the specific issues for which they were fighting seemed so morally unambiguous. Both civil rights and the empowerment of America's poor required such idealism and personal sacrifice of those who fought for them that the Movement's latent weaknesses were of relatively little significance. It was not until liberalism and the Democratic Party "betrayed" these causes and, a little later, championed what the New Left perceived as an imperialistic policy in Southeast Asia that they began to emerge in forms that would eventually destroy the Movement altogether. New Left elitism eventually spawned the violence-prone vanguardism of groups such as the one to which Jane Alpert belonged. Sexism within the Movement in turn led to the defection of large numbers of women, many of whom left to fight for women's rights (Gitlin devotes an entire chapter to this "revolution within the revolution"). The angry rejection of liberalism drove the Movement increasingly toward more extreme forms of radicalism. The vagueness of "participatory democracy" and the illusion that the New Left had no leaders allowed Movement demagogues to evade responsibility for their acts (Gitlin suggests that both Hayden and Hoffman are examples). The emphasis on "expressive politics" left the Movement open to a subculture whose main priorities were the self-indulgent consumption of self-actualization therapies, drugs, music, and physical pleasure. The soft stance on communism made possible the SDS's takeover by Marxist sectarians after Gitlin's coterie were replaced by a new "generation" of members unfamiliar with the history of Old Left anticommunism. And, finally, the early New Left's tendency to idealize third world revolutions led not only to a moral blindness to the repressive side of these revolutions, but also to an unpopular identification with America's "enemies" and a flirtation with domestic terrorism.

These weaknesses may sound familiar since we have already seen them catalogued by the renunciatory writers examined in the last chapter. In Horowitz and Collier's narratives, for example, these tendencies are claimed as sufficient grounds for renouncing the authors' earlier sixties identities outright. Gitlin responds to this by isolating and explaining the bad aspects of the generation's earlier self, so that in one sense Horowitz and Collier are correct in seeing him as "unreconstructed," even though they are wrong in their claim that his narrative is wholly lacking in irony. Something Gitlin says of Irving Howe's relationship with the New Left might just as easily be said about himself in this book: "he couldn't say anything generous about the New Left without quickly canceling it, even in the same sentence" (176). But in spite of his acknowledgment of its inherent "paradoxes and tensions," Gitlin continues to see the period of the early SDS as a golden age, and those who participated in it as a very special group. Whatever later problems arose from weaknesses in their style, the early New Left group is, in Gitlin's plot, representative of a good sixties that has to be rehabilitated from mistaken constructions of the sixties as a monolithic whole. The language he uses to describe the Old Guard that came together to write *The Port Huron Statement* verges, as he admits, on the "mawkish" (106):

> They were at once analytically keen and politically committed, but also, with a thousand gestures of affection, these unabashed moralists cared about one another. They lived as if life mattered profoundly, as if . . . you could actually take life in your hands and live it deliberately, as if it were an artwork. They seemed to live as if life were all of a piece, love and commitment indivisible. (106)

Gitlin implies that this group, in spite of their faults, would have avoided the descent into the "maelstrom" had it not been for the late sixties generation's proclivity for violence, anarchy, and hedonism.

This plotting of the generational trajectory, then, suggests that the real problems of the late sixties were the fault of younger siblings intent on leaving their older brothers and sisters behind as they charged reck-

lessly forward with their doomed "revolution." In the process of suffering that, the Old Guard underwent an ironic transformation. As Gitlin
reconstructs the process, his beloved group's "moment had passed"
(229), and their relationship with their younger siblings was beginning to
look suspiciously like their previous relationship with their own parents:
"a generation chasm was opening up within the student movement, re-
producing the one that was opening up in the wider society" (186). This
is a curious change of role for a group that conceived of itself as a vanguard for youth, but in Gitlin's retrospective view, it partially rehabilitates
the Old Guard from a past about which he clearly has mixed feelings.

Just as the annunciatory narrative conventionally ends with a prospectus
for generational action, elegiac narratives conventionally include, and
often end with, a summary of the departed generational self's legacy to
society. Maynard, conducting her post mortem on the sixties in 1973,
was still too close to the decade to offer anything more than the observation that her generation, prematurely geriatric at the time of her writing,
was simply looking for a place to which they could make their retreat.
Rossman, writing throughout the course of the seventies, identifies a
"schizogenic" legacy of authoritarianism in politics and self-indulgent
therapeutics in culture. In spite of this, he still maintains the belief in a
good sixties that contributed to American culture the necessary insight
that all aspects of life are essentially political. For Rossman, this good
sixties is embodied in the 1964 FSM, just as for Gitlin it is embodied in
the SDS of Port Huron. Harris is succinctly metonymic; the legacy of the
sixties in his book is embodied in the demons that drove Dennis Sweeney
to corner Allard Lowenstein in his office and shoot "half his heart and
lungs away" (50). Those demons, Harris suggests, are the betrayed
dreams of the generation. In place of a legacy, therefore, he includes a description of the decade's "aftermath," in which he brings the reader up-
to-date (circa 1981) on the major characters and social issues covered in
his text.

In Hayden's final chapter, however, one can see the first full-fledged
attempt to describe the sixties legacy. Among the generation's accomplishments, he lists the enfranchisement of twenty million blacks, the
government's abandonment of the Vietnam War and reconsideration of
cold war policy, the end of university paternalism, the downfall of Lyndon Johnson, the reformation of the Democratic Party, the eighteen-year-
old vote, the women's movement, and environmentalism. Gitlin followed
suit in the final chapter of his book's hardcover edition, but feeling later
that it was inadequate, he added a preface to the paperback edition that
offers a bulleted list of eight generational accomplishments. Some of
them—the enfranchisement of blacks and women, the move to end the
cold war, the end of the Vietnam War, environmentalism—echo Hay-

den's. But he also includes the change in sexual mores, the move to make authorities in all institutions accountable to their constituencies, and the continuing pursuit of ideals by sixties activists in diverse movements.

Such eulogistic conventions serve as a part of the discursive apologetic frame that positions Gitlin politically and signals his continuing belief in the generational movement despite its many grotesque mistakes. Hayden and Harris both end their narratives in the nostalgic mode, remarking that they will "miss" the sixties; Gitlin ends his in the hortative: "'It was not granted you to complete the task,' said Rabbi Tarfon nineteen hundred years ago, 'and yet you may not give it up'" (438). Given the ambivalence that marks most of the pages of his memoir, the reader may be pardoned for wondering just what that task is and how Gitlin thinks the generation should now pursue it.

Epilogue: Autobiography as Generational Dialogue

In 1997, when I first sat down to write this epilogue, my mother had just finished celebrating her seventieth birthday. As a surprise gift for her, my sister Theresa had written to dozens of people whose lives had crossed my mother's requesting a short account of their relationship with her. They were people whose contact with her had spanned her entire life—from her childhood and youth in England, through the war years and her marriage to a young American soldier, through her adaptation to life in the American Midwest and the raising of a large family, through her later move to California and new beginnings there. The resulting volume, composed of almost a hundred pages of memories about her written by others, was an impressive, and perhaps overwhelming, anecdotal and expository account of the impact she had had on the world in which she lived. Listening to her talk about it, I was struck by the thought that perhaps autobiography should more often be constructed in this way, communally and dialogically, and that the voice of the subject should be but one of many voices contributing to the conversation. After all, there are so many areas of our lives and our characters that others seem to know far better than we do ourselves, and perhaps identity is always more truly the product of communal rather than individual invention.

However desirable such dialogical autobiography may be for individuals, it is indispensable for the kind of collective identity that has been the subject of this book. Collective identity is always a relationship, a conversation among those who feel themselves a part of it. It must be spoken and willed by those people before it can exist. One of the things that this book has argued is that generational identity, if it can be said to exist at all, exists only within the kind of dialogue I have reconstructed across and between autobiographical texts. In that sense, my book has something in common with the works that it has examined, for not only have I surveyed the form of this dialogue, but in my comments on each text I have also contributed my own voice to it. For that reason, I should perhaps say something about my relationship to this generation and to these writers. I was born in 1949, just three years after the beginning of the baby boom, so I am younger than every writer I treat here, with the exception of Joyce Maynard, whose complaint about her own tardy birth had my sympathy in 1973, when I first read her. Having been raised in evangelical Protestant churches whose narrow pietism insisted upon the believer's complete removal from secular concerns, my initial reaction to the public attitudes of the "sixties generation" was not entirely positive. In 1968, however, I began to change my mind as both the absurdity and the tragedy of the Vietnam War became, to me, inescapably transparent. Over the course of that eventful year, I began to suspect that the contradiction inherent in my co-religionists' denunciation of secularism and simultaneous celebration of American militarism no longer deserved my allegiance. Partly as a result of that, I experienced in my nineteenth year what I have discussed in this book as a conversion; in my case, it was a conversion from the pietistic belief that meaning resides only in transcendent Truth to the secularist belief that meaning emerges from one's active engagement with the issues of one's times. In that belief lies the genesis of this book, for like many members of my immediate cohort— too young to have been present at the founding events of the generational moment and yet too old to have already adopted Maynard's valedictory attitude—I fell willing victim to the then widespread anxiety about where the train of generational history was going and whether or not I might not be on it. Many of the texts I have talked about in this book played a significant role in my attempts to keep up with the way stations on that train's trajectory through time, and, as such, my relationship with them is a personal one. But I also think that the attitudes and ideas that they represent were widespread and typical of many people who grew up during those years. For that reason, if not for specifically literary ones, each of these books has value. Eventually, as everyone knows, the notion of generational history as purposive and teleological lost its currency, for the rails it rode upon, like the concept of the generation itself, depended upon a kind of collective fantasy. By the mid-1970s, a good many people, myself included, found themselves floating in mid-air, the historicist fiction having proven to be a kind of ghost train. But however ill-founded that idea was, the issues of identity, politics, and values that confronted the people who came of age during that period, and which informed the dialogue between these autobiographers, persisted and continues to persist to this day.

Something else in the experience of moving from evangelical Protestantism to the secularist historicism of the sixties helped to prepare me for the writing of this book and had a strong influence on its method. One of the most conspicuous elements of American evangelicalism is the formulaic conversion tale, adopted and modified by generation after generation of born-again believers. Growing up among these stories, I had an excellent opportunity to witness at first hand people who suddenly found dramatic meaning in their lives by adopting the life plot offered by the church. Whatever truth or reality there might be in the act of grace that is said to accompany religious conversion, it always seemed to me that the most impressive power operating on the new believer was the power of a story to give shape to a person's existence. And of course not just any story could perform this function: the story had to be the same one that had been shared by thousands of millions of people over the history of Christian culture. As the refrain of an old gospel hymn has it: "Once I was lost, but now I am found. Once I was blind, but now I see." What has been "found" in these cases, it seems to me, is a satisfying story. What is "seen" is a coherent plot that explains the confusions and errors of the past and provides a morally satisfying and happy outcome. Long before I ever read any narrative psychology or looked into constructionist theory, then, I had grown accustomed to the idea of the "narrative construction of meaning."

Almost as soon as I immersed myself in the literature and culture of the Movement, I recognized the same stories and plots at work again. In fact, as this book has demonstrated, and as many writers before me have recognized, leftist conversions, both in terms of plot construction and rhetoric, bear a remarkable resemblance to those experienced by the religious right. At first that similarity struck me as grounds for skepticism, since I had the natural reaction of thinking that what I was seeing and experiencing was "the same old story." Eventually, in fact, that skepticism became more or less habitual and explains what I take to be my general stance toward most of the writers in this book. I do not see myself as an advocate for the sixties, nor for the politics of any of the writers I discuss here, though I do confess to a sympathy for some of their ideas (left, right, and elsewhere) and to a profound identification with the issues that they address. The skepticism also eventually led me to stop thinking about my own transformation as a conversion at all, as I began to see more continuity than difference between the two periods of my life. It didn't take me long, however, to notice something in the secular world that was lacking in the narrow religious one that I had left. In the secular world, many more kinds of life plots were available and fewer people seemed to be certain that any one story explained everything. I liked that heterogeneity, and I also liked the way in which stories in the secular world live in uncomfortable competition with one another. In the writing of this book, I have had an enlightening opportunity to examine more closely some of the jostling plots that members of my generation have adopted to explain our "self" to ourselves.

Like many of the authors whose texts I have examined in this book, I should perhaps end by apologizing for not having been sufficiently inclusive. I have an advantage over my authors, however, since I have limited myself to a descriptive and critical reading of selected works within an autobiographical tradition, while they sought, much more ambitiously, to construct a generational identity.

This book has reviewed many kinds of generational autobiographies: the generational manifesto of SDS; the generational advertisements of Abbie Hoffman and Jerry Rubin; the windows-in-time narratives of Michael Rossman and Julius Lester; the conversion narratives of Raymond Mungo, Peter Collier, and David Horowitz; the renunciatory narratives of Dotson Rader, Jane Alpert, and Martha Bayles; the generational elegies of Joyce Maynard, Tom Hayden, and Todd Gitlin. But the books I have examined by no means exhaust the range of autobiographical works that attempt to construct the sixties generation. They do not include, for example, this age group's self-portraiture in other media (such as television, magazine and newspaper articles, theater, painting, or films), nor do they include much of the work produced by members of other age groups about the sixties narrative. Naturally, a full account of the autobiographical work generated by the cohort born between 1935 and 1955 would take as many of these into consideration as possible. Such an extensive work, however, lay outside the scope of my intention here, which has been to demonstrate that the process of generation construction has contributed to the development of a distinctive tradition of autobiography.

This tradition has several salient features, but there are two that stand out from the rest. First, the works in this tradition all construct identities that are collective rather than individualized. In this respect, they represent a radical departure both from mainstream autobiography, which conventionally emphasizes an author's individual identity, and from popular myths about American character, which insist on the ideal of individualism. The second feature is perhaps the inevitable outgrowth of the first: no single work within the tradition can be fully understood or appreciated outside of the larger intertextual dialogue to which it contributes. All books, of course, are engaged in dialogue with other texts, but critics, tending to grant autobiographers dominion over their own identities and narratives, have often ignored the degree to which negotiation and compromise are central facets of autobiography. In generational autobiographies, the illusion of self-possession is more difficult, if not impossible, to maintain. The works I have examined here have from the beginning offered their version of the collective self as a construction. The authors of *The Port Huron Statement*, which opened the dialogue, defined the manifesto and their intentions in precisely these terms. It is a "living document," they wrote, "open to change with our times and experiences. It is a beginning: in our own debate and education, in our dialogue with society."[1] Even when these autobiographers aggressively assert a generational identity, they do so with an eye to its possible detractors and challengers. More often than not, they engage in a kind of anticipatory negotiation with other generational voices within the body of their own texts.

The autobiographical dialogue that was constructed by people born between 1935 and 1955, as we have seen, breaks down into three overlapping phases or modes of generational writing. Works that appeared between 1960 and 1971—in the midst of the generation's coming-of-age—were highly politicized, "annunciatory" works. In the Students for a Democratic Society's *The Port Huron Statement* (1962), Abbie Hoffman's *Revolution for the Hell of It* (1968), Jerry Rubin's *Do It!* (1970) and *We Are Everywhere* (1971), Tom Hayden's *Trial* (1970), or Michael Rossman's *The Wedding within the War* (1971), the collective self is announced, celebrated, advertised, mythified, and launched on its historical path. These early manifesto writers address themselves both to the previous generation, whose model of identity they reject first in confrontational and, finally, in apocalyptic tones, and to other members of their own age group, to whom they offer themselves as an elite that can guide and direct the generation as it seeks to fulfill its historical destiny.

After 1969, the year that almost all obituary writers of this age group mark as the end of the generational heyday, two new kinds of autobiography joined the dialogue. In the first kind, writers turn their attention away from the previous generation in order to engage themselves in various intragenerational arguments over identity. In general, these autobiographers are no less polemical than the annunciatory writers, but they address themselves much more actively to their peers. Their narrative stance expresses itself in reactive autobiographical modes: narratives of renunciation or conversion that provide a literary vehicle for the eradication of the author's earlier generational identity. Like the narrators of older Christian conversion stories, these modern narrators have embraced a new faith that provides a vantage point from which the errors of the old generational self may be reconstructed, judged, and condemned. The narrators in Raymond Mungo's *Famous Long Ago* (1970) and *Total Loss Farm* (1970) are of this type, as are the later narrators of Collier and Horowitz's *Destructive Generation* (1989). The narrator of the renunciation narrative, on the other hand, simply renounces the old self without the benefit of a wholly rejuvenating new faith. The narrators in Dotson Rader's *I Ain't Marchin' Anymore!* (1969) and *Blood Dues* (1973) and Jane Alpert's *Growing Up Underground* (1981) remain obsessed by an old generational self even as they enact their repudiation of it.

The latest voices in this generational dialogue are characterized by the elegiac mode. Although Joyce Maynard's precocious (and historically premature) *Looking Back* (1972) marks the first appearance of this mode, its most characteristic productions did not emerge until the end of the seventies. The narrators of Michael Rossman's *New Age Blues* (1979), David Harris' *Dreams Die Hard* (1982), Todd Gitlin's *The Sixties* (1987), and Tom Hayden's *Reunion* (1988) all indicate that the stance achieved in their books has required the passage of time. These narrators also tend to be more individualized than those of the earlier works, often constructing themselves as survivors of a generational diaspora. Although they have abandoned notions of themselves as members of a generational vanguard, they maintain their representative self-constructions by putting themselves forward as typical children of the Zeitgeist. Their focus now is memorial, or even eulogistic, even though some of them still employ the apologetic mode to respond, usually indirectly, to reactive texts written by their converted peers. Their tone is often nostalgic, marked by wistfulness and melancholy, in spite of their chastened knowledge that the younger self's moral certitude often disguised a retrospectively unattractive arrogance. The overt intention of such authors, therefore, is to achieve a detached understanding of the generational experience.

A number of observations can be made about this autobiographical dialogue, with its characteristic announcements, alliances, repudiations, and feuds. First, it takes place among persons who put themselves forward as representatives of the generation, either as typical members of the generational mass or as members of a generational elite. Second, all of these autobiographers engage with other autobiographers and potential representatives in a struggle to control public discourse over generational identity. Although this struggle initially took shape primarily in the form of an intergenerational argument, by the 1980s it had reshaped itself as an intragenerational dispute. Writers like Collier and Horowitz, intent on fixing the generational identity and its narrative in the most negative light possible, applied cold war mythologies to the sixties-generation narrative in ways that would justify President Reagan's international and domestic policies, while writers like Gitlin and Hayden took the opposite tack, and often did so in order to support their own positions on those same policies. And finally, the self in these autobiographies is, by dint of its collective nature, its utility as a tool in identity politics, and its frequent revisionings, an overt and negotiable product of communal construction.

The generational autobiographers' conviction that their own stories are *the* story of the generation is already visible in Bourne's and Ortega's notion that the generational elite interprets the spirit of the times, characterizes the generational identity, and leads the generational mass. Occasionally, such autobiographers qualify their efforts by vacillating between the construction of a collective identity and nagging doubts about their right to represent that identity. Joyce Maynard, for example, disclaims the very task she has set out to accomplish: "I should perhaps temper my statements with apologies, for saying 'we' all through this book, when there are so many people I've no right to speak for (where are the blacks? the teen-age dropouts? the people of my generation who read— really read—books? I cannot speak for them). . . . Ten years cannot be summed up; a generation can't be generalized about."[2] But such disclaimers are, as we have seen in several cases, at least partially disingenuous, for Maynard's book, like those of all generational autobiographers, is fundamentally grounded in an effort to convince its readers of the representative status of its author.

One can, however, detect a distinct falling off in these claims of representativeness over the course of the dialogue. In annunciatory narratives, such claims are as pervasive (though often implicit) as the political agenda that dominates the surface of the texts. The authors of *The Port Huron Statement* can begin with the assertion that "we are the people of this generation" without having to devote textual space to those who may think themselves inadequately represented by the writers of that document. In reactive and elegiac narratives, on the other hand, disclaimers such as Maynard's become more common as the authors demonstrate an increasing uncertainty about the possibility of a coherent "we." A comparison between the first and second autobiographical works of Michael Rossman provides a telling example of such a shift. In the first, *The Wedding within the War* (1971), Rossman aggressively speaks of the Movement as the vanguard of the generation, claiming that it "had become a presence, forcing all the young to begin in some way to define themselves with respect to it." But at the end of the seventies, he prefaces the essays that make up *New Age Blues* (1979) by saying that unlike the first book, whose ideas he took to be "in fair part the product of many minds and people," this one "has been lonely—for this decade has left me, like many others, more alone than I would like to be to shape my understanding from its conflicting evidences."[3] In large part, of course, this falling off of claims to representative status merely reflects the development of differences within the group as its external political goals were met.

In Chapter 2, I argued that Cowley's use of the generational idea inevitably led to an autobiographical form that was both a bid for control of generational identity and an invitation to polemic. The same is true of later generational autobiographies. All of the sixties-generation autobiographers in this tradition were either members of the New Left and the counterculture or heavily influenced by these movements. In spite of the fact that the majority of them were white, male, and middle-class, the generational self they defined was often characterized both by a consciousness of its own exclusion from public discourse and by its own kind of exclusiveness. For example, when Jerry Rubin titled one of his early generational works *We Are Everywhere*, it was understood that the generational "we" to which the title referred comprised alienated youths who were besieging an establishment controlled by their elders; at the same time, however, that ubiquitous "we" did not include the American soldier in Vietnam, even if he did belong to Rubin's age group.

By firing off the first autobiographical annunciations of generational identity, early Movement writers like Rubin sought to determine who would carry the moral banner of youth. It was not until the mid-seventies that the excluded groups began to construct their own autobiographical narrative. After 1975, for example, there appeared a profusion of memoirs written by Vietnam War veterans that reflect their authors' awareness of an audience familiar with the moral outlines of an already existing narrative in which the veteran is assigned the role of generational Other, the excluded brother who too readily conformed to parental expectations.[4] Frederick Downs' memoir *The Killing Zone* (1978) is typical when it begins with an account of the narrator's return to the United States after his tour of duty in Vietnam. Walking across a university campus on his way to class, he is stopped by a peer who asks him how he lost his arm. When Downs replies that he lost it fighting "up near Tam Ky in I Corps," his questioner tells him that it serves him right. Downs' book, written ten years after that encounter, is the result of his feeling that "it is necessary now to give another view of Vietnam, that of the day-to-day life of an infantryman on the ground."[5] What he means by this, as his narrative reveals, is not that he really wants us to see *Vietnam* in another light, but that he wants us to see the generational subgroup comprising American soldiers who fought there in another light. And in this, he typifies other Vietnam War memoirists. The one motive that unifies them, even when they differ widely on the political meaning of the war, is the desire to take back their identity both from other writers of their own generation and from anyone who presumes to speak of or for them, much as Karl Pretshold had tried to do in his argument with Malcolm Cowley almost half a century earlier.

Ron Kovic's *Born on the Fourth of July* (1976) offers a more complicated instance of this motive. For Downs, the reclaiming of the veterans' identity stops at showing that the soldiers were heroes in the specific context of combat, whatever the political and moral value of the war itself. Kovic's book, on the other hand, reveals how the veterans were caught in a rhetorical crossfire over the soldiers' identity. The Movement had demonized them; the older generation had cast them as heroes. On the surface, Kovic's book appears to be directed mainly at the older generation, rather than at other members of his own age group. In one revealing scene, the paraplegic Kovic and another veteran attend a Memorial Day parade at the request of officials in their hometown. Listening to these officials make speeches about him, Kovic grasps how his identity as an American hero is being constructed for him by his elders, who have a stake in seeing veterans in that role. It is a role that confirms their support for the war and their vision—determined largely by their own generational experience—of a world in which the forces of democracy and goodness are engaged in a Manichaean struggle with the forces of communism and evil. Kovic becomes aware at the same time that he can accept that self-construction only at the cost of suppressing his "real" self, with its overwhelming sense of anger and loss. The awareness leads him to reject his hero status and to reassert his own voice:

> These people had never been to his war, and they had been talking like they knew everything, like they were experts on the whole goddamn thing, like he and Eddie didn't know how to speak for themselves because there was something wrong now with both of them. They couldn't speak because of the war and had to have others define for them with their lovely words what they didn't know anything about.[6]

Books like *Born on the Fourth of July* are often, at least in part, a response to precisely this feeling. Their authors want to define themselves to the world in their own terms and to shake off the terms imposed on them by their parents.

Although Kovic avoids the pitfall of this parentally imposed self, he seems to have fallen victim to another. For much of the book's pathos results from Kovic's having come to accept implicitly his contemporaries' (that is, the Movement's) explanation of his experience; his narrative is pervaded by self-loathing, and some of the central events in the narrative actually confirm the Movement stereotype of the Vietnam soldier as baby killer. Although the older generation cannot speak for Kovic, he readily recognizes himself in the words of another returned Vietnam veteran, Charlie, who screams out in a drunken rage, "They made me kill babies! They made me kill babies!" (125). Charlie's words, Kovic says, expressed what he "had been feeling for a long time" (126). One senses, in fact, that Kovic doesn't manage to find his own voice until the narrative's final sections, in which he speaks fully, for the first time, of his involvement in the killing of Vietnamese civilians and children. As a rehabilitative strategy, therefore, Kovic must cast himself first as a victim—someone to whom history has "happened"—in order to become an active member of what he takes to be his generation's political vanguard, the antiwar movement. Even after becoming an activist, however, Kovic continues to see himself as victim, as one can see in the way he characterizes his presence at the 1972 Republican National Convention in Miami:

> This was the moment I had come three thousand miles for, this was it, all the pain and the rage, all the trials and the death of the war and what had been done to me and a generation of Americans by all the men who had lied to us and tricked us, by the man [Nixon] who stood before us in the convention hall that night, while men who had fought for their country were being gassed and beaten in the street outside the hall. (182–83)

In spite of Kovic's final acceptance of the antiwar movement's assessment of the soldiers' morality, he does not articulate a clear political agenda, for the narrative focuses exclusively on the destruction of the cultural myths that provided its author with meaning in the past. In this Kovic has much in common with other veteran memoirists, for over and over in their memoirs, the narrators recount their youthful fascination with John Wayne and Audie Murphy war movies and with the various patriotic myths that these films were intended to evoke—of America as a country with unimpeachable ideals and pure intentions, of American soldiers as romantic heroes of democracy, and of war as a glorious sport in which young men could assert and prove their manhood. And over and over, the narrators write of the collapse of one or more of these myths in the face of actual experience. Given that disillusionment, Kovic and many other veteran memoirists have much in common with the authors of autobiographies of renunciation. Like them, he recounts the destruction of his own younger self and its validating myths, and like them, he is left without a clearly enunciated set of alternative values or any blueprint for constructing a future self. One result of this failure to articulate an ideology around which a future self might be constructed is that Kovic's and other veterans' memoirs only occasionally move beyond an account of victimization to address the author's place in the larger generational and national narrative. Because of this, veterans' memoirs are only marginally, though powerfully, involved in the generational dialogue.

Besides excluding Vietnam soldiers and veterans, early attempts to construct the generational self also largely excluded women. The struggle over generational identity in the 1960s and early 1970s was carried out primarily by men who, on both the right and the left of the political spectrum, ignored the gender bias of narratives that constructed the generational war as a struggle between fathers and sons. The growth of the women's movement in the early 1970s was partly the result of an awareness of a gap between the egalitarian rhetoric of male New Leftists and their treatment of the women within their own ranks. The subsequent development of group consciousness among women produced the need to define themselves in their own terms, and an outpouring of women's writing devoted to this end ensued. Their primary group identification, however, was usually not the generation (there were only a few female writers in the later stages of this group's generational dialogue), but *all women*, past, present, and future.[7]

Besides their common reliance upon generationalism for their concept of a collective self, then, these later autobiographies have in common with Cowley's an ambivalent relation to power that derives both from their sense that the powerless (with whom they identify) are morally superior to the powerful and from their often unarticulated desire to attain power at the expense of their rivals. All of their texts are ostensibly about selves excluded from power; all of them are at the same time efforts to attain power by advancing their own narratives as *the* narrative of the generational self;[8] and all of them attempt to exclude other, often weaker, selves within the generation by omitting them from the generational narrative or by rejecting them as unrepresentative.

The rejection of other selves as unrepresentative is so pervasive among generational writers that they often practice it, as we have seen in Chapter 4, on their own former selves. Cowley's two editions of *Exile's Return* again provide the first example of such self-revision. That author's dismissal of Karl Pretshold in the 1934 edition of his generational autobiography was followed up in the 1951 revision by the complete erasure of Pretshold and the generational narrative he represented. What Cowley did to Pretshold, however, he also did to portions of his earlier version of his own self. Following anticommunist harassment during the 1940s and the failure of his own proletarian fantasies, Cowley removed all trace of his Marxist conversion from the 1951 narrative. For the sixties generation, such revisions are common, though the rejection of a former self is carried out more often through reactive sequels than through simple erasure or textual revisions. Rader's *Blood Dues* and Mungo's *Total Loss Farm* each represents not merely an update of the collective narrative, but a renunciation of the author's first formulation of generational identity in an earlier text. In Rader's case, the sequel rejects the radical politics of the first text without clearly defining the character of the author's new self. Mungo's second text, however, not only denounces the author's earlier radical politics, but clearly outlines his movement toward an even more thorough rejection of the identities available in the mainstream culture.

This malleability of the collective self in all generational autobiographies serves not only to undermine the assumption that autobiography is dependent upon the concept of the individualized self; it also practically ensures that generational authors acknowledge the self's artifactual nature. Anyone who presumes to construct an autobiographical "we" does so fully conscious that it will be contested by others who have a stake in it. If those who take issue possess power or, perhaps more important, access to publishers, they will construct another version of the generational narrative that will be advantageous to their own position. Autobiographical maneuvering of this sort highlights the self's political and social construction in a way that is rarely found in individualist works. In this book, we have seen this dialogue in operation among members of two American generations. For all of these writers, generational autobiography is an instrument in the struggle to control collective memory of the past and present. For most of them, controlling collective memory is also a means of directing the social and political future of their culture.

I began this book by calling into question the belief that the individual self is one of the constitutive principles of autobiography. By now, I hope it is clear that the radical revisioning of the self in the works I have surveyed here has some far-reaching implications for the genre. I have already stated what that relevance might be for theories that make individuality the sine qua non of American autobiography. Generational autobiography is also relevant, however, to theories that assert that the primary distinction between male- and female-authored autobiographies lies in the latter's inclusion of the "other" in the autobiographer's conception of the self.[9] Most of the autobiographies examined in this book are written by young men, and all of them manifest a remarkably fluid notion of the boundaries between self and other. This may suggest that emphasis on individuality is as age-dependent as it is gender-dependent. Or, since most of the autobiographies considered here were written by persons with leftist political inclinations, it may suggest that political orientation is an important factor. Or finally, it may suggest that one's status in the world is the determining factor since marginality and powerlessness also characterize many of these writers' self-constructions. Any or all of these may be as important as gender in influencing a writer's attitude toward the role of others in his or her sense of identity.

In any case, the orientation of generational autobiography toward communal dialogue demonstrates the soundness of what theorists in the fields of social constructivism and narrative psychology have been saying for some time: whatever may be the case with temperament or character, *identity* is not innate or god-given, nor is it the product of individual genius. It is, rather, socially or collectively constructed, and its most fundamental manifestations are to be found in the kinds of stories we tell about ourselves to each other. Not even Jean-Jacques Rousseau, who called modern Romantic and individualistic autobiography into being by insisting on his uniqueness, actually produces an autonomous self in his *Confessions*. Rousseau's text everywhere demonstrates the author's consciousness that his identity is a contested one and that he must enter into dialogue with others if he hopes to have any control over its construction. Nowhere is this more obvious than in the book's final pages. In a scene that is emblematic of Rousseau's fantasy of self-determination, the author describes himself reading a copy of his just completed manuscript to a group of listeners. When he finishes, they react with an awkward silence that poignantly confirms the author's wish that his narrative will render his readers (and his detractors) speechless.[10] Most autobiographies are just such attempts to forestall alternative constructions of the autobiographer's self; they share Rousseau's candidly confessed desire that those who espouse variant readings of the author's self be "stifled." But, in fact, such wishes are compromised from the outset. Everything autobiographers say about themselves is already conditioned by what others have said before, by the voices and narratives already in existence concerning the author's self, and by what Jerome Bruner calls the "canons" of self-writing. These shared canons, he argues, determine what does and what does not make for viable identity narratives within a given culture: "even our individual autobiographies . . . depend on being placed within a continuity provided by a constructed and shared social history in which we locate our Selves and our individual continuities. It is a sense of belonging to this canonical past that permits us to form our own narratives of deviation while maintaining complicity with the canon."[11]

Generational autobiographies are frequently explicit about this process and context. Because of this, no group of autobiographies more clearly demonstrates the arguments of constructivists about the social nature of identity narratives. As Mary and Kenneth Gergen have contended, the stories individuals tell in order to make sense of their experiences "are inherently a product not of individuals but of interacting persons."[12] When individuals construct their life stories, they inevitably make reference to other individuals with whom they have relationships. "Others' actions," the Gergens assert, "contribute vitally to the events to be linked in narrative sequence." But just as the

> individual feels that he or she has priority in self-definition, others also feel themselves to have primary jurisdiction over the definition of their own actions. Thus one's understanding of the supporting role played by another cannot easily proceed without the acquiescence of the other. If others are not willing to accede to their assigned parts, then one can ill afford to rely on their actions within a narrative. (186)

When individuals are in conflict over a narrative, "who gains superiority, in what manner, and for what purpose become paramount. . . . In any case, the emerging reality is a joint or communal product" (184). Such observations about an individual's self-narrative are doubly true of the collectivized narrative I have looked at in this book, where not a single text, but batteries of texts have been written to contest a group identity. If the "supporting cast" in an individual's self-narrative must acquiesce in order for the narrative to have legitimacy, that is even more certain of the cast making up a narrative of collective identity. In generational autobiographies, the legitimacy of the collective self requires not only the cooperation of narrative "others," but even more important, it demands the cooperation of the individuals who constitute the group itself. When that cooperation is not forthcoming, as in the case of disputes between unreconstructed Movement writers and their neoconservative rivals, generational autobiographers, as we have seen, employ various strategies to negotiate the problem. They may, for example, feign abandonment of the collective narrative altogether (e.g., "we of the sixties generation mistakenly believed that there was a sixties generation"); they may incorporate aspects of the challenge offered by noncooperative members (e.g., "the sixties generation did overreact to the repression of the establishment, but their intentions were above reproach"); they may deny the truthfulness of dissenting versions of the collective narrative (e.g., "our detractors are distorting the past for their own political ends"); they may deny the authenticity of the dissenter's membership in the collective (e.g., "our rivals possess the generational mind-set of cold war warriors"); they may try to demonstrate the greater viability of their version of the collective self (e.g., "statistics show that few people who identified with Movement values during the sixties later abandoned them for economic security"); and so on.

The autobiographies I have examined in this book not only clarify the communal and dialogical construction of identity narratives; they also make clear the way in which these narratives are given cultural coherence. Every historian is familiar with George Santayana's famous caveat "Those who cannot remember the past are condemned to fulfil it," and most lay readers are familiar with this caveat in its more popular form: "Those who forget the past are condemned to repeat it."[13] If anything, however, the texts examined in this study suggest that the opposite is true, for they have shown that those persons most familiar with the past are precisely the ones most likely to repeat it when they attempt to provide a narrative of their own lives. Almost all of the authors treated in this book construct their lives and times by borrowing their plots and characters from earlier narratives. Some of these earlier narratives are very old. For the annunciatory writers of Chapter 3, for example, the sixties narrative begins with the betrayal of youthful idealism and energy by the settled cynicism and compromise of adult institutions. That plot has respectable roots, already visible in Hamlet's disgust with his mother's unprincipled alliance with the scheming Claudius, but it is the central element of many Romantic narratives, which contrast the vibrancy and godliness of youth with the faded expectations and diminished idealism of adult society. It was also, as we have seen, the underlying plot of several popular films about youthful rebellion in the fifties. Situating themselves in this plot, it is no wonder that the sixties generation rebelled. All of the reactive narratives examined in Chapter 4 owe much to the long tradition of the conversion narrative, beginning with Saint Paul and Saint Augustine and evolving through John Bunyan's *Grace Abounding*. For such autobiographers, the conversion of Saul on the road to Damascus is a figure of almost universal applicability. Looking back on the sixties with this plot in mind, these autobiographers find that the road to the 1970s was a road leading to perdition. One after another they are struck to the ground by the sobering realization that they have sinned greatly, that they stand in need of repentance, and that they must be born again. The elegiac narrators of Chapter 5 invoke a variety of older plots. In 1980, David Harris characterizes the problem he and his generation face as they look back at the sixties by alluding to the story of God's warning to Lot that he must not look back at the past. Identifying himself with those who would look back, Harris is aware that to break the taboo is to elicit the damnation of the regnant gods of culture. Nonetheless, his narrative affirms that such a backward glance is necessary, even if painful, if the generation is ever to understand its present situation. For Tom Hayden, by contrast, the return to the nuclear family and its ideals after a period of intergenerational feuding and failed communication represents a variation on another biblical tale, the narrative of the prodigal son's return. To him, the sixties were a period of error for both fathers *and* sons, and the eighties are a time for reconciliation and fresh beginnings.

Other sixties narratives have more recent plot antecedents. Raymond Mungo's conversion narratives, for example, rely heavily on Henry David Thoreau's writings, to construct the tale of his generation's return to a simple life in the woods. Jane Alpert's renunciatory autobiography provides an example of multiple plot and character imitations. The younger self she constructs in her narrative thought she was living her life in imitation of the strong heroines of Ayn Rand's novels, but Alpert reconstructs that character (à la Freud) as a weak and misguided child seeking and resisting paternal authority and approval. David Horowitz and Peter Collier's conversion narratives of the eighties similarly borrow their generational plot from the confessions of Whittaker Chambers and Louis Budenz, repentant ex-communists of the forties and fifties. While Horowitz and Collier believe that the sixties generation was doomed to repeat the sins of the thirties generation because of their ignorance of the past, one might equally argue that Horowitz and Collier, mesmerized by Chambers' plot, impose its Manichaean simplicities on their sixties narrative without recognizing the ways in which the two periods and groups differ. Looking for a plot with somewhat more sympathy for the "revolutionaries," Todd Gitlin goes further back in time than his neoconservative detractors. In this elegiac book, the inevitable, understandable, and lamentable outcome of the sixties narrative is an echo of the denouement of Charles Dickens' version of the French Revolution in *A Tale of Two Cities*.

The implications of such borrowings and repetitions are suggestive. Santayana's caveat notwithstanding, the past is, of course, literally unrepeatable. However, if we look at history not as what "really happened in the past," but as a narrative interpretation of past events, then we can begin to determine not only the conventions that govern these narratives, but also the kinds of narratives that are available to writers in the first place. Social constructivists argue that viable autobiographical plots are limited in number. As Jerome Bruner writes,

> one important way of characterizing a culture is by the narrative models it makes available for describing the course of a life. And the tool kit of any culture is replete not only with a stock of canonical life narratives (heroes,

Marthas, tricksters, etc.), but with combinable formal constituents from which its members can construct their own life narratives. . . .[14]

If the kinds of plots we can impose on experience are limited in number, those who write history will inevitably repeat already existing plots, recycled with new characters and new settings and new historical circumstances. We are bound, in other words, by the limited fund of viable plots to an eternal repetition of the past. While this might seem depressing, in practice neither autobiographers nor their readers appear to find it so. On the contrary, it is the repetition itself that renders narrative events recognizably human and that allows writers and their readers to make sense of the disorder of real experience. It means that one's life is *not* unique, but shared and directed by universal patterns toward meaningful ends.

The construction of generational autobiography, as we have seen it here, is carried out by individuals whose narratives compete with each other to fix the generation's identity and its place in the world. What is at stake in this struggle, of course, is not merely the past itself, but the valuation of the present and the proper resolution of the issues that define it. When these authors consciously or unconsciously construct the sixties plot out of older, more familiar stories— the culture's "stock of canonical life narratives"—they draw upon the cultural weight of the latter to shape the ways in which present-day readers both see the sixties and apply its lessons to the conduct of the present moment.

Notes
Bibliography
Index

Notes

Chapter 1. Generationalism and Collective Autobiography

1. The phrases "coming-of-age experience" and "generational experience" will be used interchangeably in this book. They refer to that stage of psychosocial development immediately following adolescence. In *Youth and Dissent: The Rise of a New Opposition* (New York: Harcourt, 1960), Kenneth Kenniston refers to the same group as "youth" (156–58). Like the writers I will examine, Erikson's study group was largely middle-class, white, and American. See his *Life History and the Historical Moment* (New York: Norton, 1975), 193–224.

2. Robert Sayre's suggestion that American autobiographers in the twentieth century could most usefully be approached from the perspective of their generational affiliation has been largely ignored. See his "The Proper Study—Autobiography in American Studies," *American Quarterly* 29 (1977): 254.

3. Susan Stanford Friedman, "Women's Autobiographical Selves: Theory and Practice," in *The Private Self: Theory and Practice of Women's Autobiographical Writings*, ed. Shari Benstock (Chapel Hill: U of North Carolina P, 1988), 34–35.

4. Karl Joachim Weintraub, *The Value of the Individual: Self and Circumstance in Autobiography* (Chicago: U of Chicago P, 1978).

5. Robert Wohl, *The Generation of 1914* (Cambridge: Harvard UP, 1979), 210. Wohl's book provides a useful summary of European generationalism in the early part of this century. Subsequent citations will be noted parenthetically.

6. Annie Kriegel, "Generational Difference: The History of an Idea," *Daedalus* 107 (Fall 1978): 23–38.

7. See Bennett M. Berger, "How Long Is a Generation?" *Looking for America: Essays on Youth, Suburbia, and Other American Obsessions* (Englewood Cliffs: Prentice-Hall, 1971), 20–37; Michael X. Delli Carpini, *Stability and Change in American Politics: The Coming of Age of the Generation of the 1960s* (New York: New York UP, 1986); Hans Jaeger, "Generations in History: Reflections on a Controversial Concept," *History and Theory: Studies in the Philosophy of History* 24 (1985): 273–92; M. Kent Jennings and Richard G. Niemi, *Generations and Politics* (Princeton: Princeton UP, 1981); T. Allen Lambert, "Generations and Change: Toward a Theory of Generations as a Force in Historical Processes," *Youth and Society* 4 (Sept. 1972): 21–46; Robert S. Laufer, "Sources of Generational Consciousness and Conflict," in *The New Pilgrims*, ed.

Philip G. Altbach and Robert S. Laufer (New York: David McKay, 1972), 218–37; Karl Mannheim, "The Problem of the Generation," in *Essays in the Sociology of Knowledge,* ed. Paul Kecskemeti (London: Routledge & Kegan Paul, 1959), 276–320; Julián Marías, *Generations: A Historical Method,* trans. Harold C. Riley (Mobile: U of Alabama P, 1970); Alan Spitzer, "The Historical Problem of Generations," *American Historical Review* 78 (1973): 1359–85.

8. See Paula Fass, *The Damned and the Beautiful: American Youth in the 1920's* (New York: Oxford UP, 1977), 1–51, 361, 487.

9. Wohl, 201–8; Marías, 18–68.

10. Quoted by Malcolm Cowley in *—And I Worked at the Writer's Trade: Chapters of Literary History, 1918–1978* (New York: Viking, 1979), 6.

11. Randolph Bourne, *Youth and Life* (Cambridge, MA: Riverside, 1913), 1–53.

12. Bourne, 12–13. See also Waldo Frank's *Our America* (New York: Liveright, 1919); Van Wyck Brooks' "Young America," *Letters and Literature* (New York: Huebsch, 1918) and "On Creating a Usable Past," *Dial,* April 11, 1918. Brooks and Frank do not outline a generational theory, but their work during this period is characterized by the generational thinking that was typical of the group in which Bourne played a leading role.

13. Bourne, 13.

14. For a discussion of primitive notions of time and reality, see Mircea Eliade, *The Myth of the Eternal Return, or, Cosmos and History* (Princeton: Princeton UP, 1954), 85–92.

15. Michael Rossman, *The Wedding within the War* (New York: Doubleday, 1971), 69.

16. Dotson Rader, *Blood Dues* (New York: Knopf, 1973), 106.

17. David Harris, *Dreams Die Hard: Three Men's Journey through the Sixties* (New York: St. Martin's/Marek, 1982), 142–43.

18. José Ortega y Gasset, *The Modern Theme,* trans. James Cleugh (New York: Harper & Row, 1961), 14–15. Subsequent citations will be noted parenthetically. This book was originally published in Spanish under the title *El tema de nuestro tiempo* in 1923; it was translated into English and published by Daniels in London in 1931.

19. José Ortega y Gasset, *Man and Crisis,* trans. Mildred Adams (New York: Norton, 1958), 42–45. This book was originally published in Spanish under the title *En torno a Galileo* in 1933.

20. Mannheim, 307.

21. The fact that large generational movements became popular in the twentieth century further confirms Patricia Spacks' observation that "stormy adolescence itself creates the conventional center of interest for a great many twentieth-century reminiscences. What happens in adolescence matters, we believe; our forefathers believed this far less fervently." Patricia M. Spacks, "Stages of Self: Notes on Autobiography and the Life Cycle," in *The American Autobiography: A Collection of Critical Essays,* ed. Albert Stone (Englewood Cliffs: Prentice-Hall, 1981), 45.

Chapter 2. An American Generational Autobiography: Collective Identity in Malcolm Cowley's *Exile's Return*

1. F. Scott Fitzgerald, *The Crack-Up,* ed. Edmund Wilson (New York: Scribner's, 1931; reprinted as New Directions Paperbook, 1956). Fitzgerald's fictional

treatments of generational experience include *This Side of Paradise* (1920), *Flappers and Philosophers* (1920), *The Beautiful and the Damned* (1922), and *Tales of the Jazz Age* (1922). For a small sampling of other magazine articles on the generational theme, see the section entitled "The Younger Generation," in *The Culture of the Twenties,* ed. Loren Baritz (New York: Bobbs-Merrill, 1970), 251–93.

2. A good list of these memoirs can be found in *McAlmon and the Lost Generation: A Self Portrait,* ed. Robert E. Knoll (Lincoln: U of Nebraska P, 1962). In an appendix entitled "Biographical Repertory" (367–82), Knoll has compiled a partial list of lost generation "members" and their works.

3. Unless otherwise noted, the text I am using is the first edition of *Exile's Return: A Narrative of Ideas* (New York: Norton, 1934); subsequent references to this work will be to this edition. This work differs considerably from its successor, the more widely read 1951 revised edition, reentitled *Exile's Return: A Literary Odyssey of the 1920's* (New York: Viking, 1951). For a discussion of the differences, see my "Conversion, Revisionism, and Revision in Malcolm Cowley's *Exile's Return," South Atlantic Quarterly* 82 (Spring 1983): 179–88.

4. *Exile's Return* (1951), 10.

5. Hayden White, *Metahistory: The Historical Imagination in Nineteenth-Century Europe* (Baltimore: Johns Hopkins UP, 1973), 5–11, 93–97.

6. Malcolm Cowley, —*And I Worked at the Writer's Trade: Chapters of Literary History, 1918–1978* (New York: Viking, 1978), 8–20.

7. Ralph Waldo Emerson, "The American Scholar," *Selections from Ralph Waldo Emerson: An Organic Anthology,* ed. Stephen E. Whicher (Boston: Houghton Mifflin, 1960), 79.

8. Randolph S. Bourne, "History of a Literary Radical," *War and the Intellectuals: Essays by Randolph S. Bourne, 1915–1919,* ed. Carl Resek (New York: Harper & Row, 1964), 184–97.

9. Emerson, 78.

10. Walt Whitman, *Democratic Vistas, The Poetry and Prose of Walt Whitman,* ed. Louis Untermeyer (New York: Simon and Schuster, 1949), 849.

11. Thorstein Veblen, *The Theory of the Leisure Class* (New York: Modern Library, 1934), 395.

12. Van Wyck Brooks, *America's Coming-of-Age* (New York: Dutton, 1915), 12. Brooks, like Bourne, combined this analysis of American culture with an appeal to youth, whom he called the "student class": "a class like this we must have, and there are, I think, many signs that such a class is rapidly coming into existence. To begin with, the sudden contraction of the national cultures of Europe during the War, owing to which many currents of thought, formerly shared by all, have been withdrawn from circulation, has thrown us unexpectedly back upon ourselves. How many drafts we have issued in the past upon European thought, unbalanced by an investment of our own! The younger generation have come to feel this obligation acutely. At the same time they have been taught to speak a certain language in common by the social movements of the last 20 years" (Brooks, *Letters and Leadership* [New York: Huebsch, 1918], 124).

13. Bourne, 185–86.

14. In England, the phrase "the lost generation" was used very differently during this same period. See Robert Wohl, *The Generation of 1914* (Cambridge: Harvard UP, 1979), 85–121.

15. For a discussion of Cowley's involvement with the League of Professional Groups, see his *The Dream of the Golden Mountains: Remembering the 1930s* (New York: Viking, 1980), 106–22.

16. For another explanation for this rhetorical style, see Sacvan Bercovitch's *The American Jeremiad* (Madison: U of Wisconsin P, 1978), which argues that American writers' vacillation between doomsaying and optimism grew out of the Puritan homiletic tradition of uttering prophetic warnings to a backsliding Elect.

17. Cowley, *Dream of the Golden Mountains*, 118.

18. For Cowley's retrospective treatment of the religious nature of his move toward the left, see the chapters entitled "Act of Conversion" and "Church on Earth" in *Dream of the Golden Mountains*, 31–50. The attempt to distance himself from dogmatic Marxism included not only the expurgation of Marxist assumptions from the revised edition of *Exile's Return*, but also the downplaying of all of the book's conversion features.

19. *Exile's Return* (1951), 3.

20. In the revised 1951 edition, Cowley says that at this point in the narrative "the author begins to disappear from his book" because his adventures began to be less "representative of what was happening to others" (207).

21. *Exile's Return* (1951), 11. Cowley's claim in the revised edition that he "had failed to show [the Crosby chapter's] connection with the rest of the [1934] narrative" (11) also seems odd. If anything, his revised edition, which excises central elements of the Marxist conversion narrative, damaged the narrative structure that justified the account of Crosby's suicide. This damage was compounded by his treatment of new "characters" in the revised version. In the 1934 edition, every character was shown in relation to a single generational identity and plot. In the 1951 revision, Cowley introduces new sections on Pound, Cummings, Dos Passos, and Hart Crane, but they have almost no connection at all to the book's original generational plot, and his treatment of them is consequently anecdotal rather than illustrative.

22. Cowley, *Dream of the Golden Mountains*, 228.

23. Bernard de Voto, "Exiles from Reality," *Saturday Review of Literature,* June 2, 1934, 721–22.

24. Quoted in Sidonie Smith, *A Poetics of Women's Autobiography: Marginality and the Fictions of Self-Representation* (Bloomington: Indiana UP, 1987), 8. It is precisely Cowley's insistence on the "barometric" metaphor that separates his book from the traditional memoir, which privileges the public selves of prominent figures. F. R. Hart notes, for example, that in *Anti-memoirs,* "the dialogues of Malraux's personal memory are with public personalities: de Gaulle, Nehru, Chou En-lai, Mao. Embodied in such men are the spirits of generations" ("History Talking to Itself," *New Literary History* 40 [Autumn 1978]: 194). By using artists and would-be artists to embody "the spirits of generations," Cowley can put forward his own relatively unknown clique as representatives of the age. See also Marcus Billson, "The Memoir: New Perspectives on a Forgotten Genre," *Genre* 10 (Summer 1977): 259–82.

25. Doris Sommer, "'Not Just a Personal Story': Women's *Testimonios* and the Plural Self," in *Life/Lines: Theorizing Women's Autobiography,* ed. Bella Brodzki and Celeste Schenck (Ithaca: Cornell UP, 1968), 108.

26. As we have already seen, Cowley's barometric metaphor also underlies

one of the differences between his notion of the generational elite and that of theorists like Bourne and Ortega. The latter writers still identify the "elite" with the qualities called for by traditionalists like de Voto.

27. An analogous phenomenon can be found in the response of those who have shared an experience with an autobiographer and do not recognize their *own* experience in the other's description of it. See Lynn Z. Bloom, "Single-Experience Autobiographies," *a/b: Auto/Biography Studies* 3 (Fall 1987): 36–45.

28. Cowley, *Dream of the Golden Mountains,* 228–31.

29. Benjamin Franklin, *The Autobiography and Other Writings* (London: Penguin, 1986), 3–4.

30. Sigmund Freud, "Analysis Terminable and Interminable," *The Standard Edition of the Complete Psychological Works of Sigmund Freud,* trans. J. Strachey and A. Freud, Vol. 23 (London: Hogarth, 1964), 236–37.

31. In spite of Cowley's mortification by the response to the 1934 edition, he eventually went on to make his career as the self-appointed autobiographer of his generation. After his 1951 revision of *Exile's Return,* he continued the saga with *A Second Flowering: Works and Days of the Lost Generation* (New York: Viking, 1973); *—And I Worked at the Writers' Trade* (1978); and *The Dream of the Golden Mountains* (1980).

Chapter 3. Generational Autobiography as Annunciatory Narrative

1. I use "hidden polemic" in the sense that Bakhtin uses it: "In hidden polemic the author's discourse is oriented toward its referential object [in this case, generational identity], as is any other discourse, but at the same time each assertion about that object is constructed in such a way that, besides its referential meaning the author's discourse brings a polemical attack to bear against another speech act, another assertion, on the same topic. Here one utterance focused on its referential object clashes with another utterance on the grounds of the referent itself. That other utterance is not reproduced; it is understood only in its import; but the whole structure of the author's speech would be completely different, if it were not for this reaction to another's unexpressed speech act." See Mikhail Bakhtin, "Discourse Typology in Prose," in *Readings in Russian Poetics: Formalist and Structuralist Views,* ed. Ladislav Matejka and Krystyna Pomorska (Ann Arbor: U of Michigan P, 1978), 187.

2. I am not claiming that these autobiographies were in dialogue only with each other. Naturally, other cultural factors and voices were also implicated in the construction of these autobiographical selves. The mass media played an enormous role, for example. So did older writers, particularly sociologists and political writers who wrote dozens of books and essays about youth during the sixties.

3. Michael Rossman, *The Wedding within the War* (New York: Doubleday, 1971), 69. Subsequent citations will be noted parenthetically in the text.

4. Joyce Maynard, *Looking Back: A Chronicle of Growing Up Old in the Sixties* (1972; New York: Avon, 1974), 13.

5. The text of *The Port Huron Statement* I am using can be found as an appendix to James Miller's *"Democracy Is in the Streets": From Port Huron to the Siege of Chicago* (New York: Simon and Schuster, 1987). Subsequent citations of the *Statement* and of Miller's commentary will be noted parenthetically in the text. Much of my discussion of the writing of the *Statement* is indebted to Miller's

exhaustive account of it. For other accounts of its writing, see Tom Hayden's *Reunion* (New York: Random, 1988) and Michael Harrington's *Fragments of a Century: A Social Autobiography* (New York: Dutton, 1973).

6. Analyses of the document and SDS's contribution to contemporary political and social debates have been amply provided by historians of the period. See, for example, Miller's *"Democracy"*; Kirkpatrick Sale, *SDS* (New York: Vintage, 1973); Milton Viorst, *Fire in the Streets: America in the 1960's* (New York: Simon and Schuster, 1979), 161–96; Allen J. Matusow, *The Unravelling of America: A History of Liberalism in the 1960s* (New York: Harper & Row, 1984), 308–44; Todd Gitlin, *The Whole World Is Watching: Mass Media in the Making and Unmaking of the New Left* (Berkeley: U of California P, 1980) and *The Sixties: Years of Hope, Days of Rage* (New York: Bantam, 1987).

7. A slightly earlier example of the "weak father" narrative can be seen in Nicholas Ray's film *Rebel without a Cause* (1955). In that narrative, the young hero's lack of a strong father leads to nihilistic sullenness rather than activism. The theme of the weak father is picked up later in all of Dotson Rader's generational autobiographies. A recent example of the use of the "betrayal" narrative in its simplest form may be seen in Oliver Stone's film version of Ron Kovic's *Born on the Fourth of July* (1990). The opening sequence in that film, which depicts Kovic's idyllic and typical American childhood, is clearly intended to recapitulate this generational plot, and the narrative justification of Kovic's later antiwar radicalism is almost entirely based on the betrayal of American myths by his elders.

8. See Jeffrey A. Ross, Ann B. Cottrell, Robert St. Cyr, Philip Rawkins, eds., *The Mobilization of Collective Identity: Comparative Perspectives* (Lanham, MA: UP of America, 1980).

9. Annie Kriegel, "Generational Difference: The History of an Idea," *Daedalus* 107 (Fall 1978): 23–38.

10. See Louis Dumont's *Homo Hierarchicus* (Chicago: U of Chicago P, 1970) and *Essays on Individualism: Modern Ideology in Anthropological Perspective* (Chicago: U of Chicago P, 1986). See also George E. Marcus and Michael M. J. Fischer, *Anthropology as Cultural Critique: An Experimental Moment in the Human Sciences* (Chicago: U of Chicago P, 1986), 45–76.

11. Tom Hayden, *Trial* (New York: Holt, Rinehart, and Winston, 1970), 138. Subsequent citations will be noted parenthetically in the text.

12. See, for example, F. R. Hart, "Notes for an Anatomy of Modern Autobiography," *New Literary History* 1 (1970): 485–511.

13. Though Ortega is not explicitly cited in the manifesto, the original draft of the *Statement* echoes his work self-consciously. It read (rather awkwardly): "Every generation inherits from the past a set of problems—and a dominant set of insights and perspectives by which the problems are to be understood and, hopefully, managed" (Miller, 110).

14. It is difficult to assess just how many people actually read the *Statement*. Its original printing in 1962 was done by mimeograph, and the number of copies made is unknown. According to Miller, 20,000 copies were reprinted in 1964 and 25,000 more in 1966. It also appeared in abridged forms in a number of anthologies, including *The New Student Left*, ed. Mitchell Cohen and Dennis Hale (Boston: Beacon, 1966); *The New Radicals: A Report with Documents*, ed. Paul Jacobs and Saul Landau (New York: Vintage, 1966); and *The New Left: A Doc-

umentary History, ed. Massimo Teodori (New York: Bobbs-Merrill, 1969). In 1967, when I entered a small, private college in the Midwest, the document was commonly known, if not read, by my classmates, even those only marginally aware of student politics.

15. I perhaps should add that the generational *and* the individualist autobiographers' efforts to present the self as unified are paralleled by the struggle of nonwriters to maintain possession of their identities. We all struggle throughout our lives with others—siblings, parents, lovers, spouses, superiors, rivals, bureaucrats, institutions—to control the language that will ultimately say who or what we are. Indeed, although we fondly imagine that we are the final authorities on our own identities, control over them eventually passes out of our hands altogether and becomes subject to others' memories and reconstructions. The one mode of individualistic autobiography that fully addresses this tendency (which pervades all instances of the genre) is apologia, but no form of autobiography makes this process so clear as the generational autobiography under consideration here.

16. Abbie Hoffman, *Revolution for the Hell of It* (New York: Dial, 1968). Subsequent references to this book will be made parenthetically in the chapter.

17. Albert Stone, *Autobiographical Occasions and Original Acts: Versions of American Identity from Henry Adams to Nate Shaw* (Philadelphia: U of Pennsylvania P, 1980), 151.

18. See Theodore Roszak, *The Making of a Counter Culture: Reflections on the Technocratic Society and Its Youthful Opposition* (New York: Doubleday, 1968).

19. Abbie Hoffman, *Soon To Be a Major Motion Picture* (New York: Putnam's, 1980). Most of the essays in Hoffman's *Square Dancing in the Ice Age* (New York: Putnam's, 1982) are also autobiographical.

20. Hayden, *Trial,* 36.

21. Hoffman, *Soon To Be a Major Motion Picture,* 164–66, 239–40.

22. Hoffman's belief in the significance of his debate(s) with Rubin continued, with perhaps greater justification, even after the two had gone in widely disparate ideological directions. Rubin eventually abandoned his revolutionary image to take up work on Wall Street; Hoffman, after years underground, resurfaced with his interest in oppositional movements intact. In the 1980s, the two ex-comrades rejoined forces to stage debates over the legacy of the 1960s on college campuses all over the country.

23. For accounts of what happened in Chicago, see Daniel Walker, *Rights in Conflict: The Violent Confrontation of Demonstrators and Police in the Parks and Streets of Chicago during the Week of the Democratic National Convention of 1968* (Washington: National Commission on the Causes and Prevention of Violence, 1968); Viorst, 421–62; Gitlin, *Sixties,* 319–40. In his exhaustive coverage of the events, Walker describes the incidents as a "police riot"; most Movement writers contend that "riot" inadequately captures the systematic nature of the violence used by the police against the demonstrators.

24. Todd Gitlin reads this same line as evidence that Hoffman seemed, at times, to think "the media were transparent channels" (*Sixties,* 236). This reading seems unwarranted to me. It is true that Hoffman, unlike his Digger friends, was usually enthusiastic about the media, but that was because myth (almost al-

ways a positive term for him) could be served only by what the media did best—distort.

25. Hoffman cites Whorf and McLuhan frequently as important influences on his thought. See Benjamin Whorf, *Language, Thought, and Reality: Selected Writings* (Cambridge: Technology Press of Massachusetts Institute of Technology, 1956); and Marshall McLuhan, *Understanding Media* (New York: McGraw-Hill, 1964).

26. Jerry Rubin, *We Are Everywhere* (New York: Harper & Row, 1971), 98. Subsequent references will be made parenthetically in the chapter.

27. Jerry Rubin, *Do It! Scenarios for the Revolution* (New York: Simon and Schuster, 1970). Subsequent references will be made parenthetically in the chapter.

28. Vance Packard, *The Hidden Persuaders* (New York: McKay, 1957); Theodore White, *The Making of the President, 1960* (New York: Atheneum, 1961); and Joe McGinniss, *The Selling of the President* (New York: Trident, 1969).

29. The shock value of this reversal is one that generational autobiographers with Yippie tendencies exploited regularly throughout the late sixties and early seventies. It was captured as well in the title of Nicholas Von Hoffman's 1968 book, *We Are the People Our Parents Warned Us About* (Chicago: Quadrangle).

30. The principal theoretical works to which generationalists turned for these ideas were Norman O. Brown's *Life against Death: The Psychoanalytic Meaning of History* (Middletown, CT: Wesleyan UP, 1959) and *Love's Body* (New York: Random, 1966) and Herbert Marcuse's *Eros and Civilization* (New York: Vintage, 1962) and *One-Dimensional Man* (Boston: Beacon, 1964). However, see also Edgar Z. Friedenberg, "The Oppression of Youth," in *Seasons of Rebellion: Protest and Radicalism in Recent America,* ed. Joseph Boskin and Robert A. Rosenstone (New York: Holt, Rinehart, and Winston, 1972), 221–36.

31. The original defendants also included an eighth person, Bobby Seale, chairman of the Black Panther Party. Seale's case was later separated from that of the other seven defendants. All of the convictions were ultimately overturned in appeals court.

32. Gitlin would argue that although the primary responsibility for the violence in Chicago must be placed on the police, the left had by 1968 developed a more cynical political strategy than *Trial,* with its insistence on the organizers' peaceful intentions, would suggest. That strategy could not have helped but contribute to the violence. According to Gitlin, Hayden and others had concluded that the only way to end the war in Vietnam was by further polarizing the country. Hayden's idea was "to raise the internal cost to such a high level that those decision-makers who only deal in cost-effectiveness terms will have to get out of Vietnam. . . . The cost in terms of internal disruption, generational conflict, choking off the number of reliable soldiers, the number of willing taxpayers" (Gitlin, *Sixties,* 289). The defendants argue that that strategy was not articulated until *after* Chicago. See Rubin, *We Are Everywhere,* 58, for an example of such thinking.

33. In a later chapter, Hayden cites some specific, if somewhat less dramatic, statistics to make the same point: "One of the best known polls, conducted by *Fortune* in 1968, showed 750,000 students who 'should know better' identifying with the New Left, while another two or three million constituted a supportive base" (*Trial,* 152).

34. Gitlin, *Sixties,* 282.

35. See, for example, Jerry Farber, *The Student as Nigger: Essays and Stories* (1967; New York: Pocket, 1970); Carl Davidson, "A Student Syndicalist Movement," SDS Pamphlet (1966).

36. Michael Rossman, *On Learning and Social Change* (New York: Random, 1972), and *New Age Blues: On the Politics of Consciousness* (New York: Dutton, 1979).

37. Two contemporary analyses of the counterculture are Keith Melville's *Communes in the Counter Culture: Origins, Theories, Styles of Life* (New York: Morrow, 1972) and Theodore Roszak's *The Making of a Counter Culture*.

38. For Rossman's notions about the relationship between collective identity, cultural change, and education, see *On Learning and Social Change*, 45–50, 69–79.

39. Raymond Mungo, *Famous Long Ago: My Life and Hard Times with Liberation News Service* (Boston: Beacon, 1970), 58. For Mungo's view of this geographical dispute, see his *Total Loss Farm: A Year in the Life* (New York: Dutton, 1970), 98.

40. Malcolm Cowley, *Exile's Return: A Narrative of Ideas* (New York: Norton, 1934), 12–13.

Chapter 4. Generational Autobiography as Reactive Narrative

1. Since such accounts are fully available elsewhere, I do not intend to give a detailed description of the historical circumstances that accompanied the second phase of generational autobiographies. See, for example, Todd Gitlin, *The Sixties: Years of Hope, Days of Rage* (New York: Bantam, 1987), for an insider's account of the breakup of the Movement.

2. Another documentary made in the early 1980s, *The War at Home*, focuses on Madison, Wisconsin, as symbolic center of Movement and generational activity. The significant ending of its narrative is the bombing of Sterling Hall at the University of Wisconsin that left a graduate student dead.

3. For a different account of the distinction I am making here, see John D. Barbour, *Versions of Deconversion: Autobiography and the Loss of Faith* (Charlottesville: UP of Virginia, 1994). Barbour's definition of "deconversion narratives" is more inclusive than the one I provide for "autobiographies of renunciation."

4. Bella Dodd, *School of Darkness* (New York: P. J. Kenedy, 1954), 245–46.

5. J. B. Matthews, *Odyssey of a Fellow Traveler* (New York: Mount Vernon, 1938); Benjamin Gitlow, *I Confess* (New York: Dutton, 1940); Louis Budenz, *This Is My Story* (New York: McGraw-Hill, 1947); Richard Crossman, ed., *The God That Failed* (New York: Harper & Row, 1950); Elizabeth Bentley, *Out of Bondage* (New York: Devon Adair, 1951); Hede Massing, *This Deception* (New York: Duell, Sloan and Pearce, 1951); Whittaker Chambers, *Witness* (New York: Random, 1952). All of these writers, incidentally, belonged to Cowley's generation (Bentley, the youngest, was born in 1910; Budenz and Gitlow in 1891; Chambers in 1901; Dodd in 1904; all but two of Crossman's authors were born in the first decade of the twentieth century). These works are not, therefore, written during the first reactive phase of generational experience (the one characterized by Cowley's own 1934 *Exile's Return*), but during a second one in which the authors reject an earlier converted self. They are not, however, generational autobiographies as I have defined this term here. Although a number of these authors write about their generation, they do not generally use the notion of the generation as

the basis for their self-construction. When they focus on collective affiliation, it is usually an ideological one—those people who adhere to the principles of capitalism or those who adhere to the principles of socialism. The effect of Marxist historicism on American writers and intellectuals during this period has been more than amply described and analyzed. For several excellent studies on the subject, see Daniel Aaron, *Writers on the Left: Episodes in American Literary Communism* (New York: Harcourt, Brace & World, 1961); David Caute, *The Fellow Travellers: A Postscript to the Enlightenment* (New York: Macmillan, 1973); and John P. Diggins, *Up from Communism: Conservative Odysseys in American Intellectual History* (New York: Harper & Row, 1975). For a semi-autobiographical study of the effect of communism on the ways in which nonwriters perceive their past selves, see Vivian Gornick, *The Romance of American Communism* (New York: Basic, 1977).

6. See also Stanley Rothman and S. Robert Lichter's *Roots of Radicalism: Jews, Christians, and the New Left* (New York: Oxford UP, 1982). This sociopsychological study of radicals supports the view that the Movement attracted some socially maladjusted types. They conclude that traits such as "inverse authoritarianism," narcissism, and a heightened power drive motivated many Movement-identified "ideological radicals." They caution, however, that their studies do not apply to the mass of nonideological antiwar protestors.

7. Dotson Rader, *I Ain't Marchin' Anymore!* (New York: David McKay, 1969) and *Blood Dues* (London: London Magazine Editions, 1974; orig. pub. New York: Knopf, 1973). Subsequent citations will be noted parenthetically in the text.

8. For Mailer's essay, "The White Negro: Superficial Reflections on the Hipster," and his ideas on the "new" rebel, see "Part Four. Hipsters," *Advertisements for Myself* (London: Deutsch, 1961), 269–314. Further references to "The White Negro" will be made parenthetically in the text.

9. Paul Goodman, *Growing Up Absurd* (New York: Random, 1960) and *Compulsory Mis-education and The Community of Scholars* (New York: Random, 1964).

10. Tom Hayden, qtd. in Godfrey Hodgson, *America in Our Time* (New York: Vantage, 1976), 280. A thorough analysis of the Movement's apocalyptic fantasies at the end of the 1960s might also usefully employ the insights of Richard Slotkin's ambitious reading of American culture in *Regeneration through Violence: The Mythology of the American Frontier* (Middletown: Wesleyan UP, 1973).

11. Besides Hall, Mailer, and Williams, Rader also considers as models of historical engagement figures such as Gore Vidal, "fueled solely by envy, cynicism, and contempt" (*Blood Dues*, 45); Max Lerner, "a parlor liberal"; and Michael Harrington. In the end, he decides that none of these alternatives can "work" for him (46).

12. Hilary Mills, *Norman Mailer: A Biography* (London: New English Library, 1983), 358.

13. Interested readers should also see Rader's later memoir of Tennessee Williams, *Tennessee: Cry of the Heart* (Garden City: Doubleday, 1985), which lifts a large section (see 79–141) directly out of *Blood Dues* with only minor revisions. The main difference between *Tennessee* and the earlier book is that the revised scenes in *Tennessee* assume that Rader's homosexuality was taken for granted, both by Rader and by his friends, during 1971 and 1972.

14. In *Blood Dues,* this division of men into "fathers" and "sons" also serves as a basis for several of the chapters. Those devoted to figures like Mailer, Williams, and David Dellinger are about Rader's "fathers." Other chapters focus on his "sons": young, handsome, working-class rebels such as Jann Eller (in the chapter "The Horse of Horses"), Derek (in "Cowboys"), and Arkansas (in "On Learning of Paul Goodman's Death").

15. Rader to author, September 9, 1993.

16. Raymond Mungo, *Famous Long Ago: My Life and Hard Times with Liberation News Service* (Boston: Beacon, 1970). Subsequent references will be made parenthetically within the text.

17. One might compare Mungo's sense of his audience with other generational writers. See pages 80–81, 161–62 in this book.

18. Raymond Mungo, *Total Loss Farm: A Year in the Life* (New York: Dutton, 1970), 96. Subsequent references will be made parenthetically within the text.

19. Mungo's emphasis on myth here recalls Abbie Hoffman's pronouncements on that theme. Just how far Mungo was willing to push his belief that myth is truer than facts is made clear in *Famous Long Ago,* where he argues that it was ethical for *Avatar,* an underground paper, to invent a story about American atrocities in Vietnam and to publish it as fact under a false byline because such stories have "happened in man's history" and are "unvarnished and plain and human." Mungo claims that telling the "truth," which he defines as "simply the way you see the world, the relationship *you* have with the whole world" (76), is the basis of both autobiography and journalism. While his mythmaking is usually clear enough in his autobiographies, the *Avatar* anecdote can only make one grateful that his conversion took him out of the business of disseminating the news.

20. Annie Dillard, *Pilgrim at Tinker Creek* (New York: Harper's, 1974).

21. Cf. Stephen Diamond's chapter "An Intermission: What the Trees Said," *What the Trees Said: Life on a New Age Farm* (New York: Delacorte, 1971). which details the author's mescaline-induced vision of trees, and Dillard's chapter "Seeing," which describes a comparable, though drug-free, vision of the same thing.

22. Jane Alpert, *Growing Up Underground* (New York: William Morrow, 1981). Subsequent references will be made parenthetically within the text.

23. See, for example, Murray Kempton, "Bombs Away," *New York Review of Books,* January 21, 1982, 48–50; Stefan Kanfer, "The Politics of the Playpen," *New Republic,* December 23, 1981, 30–32; Midge Decter, "Notes from the American Underground," *Commentary,* January 22, 1982, 27–33; and Eden Ross Lipson, "A Bomber's Confessions," *New York Times Book Review,* October 25, 1981, 12–13. Lipson's is the only review in this group that does not discuss Alpert's representative status. None of the reviews is favorable.

24. A fruitful comparison could be made between Alpert's narrative and Elizabeth Bentley's 1951 *Out of Bondage.* Both are narratives of women drawn into a subversive underground movement from liberal backgrounds by men with whom they fall in love. But where Alpert's assessment of her subjugation to her lover is doggedly psychological, Bentley never questions either her lover's motivations or her own subjugation to his instructions. Bentley constructs a self consistently shaped by political ideas and neglects precisely those areas of unconscious motivation that Alpert identifies as the most crucial factors in her behavior.

25. Kanfer, 32.

26. Jerry Rubin understood this principle when he undertook the public shedding of his radical self in *Growing (Up) at 37* (New York: M. Evans, 1976). Subsequent references to Rubin's book will be made parenthetically in the text.

27. Other writers cite slightly different figures. In *Destructive Generation: Second Thoughts about the Sixties* (New York: Summit, 1989), Peter Collier and David Horowitz write that "the Treasury Department estimated that there were over five thousand bombings across the country from January 1969 through April 1970 alone" (106). In *The Sixties* (New York: Bantam, 1989), Todd Gitlin cites a much smaller number. He writes, "By conservative estimate, between September 1969 and May 1970 there were some two hundred fifty major bombings and attempts linkable with the white left—about one a day. (By government figures, the actual number may have been as many as six times as great)" (401). Gitlin's source for the government figures is Kirkpatrick Sale's book *SDS* (New York: Vintage, 1973). Subsequent references to *Destructive Generation* will be made parenthetically in the text.

28. John H. Bunzel, ed. *Political Passages: Journeys of Change through Two Decades, 1968–1988* (New York: Free Press, 1988). Although Bunzel's text comprises narratives written primarily by members of the sixties generation, he was himself born in 1924. Subsequent references to his book will be made parenthetically within the text.

29. *The God That Failed,* ed. Richard Crossman. The authors—Arthur Koestler, Ignazio Stone, Richard Wright, André Gide, Louis Fischer, and Stephen Spender—were all, with the exception of Fischer, well-known international literary figures. Bunzel's twelve authors are primarily American academics.

30. Not surprisingly, most reviewers of Bunzel's book responded to it on the level of its authors' political views. The result is that left-leaning reviewers hate the book, while conservative reviewers find it profound reading. Negative reviews include Leonard Bushkoff, "Memoir and Myth: Remembering the Way It Was in the '60s," *Christian Science Monitor,* June 3, 1988, B3; J. B. Lane, [book review], *Choice,* October 1988, 26; and Charles Freund, "The View from Over Thirty," *New York Times Book Review,* August 14, 1988, 7. Favorable reviews came from Joseph Shattan, [book review], *American Spectator,* July 1988, 45–46; and Chilton Williamson, "The Right Books," *National Review,* June 24, 1988, 48–49. Richard Gid Powers provides an academic, generally nonpolitical analysis in his "Anticommunist Lives," *American Quarterly* 41 (December 1989): 714–23.

31. *The Confessions of St. Augustine,* trans. Rex Warner (New York: New American Library, 1963), 173.

32. "Kronstadt" refers to a revolt of Russian sailors violently repressed by the young Bolshevik regime. The name "Kronstadt" has since become a shorthand way of referring to the moment of political disillusionment among people attracted to the radical left.

33. The most conspicuous exception to the pattern of self-renunciation is the introductory autobiographical essay by sociologist Edward Shils, who is called in to pronounce damnation on the sixties generation from an outsider's viewpoint (he was born in 1911). Shils claims he never had any trouble seeing that the sixties generation, like the left-leaning thirties generation, was concerned with goals that "were for the most part valueless, that the account which it gave of the world

was wrong, and that the motives of those who saw and judged the world according to the antinomian world view [his term for the sixties ethos] were discreditable" (Bunzel, 14).

34. Among the older writers are John Bunzel (b. 1924), James Finn (b. 1924), and Michael Novak (b. 1934). Their age prevented them from fully identifying with what they see as the worst excesses of the sixties and although they all abandon beliefs they adopted during that period, none of them produces a full-blown renunciation narrative with its typical loathing of the former self.

35. The degree to which this take on the sixties generation has become a cultural cliché was recently made abundantly clear in the popular Robert Zemeckis film *Forrest Gump* (1994). In that movie, the character most clearly intended to represent the sixties ethos is Jenny, a woman for whom Gump harbors a lifelong love. Jenny's predilection for drugs, her involvement in civil rights, her protests against the Vietnam War, and her sexual waywardness are all explained narratively as the consequence of childhood sexual abuse and dysfunctional family relationships. This lost and wayward child of the sixties must be rescued from these destructive proclivities by the simpleton hero, Gump. In a television interview, Tom Hanks, who won an Oscar award for his portrayal of the titular hero, praised the movie for its complete lack of political bias.

36. Peter Collier and David Horowitz, eds., *Second Thoughts: Former Radicals Look Back at the Sixties* (New York: Madison Books, 1989). Subsequent references will be made parenthetically in the text.

37. Compare, for example, Medved's comment with Michael Rossman's remarks, addressed to younger members of his generation, in *The Wedding within the War* (New York: Doubleday, 1971): "these tales are scraps from our common history. You will recognize their experience, archaic as some of its aspects may seem. You are not alone, least of all in Time. You share a heritage of developing struggle which stretches back continuously through these events . . ." (31–32).

38. Response to this book, like the response to Bunzel's, split along political lines. For a sampling of negative reviews, see Paul Berman, "The Last New Leftists," *New Republic,* April 24, 1989, 26–32; Winifred Breines, "A Couple of White Guys . . ." *Nation,* November 27, 1989, 630–32; Hendrik Hertzberg, "A Tale of Two Hippies," *Washington Monthly,* May 1989, 44–46; Todd Gitlin, "Muddled Thoughts," *Dissent,* Fall 1989, 569–71; David Burner, "We Were Disinformed," *New York Times Book Review,* April 23, 1989, 18. Positive reviews included the following: George Gilder, "The '60s: A Look Back in Anger," *Washington Post Book World,* March 19, 1989, 1, 10; Joseph Sobran, "Lost Generation," *National Review,* March 24, 1989, 43–44; George Szamuely, [review of *Destructive Generation*], *American Spectator,* August 1989, 42–43. Finally, one genuinely mixed review: Bruce Nussbaum, "This Is the Damning of the Age of Aquarius," *Business Week,* April 3, 1989, 16–17.

39. After using Rudd as a model of proper penitence, Collier and Horowitz later inexplicably lump him together with Gitlin and Hayden as someone totally lacking in "self-irony" and all too ready to use the "radical alibi" of the Vietnam War (*Destructive Generation,* 241).

40. Collier's autobiographical essay "Something Happened to Me Yesterday" is a retitled version of "Looking Backward: Memories of the Sixties Left" (his contribution to Bunzel's book), and both are reworked versions of the con-

ference speech "Coming Home" from *Second Thoughts.* Thus, Collier sustains his peers' predilection for multiple autobiographies, but with a difference: he simply publishes the same autobiography under three different titles. Horowitz's autobiographical essay "Letter to a Political Friend" is likewise a reprint of his contribution to Bunzel's anthology, and both are a much-expanded version of his short piece "Why I Am No Longer a Leftist" in *Second Thoughts.*

41. Tom Hayden, *Reunion* (New York: Random, 1988), 422.

42. Whittaker Chambers, *Witness* (New York: Random, 1952). Subsequent references will be made parenthetically within the text.

43. The statute of limitations had expired on the charge of treason (the actions of which Chambers accused Hiss in 1948 had occurred in the mid-1930s), and Hiss, having denied the accusations under oath, could be tried only for perjury.

44. Horowitz and Collier's specific claims about the technological intensification of torture methods under the Sandinistas are refuted by Paul Berman in his *New Republic* article.

Chapter 5. Generational Autobiography as Elegiac Narrative

1. Northrop Frye, *The Anatomy of Criticism* (Princeton: Princeton UP, 1971), 36–37.

2. Michael Rossman, *New Age Blues: On the Politics of Consciousness* (New York: Dutton, 1979), 61. Subsequent references will be made parenthetically within the text.

3. David Harris, *Dreams Die Hard: Three Men's Journey through the Sixties* (New York: St. Martin's/Marek, 1982), 142. Subsequent references will be made parenthetically within the text.

4. Todd Gitlin, *The Sixties: Years of Hope, Days of Rage* (New York: Bantam, 1987), 241. Subsequent references will be made parenthetically within the text.

5. For a discussion of "possessive memory" in intergenerational discussions of generational experience, see "Possessive Memory: In Search of a Methodology." *H-Amstdy American Studies List* (30 August–5 September 1995). n. pag. Online. Internet. 7 September 1995.

6. F. Scott Fitzgerald, *The Crack-Up* (New York: New Directions Paperbook, 1956), 13; and John Glassco, *Memoirs of Montparnasse* (New York: Viking, 1973), 72, 27.

7. Joyce Maynard, *Looking Back: A Chronicle of Growing Up Old in the Sixties* (New York: Avon, 1972), 18. Subsequent references will be made parenthetically within the text.

8. For Rossman's use of this phrase, see *The Wedding within the War* (3) and *New Age Blues* (100).

9. The difficulty of recapturing the feelings he shared with other members of his generation is a repeated refrain in Harris' book (see, for example, 142).

10. Todd Gitlin also cites Marshall Bloom's death as a milestone in his life, adding that "for me, Marshall Bloom died of the movement's sins" (*Sixties,* 406).

11. Harris writes, "Everyone involved in the decade would have their own date for when the Sixties ended" (281). His own date coincided with Allard Lowenstein's visit to his federal prison cell in 1970.

12. Tom Hayden, *Reunion* (New York: Random, 1988), xvi. Subsequent references will be made parenthetically within the text.

13. Critical response to Hayden's book was typically determined by review-

ers' political sympathies, but even those whom one would expect to appreciate Hayden's politics see the book as a ploy to woo voters and are wary of what they see as his opportunism. Leonard Bushkoff ("Memoir and Myth: Remembering the Way It Was in the '60s," *Christian Science Monitor,* June 3, 1988, B3) praises the memoir as a serious contribution to the "struggle for the memory of the 1960s" and calls it a *"brilliant* book," written with "unusual grace and impact." However, he warns readers to be skeptical of the portrait's self-serving elements, advising them to read James Miller's *Democracy Is in the Streets* (New York: Simon & Schuster, 1987), "which presents Hayden's other face." Mary E. King ("Hayden's Workout Book," *Nation,* October 3, 1988, 281–82) also gives the book a positive review for its nonjudgmental tone and its historical accuracy, but she faults Hayden for relying too much on analysis and too little on emotions (especially in his relations with women). Ms. King, briefly married to Dennis Sweeney, was an important white worker in the early SNCC and a close friend of Hayden's first wife, Sandra Cason. Paul Berman ("At the Center of the 60's," *New York Times Book Review,* June 12, 1988, 7) sees the book as self-serving. He accuses Hayden of a nonthinking emotionalism and wildly inconsistent politics and sneers at him for reversing "the conservative view of New Leftists as nasty children rebelling against too-nice parents. New Leftists in Mr. Hayden's recollection were very nice children, and if only the nasty parents—meaning the liberal establishment and the government, plus the flesh-and-blood parents—had spared the rod, New Left desperation could have been avoided." Taylor Branch, author of *Parting the Waters: America in the King Years, 1954–63* (New York: Simon & Schuster, 1988), is also critical of Hayden in "If I Had a Hammer . . . I'd Make Tom Hayden Stop Issuing Manifestos" (*Washington Monthly,* May 1988, 51–54). He sees Hayden as a bombastic egotist, given to writing pompous manifestos noted for their "apocalyptic vagueness." The passage of time, he says, has contributed little to Hayden's historical perspective, and his apologies for the movement's excesses fail to "go far enough." "Those who led or tolerated the Yippie-Zippie-Panther period might well have lengthened rather than shortened the war by feeding Nixon's middle-American Thermidor. On into the Reagan years and beyond, those impolitic excesses will discredit the remarkable, democratic courage of young people in the 1960s. They may have hastened the return of an atmosphere in which most Americans find it difficult to imagine a positive contribution from the young" (54). Probably the best of the reviews is Maurice Isserman's "Spin Control" (*Dissent,* Fall 1988, 501–03). Isserman accurately describes the book's primary structural features and narrative strategies, but like other reviewers, he sees Hayden as an opportunist willing to slide from one political position to another to suit his ambitions of the moment. Isserman writes that Hayden tries "to produce a balanced treatment of the New Left in *Reunion,* which is all to the good, but does so in a way that allows him to take credit for its virtues while exculpating himself from responsibility for its worst excesses" (502).

14. Malcolm Cowley, *Exile's Return: A Literary Odyssey of the 1920s* (New York: Viking, 1951), 289. Subsequent references to this edition of Cowley's book will be made parenthetically within the text.

15. Gitlin's reviewers include the following: Stanley Aronowitz, *Zeta Magazine,* January 1988, 57–58; Paul Berman, "Don't Follow Leaders," *New Republic,* August 10–17, 1987, 28–35; Winifred Breines, "Whose New Left?" *Journal of*

American History 75 (September 1988): 528–45; Alan Brinkley, "Dreams of the Sixties," *New York Review of Books,* October 22, 1987, 10, 12–16; Paul Buhle, "Remembering the Sixties," *Oral History Review* 17 (Spring 1989): 137–42; Paul Garver and George Abbott White, "What Was Old, What Was New? The New Left and American Exceptionalism," *Journal of American Studies* 22 (1988): 67–76; Murray Hausknecht, "Generational Conflict and Left Politics," *Dissent,* Fall 1988, 497–500; David Henry, "Recalling the 1960s: The New Left and Social Movement Criticism," *Quarterly Journal of Speech* 75 (February 1989): 97–112; Charles W. Hunt, "The Old Left, the New Left, and the Uses of History," *Monthly Review* (New York) 41 (September 1989): 58–61; Maurice Isserman, "The Not-So-Dark and Bloody Ground: New Works on the 1960s," *American Historical Review* 94 (October 1989): 990–1010; Marty Jezer, *Progressive,* July 1988, 30–31; Scott McConnell, "Resurrecting the New Left," *Commentary,* October 1987, 31–38; Louis Menand, "You Say It's Your Birthday," *New Republic,* April 18, 1988, 34–40; James Miller, "Tears and Riots, Love and Regrets," *New York Times Book Review,* November 8, 1987, 13–14; Herbert Parmet, "Yesterday's Rebels," *New Leader,* March 7, 1988, 17–18. Subsequent references to these reviews will be made parenthetically within the text.

16. Peter Collier and David Horowitz, *Destructive Generation: Second Thoughts about the Sixties* (New York: Summit, 1989), 248. Subsequent references will be made parenthetically within the text.

17. Some reviewers, however, fault the book precisely for its univocality. See, for example, Paul Buhle's review, listed above.

18. Charles Dickens, *A Tale of Two Cities* (London: Thomas Nelson, n.d.), 378.

19. See Isserman's review, listed above. Isserman, who wrote his own account of the period, faults both Gitlin and James Miller for the tendency to employ the predestination trope.

20. This is one of the ways in which the New Left generationalists differ markedly from traditional theoretical generationalists like José Ortega y Gasset and Karl Mannheim, who argue that a generation lasts between fifteen and thirty years. Gitlin's position here is similar to the one Maynard takes in her memoir, which identifies a generation as consisting of two or three high school graduating classes.

21. Both Gitlin and one of his readers, Louis Menand (listed above), remind us that the sixties generation is distinct from the baby boomers. As Menand points out, the birth boom, a strictly demographic phenomenon, began in "the middle of 1946, when the U.S. birthrate began to take off, nine months after V-J day" and lasted until 1964, "the last year in which births exceeded 4 million" (36). By this reckoning, only Raymond Mungo (1946), David Harris (1946), Jane Alpert (1947), and Joyce Maynard (1953) are boomers. The sixties generation, on the other hand, was a social and political construct put together by members of the New Left, the Movement, and the major spokespersons and artists of the counterculture, and they were mostly born between 1935 and 1945. They also include many of the figures discussed in this book: Carl Oglesby (1935), Bob Moses (1935), Abbie Hoffman (1936), Jerry Rubin (1938), Richard Flacks (1938), Tom Hayden (1939), Michael Rossman (1939), David Horowitz (1939), Rennie Davis (1940), Peter Collier (1941), Bob Dylan (1941), Mario Savio (1942), Dotson Rader (1942), Jonah Raskin (1942), Todd Gitlin (1943). As Menand argues, "Far

from being a part of the pig in the demographer's python, the phalanx of young people that is supposed to have burst by sheer size every social bond as it passed through the decade, most '60s radicals belonged to a generation that was the product of one of the lowest birth rates in the nation's history. They were baby busters. They moved through the system in unusually small cohorts; by the time the '60s arrived, they were ready for graduate school" (36).

Epilogue: Autobiography as Generational Dialogue

1. *The Port Huron Statement*, in James Miller, *"Democracy Is in the Streets"*: *From Port Huron to the Siege of Chicago* (New York: Simon & Schuster, 1987), 329.

2. Joyce Maynard, *Looking Back: A Chronicle of Growing Up Old in the Sixties* (New York: Avon, 1973), 151.

3. Michael Rossman, *The Wedding within the War* (New York: Doubleday, 1971), 75; *New Age Blues: On the Politics of Consciousness* (New York: Dutton, 1979), xiii.

4. A very incomplete listing of Vietnam era memoirs would include, besides the books discussed in this epilogue, the following individually authored narratives: Michael Herr, *Dispatches* (1968); Tim O'Brien, *If I Die in a Combat Zone* (1973); Philip Caputo, *A Rumor of War* (1977); Robert Mason, *Chickenhawk* (1983); Rick Eilert, *For Self and Country* (1983). It would also include the following oral and collective narratives: Mark Baker, *Nam* (1981); Al Santoli, *Everything We Had* (1981); Peter Goldman and Tony Fuller, *Charlie Company: What Vietnam Did to Us* (1983); Wallace Terry, *Bloods: An Oral History of the Vietnam War by Black Veterans* (1984).

5. Frederick Downs, *The Killing Zone: My Life in the Vietnam War* (New York: Berkley, 1978), preface.

6. Ron Kovic, *Born on the Fourth of July* (New York: McGraw-Hill, 1976), 107–8.

7. For an overview of the development of interest in women's autobiographical narratives, see Phyllis Rose, Introduction, *The Norton Book of Women's Lives,* ed. Phyllis Rose (New York: Norton, 1993), 11–37.

8. For this reason, generational autobiographies can be usefully compared with autobiographies written by members of other marginalized groups. For a discussion of women's and African Americans' autobiographies, see Estelle C. Jelinek, ed., *Women's Autobiography: Essays in Criticism* (Bloomington: Indiana UP, 1980); Domna Stanton, ed., *The Female Autograph* (New York: New York Literary Forum, 1984); Estelle C. Jelinek, *The Tradition of Women's Autobiography: From Antiquity to the Present* (Boston: Twayne, 1986); Sidonie Smith, *A Poetics of Women's Autobiography: Marginality and the Fictions of Self-Representation* (Bloomington: Indiana UP, 1987); Bella Brodzki and Celeste Schenck, eds , *Life/Lines: Theorizing Women's Autobiography* (Ithaca: Cornell UP, 1988); Shari Benstock, ed., *The Private Self: Theory and Practice of Women's Autobiographical Writings* (Chapel Hill: U of North Carolina P, 1988); Françoise Lionnet, *Autobiographical Voices: Race, Gender, Self-Portraiture* (Ithaca: Cornell UP, 1989); Personal Narratives Group, eds., *Interpreting Women's Lives: Feminist Theory and Personal Narrative* (Bloomington: Indiana UP, 1989); Margo Culley, ed. *American Women's Autobiography: Fea(s)ts of Memory* (Madison: U of Wisconsin P, 1992); Sidonie Smith and Julia Watson, eds., *De/Colonizing the Subject: The Pol-*

itics of Gender in Women's Autobiography (Minneapolis: U of Minnesota P, 1992); Sidonie Smith, *Where I'm Bound: Patterns of Slavery and Freedom in Black American Autobiography* (Westport, CT: Greenwood, 1974); Robert B. Stepto, *From behind the Veil: A Study of Afro-American Narrative* (Urbana: U of Illinois P, 1979); William Andrews, *To Tell a Free Story: The First Century of Afro-American Autobiography, 1760–1865* (Urbana: U of Illinois P, 1986); William Andrews, ed. *African American Autobiography: A Collection of Critical Essays* (Englewood Cliffs: Prentice-Hall, 1993); and Vincent P. Franklin, *Living Our Stories, Telling Our Truths: Autobiography and the Making of the African-American Intellectual Tradition* (New York: Scribner, 1995). For particularly relevant work on the ways in which marginalization has affected genre, see Caren Kaplan, "Resisting Autobiography: Out-Law Genres and Transnational Feminist Subjects," and John Beverley, "The Margin at the Center: On *Testimonio* (Testimonial Narrative)," in Smith and Watson's anthology *De/Colonizing the Subject.*

9. Mary G. Mason, for example, having examined four archetypal female autobiographies, writes that "one element . . . that seems more or less constant in women's life-writing—and this is not the case in men's life-writing—is the sort of evolution and delineation of an identity by way of alterity" (231), in "The Other Voice: Autobiographies of Women Writers," *Autobiography: Essays Theoretical and Critical,* ed. James Olney (Princeton: Princeton UP, 1980), 207–35. Mason's essay has had an important impact on much writing about gender-based differences in autobiographical writing.

10. The final paragraph of Rousseau's *Confessions* reads: "Thus I concluded my reading, and everyone was silent. Mme d'Egmont was the only person who seemed moved. She trembled visibly but quickly controlled herself, and remained quiet, as did the rest of the company. Such was the advantage I derived from my reading and my declaration." Trans. J. M. Cohen (London: Penguin, 1953), 606.

11. Jerome Bruner, "The Narrative Construction of Reality," *Critical Inquiry* 18 (Autumn 1991): 20.

12. Mary M. Gergen and Kenneth J. Gergen, "Social Construction of Narrative Accounts," in *Historical Social Psychology,* ed. Gergen and Gergen (Hillsdale, NJ: Erlbaum, 1984), 173–89. Subsequent references to this essay will be made parenthetically within the text. Other constructionist and narratological studies of identity include the following works: Thomas O. Blank, "The Social Constructionist Movement in Modern Psychology," *Personality and Social Psychology Bulletin* 14 (1988): 651–63; Jerome Bruner, *Acts of Meaning* (Boston: Harvard UP, 1990); D. D. V. Fisher, "Experiential Being and the Inherent Self: Towards a Constructivist Theory of the Self," *Journal for the Theory of Social Behaviour* 18 (1988): 149–67; Mark Freeman, *Rewriting the Self: History, Memory, Narrative* (Boston: Routledge, 1993); Kenneth Gergen, *The Social Construction of the Person* (New York: Springer-Verlag, 1985); H. J. M. Hermans and H. J. G. Kempen, *The Dialogical Self: Meaning as Movement* (New York: Academic P, 1993); Anthony Paul Kerby, *Narrative and Self* (Bloomington: Indiana UP, 1991); D. Middleton and D. Edwards, eds., *Collective Remembering* (London: Sage, 1990); Paul Ricoeur, "Narrative Identity," *Philosophy Today* 35 (1991): 73–81; George Rosenwald and Richard Ochberg, *Storied Lives: The Cultural Politics of Self Understanding* (New Haven: Yale UP, 1992); T. R. Sarbin and J. I. Kitsuse, eds., *Constructing the Social* (London: Sage, 1994); J. Shotter and Kenneth Ger-

gen, eds., *Texts of Identity* (London: Sage, 1989); Margaret Somers, "The Narrative Constitution of Identity: A Relational and Network Approach," *Theory and Society* 23 (1994): 605–49.

13. George Santayana, *Life of Reason* (1905–6), vol. I., chap. xii. *Flux and Constancy in Human Nature*. A recent newspaper article on the importance of freeing oneself from the past contains an instance of the popularized version of the phrase: "It's important to remember the old saying, 'Those who forget the past are condemned to repeat it.' But an important freedom is to be free of the weight, or 'emotional charge' of the past." Jeff Herring, "Let Psychological Freedom Ring," *New Orleans Times-Picayune,* July 11, 1996, E-5.

14. Jerome Bruner, "Life as Narrative," *Social Research* 54 (Spring 1987): 15.

Bibliography

Aaron, Daniel. *Writers on the Left: Episodes in American Literary Communism.* New York: Harcourt, Brace & World, 1961.

Alpert, Jane. *Growing Up Underground.* New York: William Morrow, 1981.

Andrews, William. *To Tell a Free Story: The First Century of Afro-American Autobiography, 1760–1865.* Urbana: U of Illinois P, 1986.

Andrews, William, ed. *African American Autobiography: A Collection of Critical Essays.* Englewood Cliffs: Prentice-Hall, 1993.

Aronowitz, Stanley. Rev. of *The Sixties,* by Todd Gitlin. *Zeta Magazine,* January 1988, 57–58.

Augustine, Saint. *The Confessions of St. Augustine.* Trans. Rex Warner. New York: New American Library, 1963.

Baker, Mark. *Nam.* New York: Berkley, 1981.

Bakhtin, Mikhail. "Discourse Typology in Prose." In *Readings in Russian Poetics: Formalist and Structuralist Views,* ed. Ladislav Matejka and Krystyna Pomorska. Ann Arbor: U of Michigan P, 1978. 176–96.

Barbour, John D. *Versions of Deconversion: Autobiography and the Loss of Faith.* Charlottesville: UP of Virginia, 1994.

Baritz, Loren, ed. *The Culture of the Twenties.* New York: Bobbs-Merrill, 1970.

Benstock, Shari, ed. *The Private Self: Theory and Practice of Women's Autobiographical Writings.* Chapel Hill: U of North Carolina P, 1988.

Bentley, Elizabeth. *Out of Bondage.* New York: Devon Adair, 1951.

Bercovitch, Sacvan. *The American Jeremiad.* Madison: U of Wisconsin P, 1978.

Berger, Bennett M. "How Long Is a Generation?" *Looking for America: Essays on Youth, Suburbia, and Other American Obsessions.* Englewood Cliffs: Prentice-Hall, 1971. 20–37.

Berman, Paul. "At the Center of the 60's." *New York Times Book Review,* 12 June 1988, 7.

Berman, Paul. "Don't Follow Leaders." *New Republic,* 10–17 August 1987, 28–35.

Berman, Paul. "The Last New Leftists." *New Republic,* 24 April 1989, 26–32.

Beverley, John. "The Margin at the Center: On *Testimonio* (Testimonial Narrative)." In *De/Colonizing the Subject: The Politics of Gender in Women's Autobiography,* ed. Sidonie Smith and Julia Watson. Minneapolis: U of Minnesota P, 1992. 91–114.

Billson, Marcus. "The Memoir: New Perspectives on a Forgotten Genre." *Genre* 10 (Summer 1977): 259–82.

Blank, Thomas O. "The Social Constructionist Movement in Modern Psychology." *Personality and Social Psychology Bulletin* 14 (1988): 651–63.

Bloom, Lynn Z. "Single-Experience Autobiographies." *a/b: Auto/Biography Studies* 3 (Fall 1987): 36–45.

Bourne, Randolph. "History of a Literary Radical." *War and the Intellectuals: Essays by Randolph S. Bourne, 1915–1919*, ed. Carl Resek. New York: Harper & Row, 1964. 184–97.

Bourne, Randolph. *Youth and Life*. Cambridge, MA: Riverside, 1913.

Branch, Taylor. "If I Had a Hammer . . . I'd Make Tom Hayden Stop Issuing Manifestos." *Washington Monthly*, May 1988, 51–54.

Branch, Taylor. *Parting the Waters: America in the King Years, 1954–63*. New York: Simon & Schuster, 1988.

Breines, Winifred. "A Couple of White Guys . . ." *Nation*, 27 November 1989, 630–32.

Breines, Winifred. "Whose New Left?" *Journal of American History* 75 (1988): 528–45.

Brinkley, Alan. "Dreams of the Sixties." *New York Review of Books*, 22 October 1987, 10, 12–16.

Brodzki, Bella, and Celeste Schenck, eds. *Life/Lines: Theorizing Women's Autobiography*. Ithaca: Cornell UP, 1988.

Brooks, Van Wyck. *America's Coming-of-Age*. New York: Dutton, 1915.

Brooks, Van Wyck. *Letters and Leadership*. New York: Huebsch, 1918.

Brooks, Van Wyck. "On Creating a Usable Past." *Dial*, 11 April 1918.

Brooks, Van Wyck. "Young America." *Letters and Literature*. New York: Huebsch, 1918.

Brown, Norman O. *Life against Death: The Psychoanalytic Meaning of History*. Middletown, CT: Wesleyan UP, 1959.

Brown, Norman O. *Love's Body*. New York: Random, 1966.

Bruner, Jerome. *Acts of Meaning*. Boston: Harvard UP, 1990.

Bruner, Jerome. "Life as Narrative." *Social Research* 54 (Spring 1987): 11–32.

Bruner, Jerome. "The Narrative Construction of Reality." *Critical Inquiry* 18 (Autumn 1991): 1–21.

Budenz, Louis. *This Is My Story*. New York: McGraw-Hill, 1947.

Buhle, Paul. "Remembering the Sixties." *Oral History Review* 17 (Spring 1989):137–42.

Bunzel, John H., ed. *Political Passages: Journeys of Change through Two Decades, 1968–1988*. New York: Free Press, 1988.

Burner, David. "We Were Disinformed." *New York Times Book Review*, 23 April 1989, 18.

Bushkoff, Leonard. "Memoir and Myth: Remembering the Way It Was in the '60s." *Christian Science Monitor*, 3 June 1988, B3.

Caputo, Philip. *A Rumor of War*. New York: Ballantine, 1977.

Caute, David. *The Fellow Travellers: A Postscript to the Enlightenment*. New York: Macmillan, 1973.

Chambers, Whittaker. *Witness*. New York: Random, 1952.

Collier, Peter, and David Horowitz. *Destructive Generation: Second Thoughts about the Sixties*. New York: Summit Books, 1989.

Collier, Peter, and David Horowitz, eds. *Second Thoughts: Former Radicals Look Back at the Sixties.* New York: Madison Books, 1989.

Cowley, Malcolm. *—And I Worked at the Writer's Trade: Chapters of Literary History, 1918–1978.* New York: Viking, 1978.

Cowley, Malcolm. *The Dream of the Golden Mountains: Remembering the 1930s.* New York: Viking, 1980.

Cowley, Malcolm. *Exile's Return: A Literary Odyssey of the 1920's.* New York: Viking, 1951.

Cowley, Malcolm. *Exile's Return: A Narrative of Ideas.* New York: Norton, 1934.

Cowley, Malcolm. *A Second Flowering: Works and Days of the Lost Generation.* New York: Viking, 1973.

Crossman, Richard, ed. *The God That Failed.* New York: Harper & Row, 1949.

Culley, Margo, ed. *American Women's Autobiography: Fea(s)ts of Memory.* Madison: U of Wisconsin P, 1992.

Decter, Midge. "Notes from the American Underground." *Commentary,* 22 January 1982, 27–33.

Delli Carpini, Michael X. *Stability and Change in American Politics: The Coming of Age of the Generation of the 1960s.* New York: New York UP, 1986.

De Voto, Bernard. "Exiles from Reality." *Saturday Review of Literature,* 2 June 1934, 721–22.

Diggins, John P. *Up from Communism: Conservative Odysseys in American Intellectual History.* New York: Harper & Row, 1975.

Dillard, Annie. *Pilgrim at Tinker Creek.* New York: Harper's, 1974.

Dodd, Bella. *School of Darkness.* New York: P. J. Kenedy, 1954.

Downs, Frederick. *The Killing Zone: My Life in the Vietnam War.* New York: Berkley, 1978.

Dumont, Louis. *Essays on Individualism: Modern Ideology in Anthropological Perspective.* Chicago: U of Chicago P, 1986.

Dumont, Louis. *Homo Hierarchicus.* Chicago: U of Chicago P, 1970.

Eilert, Rick. *For Self and Country.* New York: Pocket Books, 1983.

Eliade, Mircea. *The Myth of the Eternal Return, or, Cosmos and History.* Princeton: Princeton UP, 1954.

Emerson, Ralph Waldo. "The American Scholar." *Selections from Ralph Waldo Emerson: An Organic Anthology,* ed. Stephen E. Whicher. Boston: Houghton Mifflin, 1960. 63–80.

Erikson, Erik. *Life History and the Historical Moment.* New York: Norton, 1975.

Farber, Jerry. *The Student as Nigger: Essays and Stories.* 1967; New York: Pocket, 1970.

Fass, Paula. *The Damned and the Beautiful: American Youth in the 1920's.* New York: Oxford UP, 1977.

Fisher, D. D. V. "Experiential Being and the Inherent Self: Towards a Constructivist Theory of the Self." *Journal for the Theory of Social Behaviour* 18 (1988): 149–67.

Fitzgerald, F. Scott. *The Crack-Up.* Ed. Edmund Wilson. New York: Scribner, 1931. New York: New Directions Paperbook, 1956.

Frank, Waldo. *Our America.* New York: Liveright, 1919.

Franklin, Vincent P. *Living Our Stories, Telling Our Truths: Autobiography and the Making of the African-American Intellectual Tradition.* New York: Scribner, 1995.

Freeman, Mark. *Rewriting the Self: History, Memory, Narrative.* Boston: Routledge, 1993.

Freud, Sigmund. "Analysis Terminable and Interminable." *The Standard Edition of the Complete Psychological Works of Sigmund Freud,* trans. J. Strachey and A. Freud. Vol. 23. London: Hogarth, 1964. 211–53.

Freund, Charles. "The View from Over Thirty." *New York Times Book Review,* 14 August 1988, 7.

Friedenberg, Edgar Z. "The Oppression of Youth." In *Seasons of Rebellion: Protest and Radicalism in Recent America,* ed. Joseph Boskin and Robert A. Rosenstone. New York: Holt, Rinehart & Winston, 1972. 221–36.

Friedman, Susan Stanford. "Women's Autobiographical Selves: Theory and Practice." In *The Private Self: Theory and Practice of Women's Autobiographical Writings,* ed. Shari Benstock. Chapel Hill: U of North Carolina P, 1988. 34–62.

Frye, Northrop. *The Anatomy of Criticism.* Princeton UP, 1971.

Garver, Paul, and George Abbott White. "What Was Old, What Was New? The New Left and American Exceptionalism." *Journal of American Studies* 22 (1988): 67–76.

Gergen, Kenneth. *The Social Construction of the Person.* New York: Springer-Verlag, 1985.

Gergen, Mary M., and Kenneth J. Gergen. "Social Construction of Narrative Accounts." In *Historical Social Psychology,* ed. Gergen and Gergen. Hillsdale, NJ: Erlbaum, 1984. 173–89.

Gilder, George. "The '60s: A Look Back in Anger." *Washington Post Book World,* 19 March 1989, 1, 10.

Gitlin, Todd. "Muddled Thoughts." *Dissent* 36 (Fall 1989): 569–71.

Gitlin, Todd. *The Sixties: Years of Hope, Days of Rage.* New York: Bantam, 1987.

Gitlin, Todd. *The Whole World Is Watching: Mass Media in the Making and Unmaking of the New Left.* Berkeley: U of California P, 1980.

Gitlow, Benjamin. *I Confess.* New York: Dutton, 1940.

Glassco, John. *Memoirs of Montparnasse.* New York: Viking, 1973.

Goldman, Peter, and Tony Fuller. *Charlie Company: What Vietnam Did to Us.* New York: Ballantine, 1983.

Goodman, Paul. *Compulsory Mis-education and The Community of Scholars.* New York: Random, 1964.

Goodman, Paul. *Growing Up Absurd.* New York: Random, 1960.

Gornick, Vivian. *The Romance of American Communism.* New York: Basic, 1977.

Harrington, Michael. *Fragments of a Century: A Social Autobiography.* New York: Dutton, 1973.

Harris, David. *Dreams Die Hard: Three Men's Journey through the Sixties.* New York: St. Martin's/Marek, 1982.

Hart, F. R. "History Talking to Itself." *New Literary History* 40 (Autumn 1978): 193–210.

Hart, F. R. "Notes for an Anatomy of Modern Autobiography." *New Literary History* 1 (1970): 485–511.

Hausknecht, Murray. "Generational Conflict and Left Politics." *Dissent,* Fall 1988, 497–500.

Hayden, Tom. *Reunion.* New York: Random, 1988.

Hayden, Tom. *Trial.* New York: Holt, Rinehart, & Winston, 1970.

Hazlett, John. "Conversion, Revisionism, and Revision in Malcolm Cowley's *Exile's Return.*" *South Atlantic Quarterly* 82 (Spring 1983): 179–88.

Hazlett, John. "The Situation of American Autobiography: Generic Blurring in 'Contemporary' Historiography." *Prose Studies: History, Theory, Criticism* 13 (September 1990): 261–77.

Henry, David. "Recalling the 1960s: The New Left and Social Movement Criticism." *Quarterly Journal of Speech* 75 (February 1989): 97–112.

Hermans, H. J. M., and H. J .G. Kempen. *The Dialogical Self: Meaning as Movement.* New York: Academic Press, 1993.

Herr, Michael. *Dispatches.* New York: Avon, 1968.

Hertzberg, Hendrik. "A Tale of Two Hippies." *Washington Monthly* 21 (May 1989): 44–46.

Hodgson, Godfrey. *America in Our Time.* New York: Vantage, 1976.

Hoffman, Abbie. *Revolution for the Hell of It.* New York: Dial, 1968.

Hoffman, Abbie. *Soon to Be a Major Motion Picture.* New York: Putnam, 1980.

Hoffman, Abbie. *Square Dancing in the Ice Age.* New York: Putnam, 1982.

Hunt, Charles W. "The Old Left, the New Left, and the Uses of History." *Monthly Review* (New York) 41 (September 1989): 58–61.

Isserman, Maurice. "The Not-So-Dark and Bloody Ground: New Works on the 1960s." *American Historical Review* 94 (October 1989): 990–1010.

Isserman, Maurice. "Spin Control." *Dissent,* Fall 1988, 501–3.

Jaeger, Hans. "Generations in History: Reflections on a Controversial Concept." *History and Theory: Studies in the Philosophy of History* 24 (1985): 273–92.

Jelinek, Estelle C. *The Tradition of Women's Autobiography: From Antiquity to the Present.* Boston: Twayne, 1986.

Jelinek, Estelle C., ed. *Women's Autobiography: Essays in Criticism.* Bloomington: Indiana UP, 1980.

Jennings, M. Kent, and Richard G. Niemi. *Generations and Politics.* Princeton: Princeton UP, 1981.

Jezer, Marty. Rev. of *The Sixties,* by Todd Gitlin. *Progressive,* July 1988, 30–31.

Kanfer, Stefan. "The Politics of the Playpen." *New Republic,* 23 December 1981, 30–32.

Kaplan, Caren. "Resisting Autobiography: Out-Law Genres and Transnational Feminist Subjects." In *De/Colonizing the Subject: The Politics of Gender in Women's Autobiography,* ed. Sidonie Smith and Julia Watson. Minneapolis: U of Minnesota P, 1992. 115–38.

Kempton, Murray. "Bombs Away." *New York Review of Books,* 21 January 1982, 48–50.

Kenniston, Kenneth. *Youth and Dissent: The Rise of a New Opposition.* New York: Harcourt, 1960.

Kerby, Anthony Paul. *Narrative and Self.* Bloomington: Indiana UP, 1991.

King, Mary E. "Hayden's Workout Book." *Nation,* 3 October 1988, 281–82.

Knoll, Robert E., ed. *McAlmon and the Lost Generation: A Self Portrait.* Lincoln: U of Nebraska P, 1962.

Kovic, Ron. *Born on the Fourth of July.* New York: McGraw-Hill, 1976.

Kriegel, Annie. "Generational Difference: The History of an Idea." *Daedalus* 107 (Fall 1978): 23–38.

Kundera, Milan. *The Book of Laughter and Forgetting.* Trans. M. H. Heim. New York: Penguin, 1981.

Lambert, T. Allen. "Generations and Change: Toward a Theory of Generations as a Force in Historical Processes." *Youth and Society* 4 (September 1972): 21–46.

Lane, J. B. Rev. of *Political Passages: Journeys of Change through Two Decades, 1968–1988,* ed. John Bunzel. *Choice,* October 1988, 26.

Laufer, Robert S. "Sources of Generational Consciousness and Conflict." In *The New Pilgrims,* ed. Philip G. Altbach and Robert S. Laufer. New York: David McKay, 1972. 218–37.

Lionnet, Françoise. *Autobiographical Voices: Race, Gender, Self-Portraiture.* Ithaca: Cornell UP, 1989.

Lipson, Eden Ross. "A Bomber's Confessions." *New York Times Book Review,* 25 October 1981, 12–13.

Mailer, Norman. "The White Negro: Superficial Reflections on the Hipster." *Advertisements for Myself.* London: Deutsch, 1961. 269–314.

Mannheim, Karl. "The Problem of the Generation." In *Essays in the Sociology of Knowledge,* ed. Paul Kecskemeti. London: Routledge & Kegan Paul, 1959. 276–320.

Marcus, George E., and Michael M. J. Fischer. *Anthropology as Cultural Critique: An Experimental Moment in the Human Sciences.* Chicago: U of Chicago P, 1986.

Marcuse, Herbert. *Eros and Civilization.* New York: Vintage, 1962.

Marcuse, Herbert. *One-Dimensional Man.* Boston: Beacon, 1964.

Marías, Julián. *Generations: A Historical Method.* Trans. Harold C. Riley. Mobile: U of Alabama P, 1970.

Mason, Mary G. "The Other Voice: Autobiographies of Women Writers." In *Autobiography: Essays Theoretical and Critical,* ed. James Olney. Princeton: Princeton UP, 1980. 207–35.

Mason, Robert. *Chickenhawk.* New York: Penguin, 1983.

Massing, Hede. *This Deception.* New York: Duell, Sloan & Pearce, 1951.

Matthews, J. B. *Odyssey of a Fellow Traveler.* New York: Mount Vernon, 1938.

Matusow, Allen J. *The Unravelling of America: A History of Liberalism in the 1960s.* New York: Harper & Row, 1984.

Maynard, Joyce. *Looking Back: A Chronicle of Growing Up Old in the Sixties.* New York: Avon, 1972.

McConnell, Scott. "Resurrecting the New Left." *Commentary* October 1987, 31–38.

McGinness, Joe. *The Selling of the President.* New York: Trident, 1969.

McLuhan, Marshall. *Understanding Media.* New York: McGraw-Hill, 1964.

Melville, Keith. *Communes in the Counter Culture: Origins, Theories, Styles of Life.* New York: Morrow, 1972.

Menand, Louis. "You Say It's Your Birthday." *New Republic,* 18 April 1988, 34–40.

Middleton, D., and D. Edwards, eds. *Collective Remembering.* London: Sage, 1990.

Miller, James. *"Democracy Is in the Streets": From Port Huron to the Siege of Chicago.* New York: Simon & Schuster, 1987.

Miller, James. "Tears and Riots, Love and Regrets." *New York Times Book Review,* 8 November 1987, 13–14.

Mills, Hilary. *Norman Mailer: A Biography.* London: New English Library, 1983.

Mungo, Raymond. *Famous Long Ago: My Life and Hard Times with Liberation News Service.* Boston: Beacon, 1970.

Mungo, Raymond. *Total Loss Farm: A Year in the Life.* New York: Dutton, 1970.

Nussbaum, Bruce. "This Is the Damning of the Age of Aquarius." *Business Week,* 3 April 1989, 16–17.

O'Brien, Tim. *If I Die in a Combat Zone.* New York: Delacorte, 1973.

Ortega y Gasset, José. *Man and Crisis.* Trans. Mildred Adams. New York: Norton, 1958. Trans. of *En torno a Galileo.* Madrid, 1933.

Ortega y Gasset, José. *The Modern Theme.* Trans. James Cleugh. New York: Harper & Row, 1961. Trans. of *El tema de nuestro tiempo.* Madrid, 1923.

Packard, Vance. *The Hidden Persuaders.* New York: McKay, 1957.

Parmet, Herbert. "Yesterday's Rebels." *New Leader,* 7 March 1988, 17–18.

Personal Narratives Group, eds. *Interpreting Women's Lives: Feminist Theory and Personal Narrative.* Bloomington: Indiana UP, 1989.

Powers, Richard Gid. "Anticommunist Lives." *American Quarterly* 41 (December 1989): 714–23.

Rader, Dotson. *Blood Dues.* New York: Knopf, 1973.

Rader, Dotson. *I Ain't Marchin' Anymore!* New York: David McKay, 1969.

Rader, Dotson. *Tennessee: Cry of the Heart.* Garden City: Doubleday, 1985.

Ricoeur, Paul. "Narrative Identity." *Philosophy Today* 35 (1991): 73–81.

Rosenwald, George, and Richard Ochberg. *Storied Lives: The Cultural Politics of Self Understanding.* New Haven: Yale UP, 1992.

Ross, Jeffrey A., et al., eds. *The Mobilization of Collective Identity: Comparative Perspectives.* Lanham, MA: UP of America, 1980.

Rossman, Michael. *New Age Blues: On the Politics of Consciousness.* New York: Dutton, 1979.

Rossman, Michael. *On Learning and Social Change.* New York: Random, 1972.

Rossman, Michael. *The Wedding within the War.* New York: Doubleday, 1971.

Roszak, Theodore. *The Making of a Counter Culture: Reflections on the Technocratic Society and Its Youthful Opposition.* New York: Doubleday, 1968.

Rothman, Stanley, and S. Robert Lichter. *Roots of Radicalism: Jews, Christians, and the New Left.* New York: Oxford UP, 1982.

Rousseau, Jean-Jacques. *Confessions.* Trans. J. M. Cohen. London: Penguin, 1953.

Rubin, Jerry. *Do It! Scenarios for the Revolution.* New York: Simon & Schuster, 1970.

Rubin, Jerry. *Growing (Up) at 37.* New York: M. Evans, 1976.

Rubin, Jerry. *We Are Everywhere.* New York: Harper & Row, 1971.

Sale, Kirkpatrick. *SDS.* New York: Vintage, 1973.

Santoli, Al. *Everything We Had: An Oral History of the Vietnam War by Thirty-Three Soldiers Who Fought It.* New York: Ballantine, 1981.

Sarbin, T. R., and J. I. Kitsuse, eds. *Constructing the Social.* London: Sage, 1994.

Sayre, Robert. "The Proper Study—Autobiography in American Studies."
    American Quarterly 29 (1977): 241–62.

Shattan, Joseph. Rev. of *Political Passages: Journeys of Change through Two
    Decades, 1968–1988,* ed. John Bunzel. *American Spectator,* July 1988,
    45–46.

Shotter, J., and Kenneth Gergen, eds. *Texts of Identity.* London: Sage. 1989.

Slotkin, Richard. *Regeneration through Violence: The Mythology of the Ameri-
    can Frontier.* Middletown: Wesleyan UP, 1973.

Smith, Sidonie. *A Poetics of Women's Autobiography: Marginality and the Fic-
    tions of Self-Representation.* Bloomington: Indiana UP, 1987.

Smith, Sidonie. *Where I'm Bound: Patterns of Slavery and Freedom in Black
    American Autobiography.* Westport, CT: Greenwood, 1974.

Smith, Sidonie, and Julia Watson, eds. *De/Colonizing the Subject: The Politics of
    Gender in Women's Autobiography.* Minneapolis: U of Minnesota P, 1992.

Sobran, Joseph. "Lost Generation." *National Review,* 24 March 1989, 43–44.

Somers, Margaret. "The Narrative Constitution of Identity: A Relational and
    Network Approach." *Theory and Society* 23 (1994): 605–49.

Sommer, Doris. "'Not Just a Personal Story': Women's *Testimonios* and the
    Plural Self." In *Life/Lines: Theorizing Women's Autobiography,* ed. Bella
    Brodzki and Celeste Schenck. Ithaca: Cornell UP, 1988. 107–30.

Spacks, Patricia M. "Stages of Self: Notes on Autobiography and the Life
    Cycle." In *The American Autobiography: A Collection of Critical Essays,* ed.
    Albert Stone. Englewood Cliffs: Prentice-Hall, 1981. 44–60.

Spitzer, Alan. "The Historical Problem of Generations." *American Historical
    Review* 78 (1973): 1359–85.

Stanton, Domna, ed. *The Female Autograph.* New York: New York Literary
    Forum, 1984.

Stepto, Robert B. *From behind the Veil: A Study of Afro-American Narrative.*
    Urbana: U of Illinois P, 1979.

Stone, Albert. *Autobiographical Occasions and Original Acts: Versions of
    American Identity from Henry Adams to Nate Shaw.* Philadelphia: U of
    Pennsylvania P, 1980.

Students for a Democratic Society. *The Port Huron Statement.* In *"Democracy
    Is in the Streets": From Port Huron to the Siege of Chicago,* by James Miller.
    New York: Simon & Schuster, 1987. 329–77.

Szamuely, George. Rev. of *Destructive Generation,* by Peter Collier and David
    Horowitz. *American Spectator,* August 1989, 42–43.

Terry, Wallace. *Bloods: An Oral History of the Vietnam War by Black Veterans.*
    New York: Ballantine, 1984.

Veblen, Thorstein. *The Theory of the Leisure Class.* New York: Modern Li-
    brary, 1934.

Viorst, Milton. *Fire in the Streets: America in the 1960's.* New York: Simon &
    Schuster, 1979.

Von Hoffman, Nicholas. *We Are the People Our Parents Warned Us About.*
    Chicago: Quadrangle, 1968.

Walker, Daniel. *Rights in Conflict: The Violent Confrontation of Demonstra-
    tors and Police in the Parks and Streets of Chicago during the Week of the*

Democratic National Convention of 1968. Washington: National Commission on the Causes and Prevention of Violence, 1968.

Weintraub, Karl Joachim. *The Value of the Individual: Self and Circumstance in Autobiography.* Chicago: U of Chicago P, 1978.

White, Hayden. *Metahistory: The Historical Imagination in Nineteenth-Century Europe.* Baltimore: Johns Hopkins UP, 1973.

White, Theodore. *The Making of the President, 1960.* New York: Atheneum, 1961.

Whitman, Walt. *Democratic Vistas. The Poetry and Prose of Walt Whitman,* ed. Louis Untermeyer. New York: Simon & Schuster, 1949. 805–64.

Whorf, Benjamin. *Language, Thought, and Reality: Selected Writings.* Cambridge: Technology Press of Massachusetts Institute of Technology, 1956.

Williamson, Chilton. "The Right Books." *National Review,* 24 June 1988, 48–49.

Wohl, Robert. *The Generation of 1914.* Cambridge: Harvard UP, 1979.

Index

Numbers in bold indicate the main discussion of the entry.

Myth: and Jane Alpert, 126–28; and annunciatory narratives, 128, 201; capitalist, 46; Chicago demonstrations as,
50–51, 54–55; Chicago Seven trial as,
69; cold war, 202; and counterculture,
73; and countermyth, 57–58; of creation, 9; defined by Hoffman, 51; of expulsion from Eden, 29; FSM as, 78;
generational, 40, 52–53, 64, 77; and
Tom Hayden, 68; historic event as,
50–52, 55, 77–78, 83; and Abbie Hoffman, 49–58, 127; of identity, 51–53,
126; individualism as, 4, 14, 46, 200;
justificatory, 41, 44; and language, 57;
and media, 57, 112, 127; and Raymond
Mungo, 114–16, 225n; national, 41, 42,
57, 206, 220n; of revolution, 54, 126–
28; right wing, 59; and Michael Rossman, 73, 77–78; and Jerry Rubin, 61,
64–65, 127; sexual, 52, 137; Third
World as, 148; versus truth, 225n; Watergate scandal as, 169; Yippie as, 64

Neoconservativism: and claims of marginalization, 150; and critique of sixties,
141–42; and *Destructive Generation,*
139; and generational dialogue, 209;
and renunciatory narratives, 134
New Age consciousness, 73, 85–86, 108,
113, 116–17, 165, 167–68, 169, 175
New Left, the: and Jane Alpert, 124; and
counterculture, 73, 78; and generational
autobiography, 203, 208; and generational identity, 64, 66, 73, 78; and generationalism, 71; as generational representatives, 222n; and Todd Gitlin, 187,
191–94; and David Harris, 173, 175;
and Tom Hayden, 183; and liberalism,
173, 193; and Raymond Mungo,
110–11, 113; and New Age, 80, 108;
and old left, 89, 190; and *Port Huron
Statement,* 55; and Dotson Rader,
92–93, 98–99; rejection of, 119,
130–33; and Michael Rossman, 168;
and Jerry Rubin, 59, 62, 64–65; and
sexism, 52, 193, 206; as vanguard,
64–65, 192–93; as voice in autobiographical dialogue, 81. *See also* Leftism
New Left autobiographers: attack on, 139,
141–42
Newton, Huey, 143
Nicaragua. *See* Sandinismo

Niemi, Richard G., 215n
Nixon, Richard: as critic of left as "fifth
column," 129; as enemy, 101, 205; as
failed father figure, 168; as fifties figure,
101; and middle-American Thermidor,
229n; and mining of Haiphong Harbor,
164; as object of protest demonstration,
99; as rigid father figure, 182; and
"Vietnamization policy," 85; and Watergate Scandal, 177
Nostalgia: and *The Big Chill,* 151–52, 155;
and Malcolm Cowley, 179–81; and elegiac narratives, 153, 202; and generational retrospectives, 9; and David Harris, 171, 186, 196; and Tom Hayden,
179–81, 196; and Joyce Maynard, 156,
162; and neoconservative rhetoric, 129,
134–35, 144; and Michael Rossman,
166, 168
Novak, Michael, 132–33, 139, 227n
Nussbaum, Bruce, 227n

O'Brien, Tim, 231n
Ochberg, Richard, 232n
Ochs, Phil, 69, 184
Oglesby, Carl, 151, 230n
Olney, James, 232n
Ortega, Daniel, 148
Ortega y Gasset, José: and generational
theory, 4, 10–12, 17–20, 47, 71, 75, 202,
216nn, 230n

Packard, Vance, 62, 222n
Parental figure(s): and Jane Alpert, 120,
121–22; and annunciatory narratives,
40, 80–81, 86, 182; and Martha Bayles,
136–37; betrayal by, 56, 65, 94, 183,
210; Chicago trial jury as, 181; and
Malcolm Cowley, 18; and Erik Erikson,
3; and generational autobiography, 38,
81, 86; and generational identity, 6, 64,
86, 90, 205; and generational plot, 129;
and generational theory, 16, 44; and
Todd Gitlin, 190, 195; and Tom Hayden, 178, 181–84; and Abbie Hoffman,
50, 57; J. Edgar Hoover as, 182, 183–
84; hypocritical, 183; as imagined audience, 80–81; and Joyce Maynard, 161–
62; old left as, 190; permissive, 121,
136–37; and *Port Huron Statement,* 56;
and "psychosocial moratorium," 3; and
Dotson Rader, 90, 94, 106; repressive,

Wisconsin Studies in American Autobiography

William L. Andrews
General Editor

Robert F. Sayre
The Examined Self: Benjamin Franklin, Henry Adams, Henry James

Daniel B. Shea
Spiritual Autobiography in Early America

Lois Mark Stalvey
The Education of a WASP

Margaret Sams
Forbidden Family: A Wartime Memoir of the Philippines, 1941–1945
Edited, with an introduction, by Lynn Z. Bloom

Journeys in New Worlds: Early American Women's Narratives
Edited by William L. Andrews

Mark Twain
Mark Twain's Own Autobiography:
The Chapters from the "North American Review"
Edited, with an introduction, by Michael J. Kiskis

American Autobiography: Retrospect and Prospect
Edited by Paul John Eakin

Charlotte Perkins Gilman
The Living of Charlotte Perkins Gilman: An Autobiography
Introduction by Ann J. Lane

Caroline Seabury
The Diary of Caroline Seabury: 1854–1863
Edited, with an introduction, by Suzanne L. Bunkers

Cornelia Peake McDonald
A Woman's Civil War: A Diary with Reminiscences of the War, from March 1862
Edited, with an introduction, by Minrose G. Gwin

Marian Anderson
My Lord, What a Morning
Introduction by Nellie Y. McKay

American Women's Autobiography: Fea(s)ts of Memory
Edited, with an introduction, by Margo Culley

Frank Marshall Davis
Livin' the Blues: Memoirs of a Black Journalist and Poet
Edited, with an introduction, by John Edgar Tidwell

Joanne Jacobson
Authority and Alliance in the Letters of Henry Adams

Kamau Brathwaite
The Zea Mexican Diary
Foreword by Sandra Pouchet Paquet

Genaro M. Padilla
My History, Not Yours:
The Formation of Mexican American Autobiography

Frances Smith Foster
Witnessing Slavery: The Development of Ante-bellum Slave Narratives

Native American Autobiography: An Anthology
Edited, with an introduction, by Arnold Krupat

American Lives: An Anthology of Autobiographical Writing
Edited, with an introduction, by Robert F. Sayre

Carol Holly
Intensely Family: The Inheritance of Family Shame and the
Autobiographies of Henry James

People of the Book: Thirty Scholars Reflect on Their Jewish Identity
Edited by Jeffrey Rubin-Dorsky and Shelley Fisher Fishkin

John Downton Hazlett
My Generation: Collective Autobiography and Identity Politics

William Herrick
Jumping the Line: The Adventures and Misadventures of an American Radical

Women, Autobiography, Theory: A Reader
Edited by Sidonie Smith and Julia Watson

www.ingramcontent.com/pod-product-compliance
Lightning Source LLC
Chambersburg PA
CBHW060255100426
42742CB00011B/1755